ESCAPE OR DIE

By the same author,
and also available in Cassell Military Paperbacks

REACH FOR THE SKY
THE GREAT ESCAPE

ESCAPE OR DIE

True stories of heroic escapes

PAUL BRICKHILL

CASSELL

Cassell Military Paperbacks

Cassell, an imprint of Orion Books Ltd, Orion House,
5 Upper St Martin's Lane, London WC2H 9EA

First published in Great Britain by Evans Brothers in 1952

This Cassell Military Paperbacks edition published 2003

A catalogue record for this book is available from the British Library

ISBN 978-1-4072-1464-1

Printed in Great Britain by Mackays of Chatham plc, Chatham, Kent

The Orion Publishing Group's policy is to use papers that are natural,
renewable and recyclable products and made from wood grown in
sustainable forests. The logging and manufacturing processes are expected to
conform to the environmental regulations of the country of origin.

www.orionbooks.co.uk

CONTENTS

LIST OF ILLUSTRATIONS

FOREWORD

THE fact that so many R.A.F. prisoners of war managed to escape in World War II and that so many shot-down airmen successfully evaded the enemy was due partly to escape training and partly to the efforts of thousands of civilian men, women and even children. Many of these civilians, living in their own countries under a regime of terror, helped our men with a most remarkable cold-blooded courage. Often they risked much more than the escaping or evading airman. If the airman were caught he would become a prisoner of war, but the civilians who helped him faced sudden death and torture.

At the end of the war the Royal Air Force Escaping Society, of which I am Chairman, was formed as an act of gratitude by those who got away. While it acts as a focus and as a means of reunion for its members, its main object is to repay some part of the debt we owe to our former civilian allies, especially to the widows and orphans of those who died trying to help us in France, Belgium, Holland, Italy and in the Far East.

Already we have brought many orphans to this country for a holiday. We have helped widows afflicted by sickness or want. We have managed to give a training for a career to some of the sons of the heroes whose sacrifice it was to help our cause. To that end Paul Brickhill has undertaken the writing of this book, to help to provide much needed funds for the society's work, and I am grateful to him for having undertaken the task.

BASIL EMBRY.

9

ESCAPE

by H. E. Bates

It is well known, I think, that when a member of the armed forces of this country is captured by an enemy in time of war it is his duty, by all possible and reasonable means, to escape. International law compels him to give the enemy no other information about himself than his name, rank and number; but when he has done this the war, for him, does not end. It begins all over again: to be fought under a new set of rules, in the new set of circumstances, and above all without the comforting assistance of lethal weapons. The captor has the guns, the bullets, the mines, the tear-gas, the searchlights, the spies, the traps, the barbed wire, the dogs and all the countless refinements of mental oppression that make life in prison compounds a special sort of hell. Against these things the captive has only his wit, his resource, his inventiveness, his brains, his endurance, his humour, his luck—if fate allows him any—and perhaps most important of all his mental attitude. This may well be of the kind that makes for heroism. It is much more likely to be of the kind that generates pure cussedness. And pure cussedness, among prisoners of war, is incontestably a weapon of the highest value. It enables the captive to make a devil of a nuisance of himself; it is his most consistent way, even if all others fail, of continuing to harass the enemy.

To these obvious facts the R.A.F., more than any other part of this country's fighting forces during the Second World War, brought a special attitude of its own. I do not think it was a braver, more ingenious, more determined, or more resourceful attitude than that shown by men in other services. It certainly excelled in pure cussedness; it was also rich in invention and defeatless humour; but above all it was shaped and governed by a special set of circumstances that had never applied to a British fighting force in war-time before. The fall of France in 1940 was in great part responsible for these circumstances, and they are so obvious that it would, for that very reason, be easy to overlook them.

When the continent of Europe became a great mass of enemy-occupied territory with only a few precarious friendly or neutral pockets, leaving Great Britain the only remaining fighting base from which the enemy could be attacked, the R.A.F. found itself in a curious position. It began to fight from its own back door. Whereas in other wars men had gone out from Britain to tackle enemies well out of sight of home, the R.A.F. now found itself having tea in the calm summer air of an English village at four o'clock, fighting in a highly specialised theatre of its own at twenty thousand feet at half-past, and returning to take a telephone call from an inquiring girl-friend at five. A man could be watching Miss Ginger Rogers' enchanting legs on a ciné screen between tea and dinner and then be dead, a prisoner or a confused shot-down wanderer, hundreds of miles away, before bed-time. The necessity of leading such a life of sandwiched peace and frenzy, love and tracer bullets, cool beers on English lawns and stratospheric bloodiness, all under pressure of violent change, had a strange effect of unworldly tautness on the faces of flying men that will never be forgotten by those who knew them well.

The effect of these circumstances on the outlook of R.A.F. fighting men was bound to be highly varied; but presently we were meeting in England with a general type—later to be met with in all other theatres of war—who had solved, at least as far as onlookers could judge, this curious problem of abnormality in living. He brought to it a refined attitude of under-statement, a desire to be casual in a low key that was well expressed in his language. He no longer crashed an aircraft; he pranged or wrapped it up. He no longer fought a gallant action; it was a good show. He no longer died; he bought it. All these things united to become a legendary synonym for acute Britishness. The more closely and harshly war impinged on life the more smoothly, casually and cryptically were the fears of it wrapped up in the veil of language and the cloak of behaviour. War was an embarrassment that simply ought not to be mentioned.

All this was really another expression of an age-old British reluctance to make a fuss about things; but its acutely specialised form among flying men had some highly interesting effects. It made them, when captured, the most reluctant of prisoners; it was suddenly very annoying not to be able to ride home to tea; it was absolutely infuriating to be keeping a date with a Nazi rifle instead of one with a brunette in a café at Canterbury. It also, I think, made the R.A.F. singularly unprepared for capture, just as they were mentally unprepared for subjection anyway. A soldier, blazing away at a local enemy from a fox-hole, must inevitably carry in his mind, however much he hates it, the idea that the situation may suddenly turn very nasty and put him behind barbed wire. The R.A.F. found the same prospect constitutionally difficult to accept: so much so that when I asked the author of this book why flying men, especially bomber pilots, did not go over Germany wearing fully prepared civilian disguise under their flying suits, so that they could begin organised escape immediately on hitting German soil instead of afterwards toiling in tunnels, he remarked that he supposed no R.A.F. man ever had a final and absolute belief that he would be shot down, and that if by some unfortunate accident he were, he would never be captured anyway. One story in this book, the excellent one by Group Captain John Whitley, is a proof of this as well as its exception. Group Captain Whitley went elaborately prepared. He was one of those who made a will while healthily refusing to accept the idea of death. " He violently rejected," says Mr. Brickhill, " the idea of being captured."

For most captured flying men, however, one simple fact did not become apparent until long afterwards. " We did not grasp until it was too late," one said, " that the moment we hit German soil was the moment for which we were afterwards to work so sweatily, bitterly and ingeniously, and often with such terrible disappointments, to re-achieve." In other words very few men grasped that their arrival on enemy soil was really a state of freedom. It was only from behind the barbed wire of compounds that they looked out and planned with such meticulous care and risk the business of getting back to the very point from which they had started. How meticulously and ingeniously they did plan it all readers of Mr. Brickhill's *The Great Escape*, with its account of masterly systems of pass forging, corruption and blackmailing of guards by sheer daylight cheek, and of Mr. Eric Williams' *The Wooden Horse*, with its astounding piece of schoolboy amateurism turned professional, will already know. They will see it all repeated and confirmed in the eight stories that follow here: stories of escape in the desert, escape through Poland and Russia, escape through the charms of women, escape by canal boat, and perhaps the most horrifying and amazing escape of a war that was probably richer in escape stories than any war that was ever fought—the escape of Squadron Leader McCormac from Malaya to Australia by way of Java. This is an epic of sheer blazing resolution that even *The Wooden Horse* does not excel.

It is not easy to define the common characteristic of these escapes, all by men of the R.A.F., in half a dozen different theatres of war, in circumstances varying from the snows of Polish forests to the scalding dust of the Libyan desert and from the quaysides of the Baltic to the horrors of jungles in Java. It seems to me to be a quality not readily definable by words like courage, resource or even determination, though determination is perhaps the most powerful common attribute these escapers share. It seems to me to amount, in each case, to something like pure cussedness, to a simple blind stubborn refusal to be subjected. There is a sort of illogical pig-headedness about it well expressed in the old phrase, " He's dead but he won't lie down." Every man in these stories was quite determined that however dead he might look or even might feel he was damn well not going to lie down; and the bolder and more brazen his determination the better, in most cases, it succeeded. It has been said, and I think with a good deal of truth, that the R.A.F. were the new Elizabethans, fighting and adventuring in air as the great navigators had fought and adventured on the seas. Both had certain qualities in common that are very English, and a kind of highly skilled amateurism—finding its highest expression, of course, in men like T. E. Lawrence, Wingate and Spencer Chapman—is not the least of them. It is that glorious flexibility, the trick of learning the rules and then of learning how to defy them, turn them upside down and finally make them of infinitely greater profit, that is somewhere at the back of all the exploits related in this book and of all the thousands like them that still lie in the files and archives of official records and personal memory.

It has been said that in the event of another war every official directive and instruction on escape will either have to be amended or abandoned altogether. The enemy knows all our tricks; we shall have to think up others. I do not know if the official escape lectures for the R.A.F. contained any reference to the trick so pleasantly played by the men in the episode *The Women Who Took a Hand;* but it is certainly one of the oldest in the world. The trick of *The Wooden Horse* was an extremely old one too; so was the trick of an irrepressible Canadian navigator friend of mine who charmed his Roman nurse until she looked the other way and he was able to walk serenely out of hospital and into the Vatican. Possibly, now that the enemy knows all the new tricks, we shall necessarily have to make do with the old ones, which are so often the best. All this is conjecture, and I do not think it will worry us. All that is certain is that as long as there are prisons men will try to escape from them; and that as long as there is an R.A.F. it will bring to the problems of escape the qualities of high resource, pure cussedness and that indefinable, damnably annoying refusal to lie down when dead, of which all the stories in this book are such excellent—and, I think, such exciting—examples.

ESCAPE—OR DIE

Charles Edward McCormac was a planter's son, born in Croydon, England, in October, 1915. In 1919 his parents took him to Malaya and he grew up there, learning to speak Malay and some Chinese, Japanese and Tamil, not realising at the time how that was going to help save his life. Educated partly in Australia, he joined the R.A.F. at eighteen and in 1937 went to No. 36 (Torpedo-bomber) Squadron in Malaya as a wireless technician in aircrew. They flew the old Vildebeestes, which had two supple wings strung together with struts and wire. One night in 1939 an aileron jammed and his plane spun ten thousand feet into the sea. The pilot was either drowned or taken by sharks, but McCormac, who was never a docile young man, kept afloat for thirteen hours, hanging on to wreckage till a flying-boat spotted him next morning and picked him up. Having an affection thereafter for flying-boats, he transferred to No. 205 Squadron (Singapore flying-boats). In 1940 he married the daughter of the postmaster at Kuching and was stationed in Singapore on the fateful December 7, 1941.

AFTER they pushed him back into the compound, bleeding, McCormac knew that the next time the Japanese took him to the Y.M.C.A. for interrogation they intended to torture him, presumably to death. What made it worse were the impossible alternatives.

The change had been so swift. A few weeks before, he and Pat had moved into their new house, married quarters near the aerodrome. He was twenty-six and she, twenty-one, was having their first baby. In that same week the Japs landed in Malaya. At first, people in Singapore did not think the Japanese would get very far. Pat was frightened when Charles, as a sergeant wireless operator-gunner, flew in the Catalinas on bombing raids, but when he was not flying he came home at night. And then the defences seemed to crumble, the Catalina squadron was wiped out in a single, devastating Jap raid and the remnants were evacuated to Java.

McCormac did not go with them. He had lived many years in Malaya, where his father had been a planter, before he joined the R.A.F., and because he was an " old hand " the C.O. gave him permission to stay behind and see Pat safely evacuated by ship ; the Japanese had unpleasant ways of dealing with Eurasian girls who married Europeans. They said they were renegades and gave them special treatment. She was lovely in the exotic Eurasian way but to McCormac, standing on the wharf, she looked tearfully forlorn leaning over the rail as the ship pulled out.

He went back briefly to the house, a sinewy man with a bitter downward twist to his mouth, moving from room to room methodically smashing all their things so the Japs would not get them. Then he put on a clean, white shirt that Pat had left out for him and went out to join up with the army in the ground fighting.

Singapore fell a week later and two days after that the Japanese caught McCormac, still on the island, fighting from the roadblocks with a band of volunteers. Out of touch with other troops they had not known the island had fallen, and that was the start of the trouble. It had pleased the Japanese to regard them as saboteurs and they shot two of the band on the spot. Then they noticed McCormac's dirty white shirt. If he had been in the R.A.F. as he claimed, they said, he would be wearing a khaki shirt. He must be a spy and they would deal with him in a suitable way quite soon.

The hell of the cage had started then. Isolated in a banana forest, the Pasir Panjang cage was a hot clearing a hundred yards square, fenced by coils of barbed wire and circled by the trunks and broad leaves of banana trees, a screen round the degradation. Inside the wire the Japanese crammed hundreds of British and Australian soldiers and civilians, giving them each a couple of spoonfuls of rice and a sliver of dried fish most days. Starvation and dysentery are an unpleasant combination and the cage was a focus of sweaty putrescence. By night, arc-lamps round the wire threw a glare over them, though by day the Japanese sent them in heavily guarded batches down to the docks to clear bomb rubble.

The Japanese commandant warned them that they could not hope to escape, but if they tried the punishment would be extreme, not only for the man who tried but for others, too, as a deterrent.

One day, three of them tried. They did not return with their party and it was rumoured that friendly Chinese had hidden them. The thin men in the cage waited for the reprisals, but nothing happened.

A few days later an army sergeant slipped away. Still nothing happened. After another few days seven more did not return from the docks one evening.

At dawn the men in the cage were paraded at attention. They were still at attention at 4 p.m., many held up by friends after collapsing and being clubbed to their feet.

At that hour a party of Japanese officers arrived and a Japanese sergeant wandered thoughtfully among the prisoners as though he were inspecting cattle and picked out eleven men, mostly Australians, all about 6 feet tall. Japanese soldiers dragged them to the middle of the parade square and lashed their hands behind them. Another squad of Japanese soldiers marched briskly up to them and bayoneted all of the eleven in the throats and stomachs. It was quite quick and they were all dead within a minute.

A growl started swelling from the captives. Some of them shuffled a pace or two forward, almost involuntarily ; the machine guns opened up and as three of them toppled to the ground an Australian lieutenant jumped forward and faced them, waving his arms and yelling : " Hold it, you fools. We can't do anything yet."

He turned and walked warily towards the Japanese officers and the captives heard him saying in English that they had violated the rules of war. A Japanese soldier hit him in the back with his rifle butt, the commandant signalled to his men and three of them grabbed the Australian and started to drag him away. The lieutenant managed to twist his head round to the parade again and shouted to them : " Mark these bastards for future reference."

They never saw him again.

The commandant announced that he would not kill any more men at random. If anyone else escaped they would execute every remaining man on his working party.

The following morning they took McCormac to the Y.M.C.A., standing him in a room in front of a Japanese officer wearing baggy khaki pants, puttees, shirt and a sword. He had a flattish head and a Mongoloid, moon-like face, and for the first hour he made McCormac walk in and out bowing and hissing to show respect. They questioned him for the next hour, beating him occasionally with fists.

In interrogations by the Japanese, Western soldiers are absolved from the normal obligation to give name, rank and number only. To avoid torture one is permitted to answer a few questions. For an hour McCormac fended off some questions and answered others. They left him (under guard) for four hours, presumably to let fear work on his morale, and then two Japanese soldiers took him into a room in front of another Japanese officer, clearly a senior one. (A long time after, McCormac discovered that his name was Teruchi, and he was the chief of the Kempei-Tai, the " thought police," in Singapore. The Kempei-Tai's methods were rather more robust than those of the Gestapo.)

Teruchi was short and very broad. He spoke English with an American accent and looked almost European

" You lived in Cairnhill Road ? " he said.

" Yes," said McCormac.

" Then your wife was Eurasian ? "

McCormac stared at Teruchi and did not answer.

" Do not deny it," Teruchi said. " We have been to the house." He took a couple of steps forward and the Japanese soldiers gripped McCormac's arms rigidly. Teruchi said coldly, " You're the curse of the East, you people. And you're a saboteur." He kicked and his boot caught McCormac in the stomach. Teruchi kicked again and again till McCormac collapsed on to his knees, arms still tightly held, feeling he was going to vomit.

" Where is your wife ? " Teruchi said.

" I don't know."

Teruchi said more slowly : " Where . . . is . . . your . . . wife ? "

" Evacuated."

" When, and how ?   And to where ? "

" By sea.   The third of February.   I don't know where to."

" Ah," said Teruchi.   " The *Wakefield*."   McCormac was startled again.   Teruchi seemed to know nearly everything.

" We sank her," Teruchi said with satisfaction, and added unemotionally, " I regret to assure you that there were no survivors.   You can believe me when I say that.   I know."

McCormac felt he wanted to be sick again.

" Where is your wife's family ? "

Pat's parents, her sister and brother were in Kuching, Sarawak, where the father was postmaster.   McCormac had a terrible certainty of what would happen to them if the Japanese located them.

" I don't know," he said.

Moving deliberately, Teruchi pulled his Samurai sword out of its bamboo scabbard.   He held it with two hands clasped round the long handle and waved the blade in front of McCormac's eyes.

" Where is your wife's family ? "

" I don't know," McCormac said stubbornly. " I just have no idea."

Teruchi jabbed but McCormac, tensed and waiting, managed to jerk his head aside in time to save his eye.   The point speared through the fold of skin at the corner of his eye, grated on the bone and tore through and out.   Teeth bared with shock, he twisted his face down and to one side, trying to hunch it protectively between his shoulders while the blood dripped on his thigh.

" Where is your wife's family ? "

" I don't know."   McCormac lifted his head to watch.

Teruchi jabbed again and once more McCormac ducked and the point sliced across his cheek by the corner of his mouth, but did not go through into the mouth.   Teruchi smiled and McCormac, reckless from rage and pain, snarled: " You do that again and I'll bloody well choke you."

Teruchi, still smiling, said gently, " I will see you again.

We will have adequate time and arrangements." He jerked
his head to the Japanese guards; they yanked McCormac to
his feet and handed him over to two guards from the Pasir
Panjang cage, a lean one with a bony face known to the
prisoners as " Kinching " (a very rude Malayan word) and a
plump one known with crude but satisfying humour as
" Fatarse." They walked him the four miles back, opened the
wire gate and kicked him through.

The working parties were back from the docks and an
Australian called Donaldson, with whom McCormac had
become friendly, swabbed the gashes on his face with a strip
torn off McCormac's shirt while he listened to what had
happened. Donaldson was not a soldier, but had been a
businessman in Singapore and was older than most of the
prisoners, about forty, tall, once burly but much thinner now.
He had a sharp nose and a hard, not unpleasant, smile. At
the end he said : " You're in a crook position. If you stay
here they'll give you the treatment all right."

" I know," said McCormac, " and I won't be coming back."
They were sitting together on the filthy dirt and McCormac
muttered : " They might find out where Pat's family are
before it's over. I don't know how long you can hold out.
I never had it before." He sounded grimly flippant.

" They mightn't harm them," suggested Donaldson.

" Pigs might fly."

" Oh God, there must be something."

" I could try and escape," McCormac said. " Not much
chance of getting far and they'd bayonet the rest of you sixteen
blokes in my working party."

" Be a bit hard to encourage you in that one," Donaldson
grunted.

" There's one other alternative," said McCormac, who had
been thinking a lot. " When they come for me they'll probably walk me by road with a couple of guards. I can jump
'em and get a quick bullet—I might be able to take one of the
bastards with me."

" That's a pretty lousy prospect, too," Donaldson said.
To McCormac it hardly seemed real. Too much had
happened that day for the full impact to hit him. He said :

" They got Pat. I wouldn't mind going out and taking one of the swine with me. At least her family might be all right then."

He realised he was probably in for an unpleasant period of waiting. So soon after the surrender the Japs were slowly working through hundreds of interrogations. It might be weeks before they sent for him again. In the morning they marched him to the docks again with the working party and on the way Donaldson edged alongside and said quietly :

" I got an idea last night. Supposing all the working party escaped, all seventeen of us. They'd have no one left to take reprisals against."

McCormac felt a moment of hope but then knew it was no good. " No go," he said. "They wouldn't do it. If they weren't killed in the break they'd die sooner or later in the jungle. Where the hell could they go ? "

" Aussie isn't a bad place."

" Over two thousand miles," McCormac said. " One in fifty might make it, though God knows how. If they stay here they've got a fair chance of being alive when our blokes come back and kick the Japs out."

(At that time, though it sounds strange, most of the prisoners thought Singapore would be freed again in three months. They so badly wanted to think that and did not know how grim the situation was in the Far East.)

" Worth trying anyway," Donaldson said. He had a few words with each member of the party at the docks that day ; two or three liked the idea, a couple were tepidly interested and the rest not interested.

A Portuguese Eurasian was in charge of the party. He was not a prisoner—Eurasians not obviously tainted by European influence were accepted by the Japanese, who wanted to use their labour and special skills. The Portuguese Eurasian directed rubble clearing and they found he was a friend, though necessarily a guarded one. When the Jap guards were watching he bellowed and snarled at the prisoners, but when the guards' backs were turned he whispered in a friendly way out of the corner of his mouth, advised them to go slow on the work and now and then slipped them a cigarette or a little rice from his pocket. He was dark and fat, about forty-five, and McCormac caught him looking at him in a strangely inquiring way several times over the next few days. The man spoke to him more than to the others, too, making excuses to come over and give him instructions.

About five days after the affair with Teruchi the man said to McCormac : " Don't you remember me . . . Rodriguez. I worked on the aerodrome."

McCormac placed him then : remembered him as one of a local, hired labour force building huts and runways and pens for the planes. They talked warmly for a while and McCormac told Rodriguez of the grim position he was in.

" Why don't you escape ? " Rodriguez asked, and McCormac told him why. Rodriguez was not particularly impressed. " If your party all stay here," he said, " their lives are not likely to be long." He hesitated before he spoke again, and then said, " My brother is in Malaya. He is with some Eurasian and Chinese guerrillas in the hills around Kuala Lipis. They raid the Japs. I could tell you where there is a boat for crossing the Johore Straits and you could probably all reach them and join them."

" Why are you offering all this ? " McCormac asked. " We can pay you nothing and only endanger you."

" I want no payment," Rodriguez said. " The Japanese raped my eldest daughter and took her away."

Fatarse and Kinching were in a good humour that night, and so were the other guards, Flatface, Lofty and Harry, the little Korean, cruellest of them all. They had been to watch the mass beheadings of some recalcitrant prisoners and of some Malayans and Chinese suspected of being anti-Japanese. They told the men in the cage that scores of heads had rolled and described the scene with gestures and laughter.

A rumour went round next day that the men in the cage were being sent to Siam, and that in Siam prisoners were dying like flies from disease.

McCormac's face was healing but he was getting edgy, waiting for the next call from Teruchi. The nightmare was becoming near and real. " It'd be funny," he said wryly to Donaldson, " if they took us all to Siam, me included, and that bastard at the Y.M.C.A. couldn't find me. I'd die laughing in Siam." He was not, at the time, conscious of the ironic humour of the last bit. Donaldson pointed it out, saying :

" We'll probably all die there. Look, let's try the gang again about escaping. If Rodriguez'll help us they might come at it."

Once more they approached the others but there were still half a dozen who refused. McCormac thought of the solution.

" Look, Don," he said, " there's no roll call here ; only numbers. So long as there're seventeen on the gang the Japs don't give a damn. There are some other tough blokes in this compound. Why not fix some changeovers till we have seventeen blokes all game for it ? "

That evening they fixed it, crawling among the wretches lying on the filthy ground, talking in whispers till they had six men willing to join them and had arranged for the six they replaced to join other parties. They would make for the hills near Kuala Lipis and join the guerrillas.

Next day they faced the problem of how to escape, and down at the docks, manhandling the crushed concrete and debris, they conspired in whispers whenever they could. Rodriguez, a little fearfully, consented to help them all, but only on condition they did not escape during the day when under his care. He had a wife and six more children to consider.

" If you can get out of the compound at night," he said, " come to my house at Paya Lebar and I'll lead you to the boat."

Back in the cage they made a plan for the following night. The lights always came on at six-thirty, and then the tropical night fell with its usual swiftness. If they could somehow smash the lighting system they could rush the gate when it was dark and scatter into the banana trees and lalang grass. The gate was only a flimsy bamboo affair strung with barbed wire, and just outside it the guards lived in a little atap hut. Other guards patrolled on the other side of the cage, but, if it was dark enough and the escapers were quick enough, most of them could probably reach the jungle before the guards could get into action.

They had all noticed the junction boxes of the electric wiring running along the ground just outside the barbed wire. McCormac said, " I've got long arms. I can reach a couple of them and yank 'em out." They were keyed up to it now, scared but resolved. There was no going back. Anyone who backed out now would be bayoneted in reprisal after the escape. Donaldson had a last grim word before they tried to sleep : " If anyone's wounded or falls behind, there's no going back for them. They'll have to be left."

They all agreed. McCormac, eyeing them, thought what a desperate team they looked—dirty and stinking all of them, with cropped heads and thick beard stubble, hungry and skinny-ribbed, dressed in filthy, ragged shorts and brutalised by circumstance.

He sweated more than usual at the docks next day in case Teruchi should send for him, but the day passed much as usual, except that most of them managed to walk back to the cage with thick sticks hidden in their shorts. Donaldson had found a lump of lead and a couple of feet of thin rope. He knotted the lead to the end of the rope to make a " bolo " club.

About a quarter past six Donaldson and a couple of others stood round McCormac while he reached through the barbed wire and yanked two electric leads out of a junction box. In ones and twos they were all wandering over to the front gate. Six-thirty came and nothing happened. Dusk was gathering in the hot clearing. A Jap soldier walked out of the atap guard hut and crossed to another little atap hutch where the power plant was to switch on the lights. He vanished inside and, presumably as he pulled the switch, a flash lit the hutch from the inside ; there was a puffing explosion and the roof burst into flame. " Christ, it's blown up ! " One of the prisoners nearly shrieked it in hysteria.

Donaldson bellowed " Now ! " and jumped forward, the others streaming after him. The bamboo gate burst in front of them as they trampled through, and at the same moment Jap soldiers came running out of the guard hut and screamed at the sight of them. Two had guns and raised them, but only three or four shots cracked before the prisoners were on them. McCormac smashed a lump of wood into the little Korean's face and the Korean dropped. McCormac brought the wood down again on his skull, which seemed soft. He tugged the bayonet out of the Korean's belt and ran for the banana trees. Dim figures were running with him. He looked back and saw bodies on the ground and Donaldson struggling with one of them. " Come on, you bloody fool," McCormac screamed, and Donaldson seemed to fiddle a while with the body and came running after him. Machine guns opened up on the other side of the cage, and then they were stumbling through the lalang grass, zigzagging between the banana trunks and the huge green leaves that slapped against their faces.

McCormac found himself with Donaldson ; they ran on for several minutes till the crashing noises near them in the jungle grew fainter. They slowed to a walk for a while, sweating, hearts pounding, and breathing noisily, probably as much from tension as the exertion. McCormac felt his mouth was dry and a frightened exultation on him. When he had enough breath to talk he said, " Why in God's name did you wait back there ? "

" Fatarse had my bolo," Donaldson said.

" Why did you let him grab it, you fool ? "

" He didn't," Donaldson said. " It was sunk in his skull and wouldn't come out. I brought his bayonet instead."

They broke into another run after a while, and then walked again till they had their breath before running once more when they came out of the banana trees into secondary jungle, endless lalang grass to their waists and the occasional stunted banana tree in the rocky ground. It was fairly dark but they could just see enough to dodge the obstacles and made good time, veering through the outskirts of Singapore town, where many Eurasians lived and where they might pass as Eurasians instead of being stopped by any Japanese they came across. Once they thought they saw a party of Japanese as they crossed a road, but they dived into the grass again on the other side and were not hailed.

It was several miles to Paya Lebar, and when they were out

of the rubber trees they moved warily, hunched low with only their heads peering nervously over the dry tips of the lalang grass, which rattled with a terrifying noise as they brushed through. Some time after ten o'clock Donaldson picked out the loom of the big tree that Rodriguez had said was about fifty yards down the track from his house. The darkness was heavy and still, almost cool after the steamy heat of the day, but they were both sweating and trembling and sat down by the trunk of the tree.

Ten minutes later the grass rustled ; they crouched silently, and as two shadows neared they recognised two of the party. During the next quarter of an hour several more arrived, and McCormac crawled off round to the back of Rodriguez's house and knocked quietly on the door. In a few seconds Rodriguez opened it, dressed in slacks and a dirty singlet. Somehow he had heard of the explosion by the cage and was nervous.

" I think there is an alarm," he whispered. " I cannot risk my family by taking you to the boat." He told McCormac exactly where it was, hauled up on the mud of the mangrove swamp near Kranji Point, about three hundred yards west of the spot where the Causeway threaded across the narrow strait to Johore. He took McCormac's hand and pressed some paper into it (it was three hundred and fifty Jap dollars), squeezed the hand, whispered " Good luck," and vanished behind the door. McCormac crawled back to the tree and found that fifteen of the party had arrived.

They waited nearly half an hour for the other two, but they never came, and three or four said they thought they had seen them shot or bayoneted in the escape. It seemed fairly sure that two of the Jap guards were dead too, and probably at least one more. They all knew now that if they were recaptured there would be no simple ceremony such as a bayonet in the stomach, but a more prolonged business— probably the bamboo treatment, where a man is lashed down, tightly spreadeagled over some young bamboo shoots. The bamboo grows some five inches a day and the tips are sharp enough to be neither stopped nor diverted by a human body. Or there were other methods, such as the bamboo driven through the rectum. Once on the way to the dock labour they had seen a pregnant native woman killed in that way.

In twos and threes they set off for Kranji Point, the groups keeping about twenty yards between them, led by McCormac, who knew the area better than anyone else. Again there were several miles to cover and McCormac tried to keep in the gloom of the rubber trees that bordered the Yio Chu Kang Road, led them by a burned-out village and around Seletar radio station. Near Kranji Point they ran across the Naval Base Road and slipped in among the twisted trunks and roots of the mangroves. They closed up to keep together and a minute later McCormac led the compact group on to the mud flats. Either by luck or judgment he had led them well ; on the mud over to the left by the water's edge lay two small boats, and almost in the same instant he and Donaldson and the others in front saw dark shapes moving about ten yards away.

Those in front tried to back ; a shout came from the dim shapes and one of the escapers yelled " Japs ! " More startled shouts, and McCormac was running with some of the others at the dark shapes. There were two or three orange flashes and the jarring cracks of point-blank rifle shots, and the two groups tangled in struggle. McCormac hacked like a maniac with his bayonet ; a Jap fired two more shots from a machine pistol and McCormac crashed into him and they both went down, the Jap underneath. McCormac was stabbing him and suddenly it was all over.

Someone they thought was a Jap was running into the fringe of the mangroves, bodies were lying on the ground and others were gasping on their feet. There were eight escapers left on their feet, and the bodies of six Japanese soldiers and several escapers on the ground. All the people lying on the ground seemed to be dead.

Someone said in a hoarse whisper, " Come on, for Christ's sake. There'll be hundreds of them here in a minute." They ran over to one of the little boats and shoved it down towards the water ; it slid fairly easily over the slime into the oily water and they tumbled in, found a paddle lying in the bottom, and one of them dug the blade into the water and drove the little boat slowly out into the strait.

After the first fumbling seconds they quietened down and were about two hundred yards out, making a little headway through the quiet sea, when a searchlight flicked into brightness on the Causeway ; one moment they had been thankfully marooned in the husk of darkness, and then, full-grown from birth, the beam lay flat and dazzling on the water. It started to sweep and McCormac whispered sharply, " Down."

Flat on the floorboards they huddled under the level of the gunwales, conscious of soft light as the beam slid across the boat, then darkness and light again as the beam swung back. It played around them for a long time and they waited in terror for the sound of an approaching launch. It seemed to be hours before the light flicked off. The Japanese must have thought it was an empty boat adrift, because no launch came. When at last they sat up again the scattered lights on the shore and the Causeway had retreated into the distance and they did not know which way they were facing.

" We've been drifting," McCormac said. " There's a hell of a strong tide here and we're probably moving out to sea."

" Thank God for that," said Donaldson. " The farther the better."

There was no point paddling when they did not know where they were going and they spent the time investigaing the boat. It was small and old, and on the floorboards up in the bows they found a small drum of water, some strips of dried fish and some rotten fruit.

Dawn seemed a long time coming and they lay quietly in the boat until the fresh pink in the east showed flat grey sea with the dead, oily look one finds in the tropics. As the light grew stronger the land showed as a dark line low on the sea in the track of the sun. In turns they tried to paddle towards it, but the tide was still running strongly and it did not seem that they were making headway. The boat had a short mast but no sail, and they all took their singlets off and were knotting them together to make a crude sail when Donaldson noticed two dots in the sky over the land. In seconds they knew that the dots were aircraft heading their way. The planes were quite low and flew steadily towards them —seemed to be passing to one side of them when both swung towards the little boat.

" Zeros," McCormac said tersely. " Overboard ! " And
he dived over the side into the water, which was quite warm.
Someone said, " Jesus, the sharks ! "   Two or three of the
others jumped over and the rest stayed in the boat, warily
watching the fighters, which curved in and slid, roaring, low
over the water to one side of the boat, dropping wing-tips to
watch.   In line astern they climbed a little, turned steeply,
slanted down and ran in for the kill.   In panic, the last men
in the boat were tumbling over the side and, as the first
flashes came from the leading fighter, McCormac, who had
swum about twenty yards from the boat, took a deep breath
and went under.   When he came up the water was lacy with
foam torn up by cannon shells and the boat was upside down.
The leading fighter was turning in again.   He saw a couple of
other heads on the water and then he went under once more.
When he surfaced with the strain of trying to hold his breath
the water was frothing again as the second fighter slammed in
a blare of noise overhead.   Each fighter made two more firing
passes; then they circled once briefly and turned off back to
the land.

McCormac swam over to the upturned keel moving slug-
gishly in the water.   Donaldson reached it at the same time,
and McCormac remembers the beads of water glistening in
his stubbly beard.   Two more heads bobbed beside them, the
owners panting and splashing.   McCormac recognised them
as two British soldiers whom he knew as Roy and Skinny.
The foam lashed up by the shells was dissolving but there
were no other heads in sight.

Donaldson panted, " Let's turn this damn thing over
again," and they reached up clumsily to the keel, heaved on
one side and the boat came slowly over, full of water and with
the gunwales just above the surface.

Someone said, " Get in, for Christ's sake, away from the
sharks," and they floundered over the gunwales, nearly turning the boat over again.   Virtually floating inside her, they
looked for the other four.   There were no signs.   McCormac
said laconically, " Sharks or bullets."   There seemed to be
nothing more to say.

When they had their breath they started bailing with their

hands and slowly the gunwales lifted so that the water stopped slopping into her. Shells had torn a chunk out of the bow, but otherwise, by some miracle, there were only two neat holes under the water-line, and McCormac plugged these roughly with strips torn off the remains of his shirt.

In half an hour the boat was riding reasonably easily. Six inches of water still sloshed over the floorboards, but they were exhausted and it was cooler to leave it there. They looked again for the missing four, but they were still missing, without trace, and it was then that they discovered that the drum of water, the paddle and the food were also missing.

Away to the east the land still lay thinly on the horizon and they hoped the turning tide would swing them in again to the Malayan coast, where they could get ashore unnoticed. By noon they knew unmistakably the line was getting fainter, and after about three hours they could not see it any more.

Now thirst was worrying them. The heat was heavy and endless and they lay in the water on the floorboards ; it was cooler like that, but by dusk McCormac could feel his tongue swelling. Darkness brought coolness but they could not sleep. Miraculously, round about midnight, rain poured for nearly an hour, fresh and cool, and they lay on their backs with their mouths open and also soaked it up in their filthy rags and squeezed it into their mouths.

At dawn they were alone on the sea. By noon their tongues were swelling again and McCormac knew that they, the last four out of the seventeen, were probably going to die too. They lay there quietly.

About four o'clock Skinny, a wiry little gunner from Wales with a broken nose and two teeth missing, said sharply, " God, here they come again." His voice was frightened and his rigid face stared over the gunwale. They looked and saw the dot low in the air. No one spoke until McCormac said, " It's coming this way." In a few seconds there was no doubt.

Someone, either Skinny or Roy, said, " Only one this time," and Donaldson growled, " That's quite enough."

They watched it growing larger, undecided whether to chance the sharks or the bullets. McCormac, the airman, suddenly said, " That's not a fighter. It's too big. It's a multi-engined job."

The plane grew swiftly and McCormac saw that it was a big flying boat. He recognised it and said, surprised, " It's a Dornier. A Jerry ! "

" With a Jap crew," Donaldson snarled.

" Japs have got their own flying boats," said McCormac.

Skinny said excitedly, " Let's wave. They might pick us up. We'll have a chance with the Jerries."

" They'll hand us over, you fool."

The big aircraft swept straight towards them, engines swelling louder. Skinny jumped up in the boat, waving his singlet and shouting. The plane swept about a hundred feet over their heads and in a few seconds it was a quarter of a mile past, going away. McCormac did not know whether to feel sorry or glad, and then the flying boat slowly turned, kept turning, right round, and came sliding back at them. A wing dipped as it roared over and then it turned very slowly again and suddenly the nose dipped. It was a mile away and it was some seconds before they heard the sound of the engines dying. It landed in a shower of glistening spray and turned towards them.

McCormac was planning to jump over the side and swim away, remembered the sharks and changed his mind. Almost hypnotically they watched the flying boat approach till they could see oil streaks under the wings, the rivets in the dull, grey metal and a face vaguely behind the windscreen. A sudden burst of engine and the hull swung against the boat. A door in the side snapped open and in the frame stood a white man. He was stocky, young and blond, dressed in a white shirt and slacks. Grinning at them, he shouted something in a foreign tongue. McCormac caught the word "*Komm.*"

" Typical —— Hun," Donaldson said.

The man leaned out and caught Skinny's arm and Skinny put a foot on the door ledge and was heaved into the plane. One by one the others scrambled after him, helped by the man in white. They all collapsed on the floor and McCormac started vomiting. He lifted his head after a while and saw the white man and a little brown man looking down at him. For a moment he did not comprehend, and then a wild thrill shot through him.

He said in Malay, " Who are you ? " and the white man answered in a language very like Malay:

" Royal Netherlands Air Force."

McCormac turned with a shout to the others: " They're not Huns and Japs. They're Dutch and Javanese." The others looked dumbly and McCormac turned back to the white man and said in Malay (which is similar to Javanese) : " I am Royal Air Force."

The white man grinned, they shook hands, and McCormac started vomiting again. The other three suddenly realised and there was a lot of excited shouting and laughing and shaking hands all round. The little Javanese wireless operator brought them mugs of coffee and then more coffee as they drank it down. Some cold rice and veal followed and in between bites McCormac told the Dutchman briefly where they had come from, and how, adding some heartfelt thanks. The Dutchman beamed sympathetically. McCormac asked him then where they were bound and the Dutchman said they were heading for a swamp near Medan, in northern Sumatra.

" Thank God ! " McCormac said. " We can get in touch with our troops there."

The Dutchman looked at him curiously and said, " Sumatra has fallen. The Japanese have overrun it." The tragedy must have shown in McCormac's face because the Dutchman went on : " There are no Japs where we are landing. We have to evacuate some people there." He added awkwardly, " A lot of people. A full load. We will have to leave you there."

McCormac asked quietly if they were returning for more and the Dutchman shook his head. He said anxiously that there were some guerrillas fighting in the mountains in central Sumatra and that the four escapers should be able to link up with them.

It was bitter news, but after the rescue from the boat the four could have taken almost anything. They never did find out where the flying boat came from ; the Dutchman would not say. All they knew was that it would never happen again in a million times. Even landing to pick them up, the Dutch-man said, was an unusual whim, a last-minute change of mind, and all the way to the swamp near Medan, Donaldson kept saying, shaking his head, " It's a miracle, a bloody miracle." And so it was.

They touched down at dusk off a dark line of man-groves, and as they taxied in, people seemed to seep out from between the tangled trees, dozens of them, white and Eurasian, the remnants of isolation, some of them weeping to see the plane. Two of the Javanese crew inflated a rubber dinghy and ferried McCormac and the other three to the mud. A very old native greeted them gravely ; he seemed to be a local official and must have been nearly seventy, bald and toothless, with an incredibly wrinkled face like an old brown prune, and a sarong with the skirt tucked between his skinny legs.

They watched the Javanese ferry the women and children to the flying boat, making about ten trips till McCormac had counted sixty passengers squeezed into the plane. The engines spun explosively and the plane ran a long way over the water till it lifted into the gloom.

The old man beckoned and they followed him into the mangroves, stumbling over twisted roots in the darkness till they came to a rough trail that led through jungle. Now the excitement was over unutterable weariness was falling on them and they walked in a kind of numb misery, almost past caring. Roy was inclined to stagger as though he had been drinking. He was a slightly-built, sallow private, almost weedy, and he had had dysentery nearly all the time for weeks, so that he was fairly weak. He endured it stoically, but had hardly said a word since the escape. McCormac and Donaldson took his arms and tried to help him and they went about two miles like this till they came out suddenly into a native kampong in a clearing.

Dimly against the stars they saw atap huts perched primly on stilts above the ground ; the native led them to one, pointed up and they climbed the rickety ladder. Inside they collapsed on the rush-strewn floor. The native lit a small oil lamp and went out again. In a few minutes he was back with a woman who was carrying a jar of water. She had to refill the jar for them three times, and then she brought a bowl of rice, though they could only swallow a few mouthfuls. Since leaving the mangroves they had hardly spoken ; everything seemed so unreal. Silent, they fell asleep.

All the next day they stayed in the hut except when the colicky cramps of dysentery forced them out into the fringes of the jungle that crowded round the kampong, tangled, thick, spongy and green, and full of still and clammy heat, though only a few pale blades of sunshine filtered through the matted foliage overhead. Roy was so weak that he took a long time to climb the ladder each time. He said his legs felt like rubber.

The old native came and squatted on his haunches and talked a long time in Javanese with McCormac. They must not stay long in the village because the Japanese might return. They had been through once. Their best plan was to make for the mountains inland where some guerrillas were thought to be living near Lake Toga. Or they might make for Java where they might find white troops still hiding in the jungle.

McCormac said to the others : " Java's five hundred miles away. Let's try the mountains first. It'll be cooler there and we can get our strength back." Everyone agreed.

Streams of natives kept climbing up the ladder to peer at them ; little brown people with soft brown eyes and red, betel-stained teeth. They were solemn and a little scared at first, but after McCormac chatted to them in Malay they giggled like children and tried to touch him. The same woman brought them chicken and rice, durians and turtle eggs.

" I hope these jokers aren't fattening us for the kill," Donaldson said. He knew almost as well as McCormac that the unwritten law of the East forbade the starving stranger to be turned away—though it said nothing about forbidding the host from knifing the stranger afterwards.

On the afternoon of the third day in the kampong the old native squatted gravely beside McCormac again and said with impassive politeness that they must leave that evening. A native, he said, could earn 400 guilders reward from the Japanese for reporting a white man and it was not good to stay too long in one place.

McCormac nodded. He had been expecting it. All of them felt better after the rest and even Roy had lost some of his haggard look. They ate a lot of rice and chicken and about two hours before dusk the old man took them to a jungle trail. He said the mountains were six days' walk away. It seemed that every native in the village clustered round, chattering and grinning, as McCormac thanked the old man, the four shook hands with him and the old man gave them a toothless grin. The villagers giggled and waved and the four were filing along the jungle trail, McCormac in front. As the man who spoke Malay and knew the jungle better than any of them he was, by tacit consent, leader of the party.

For the past two days he had been lecturing them on the jungles and native customs. The jungle could be a friend as well as an enemy, he had told them. It could hide them and give them food and water. And it could kill them if they let it. The worst enemy was the kraut, the little black and gold snake about eighteen inches long and as thick as an index finger. It was supposed to go for the eyes, and then you'd had it. He had warned them, too, about scorpions, spiders, pythons and wild boars.

They were quiet for the first quarter of an hour as they padded along, wary eyes on every hanging creeper and bush that brushed across the trail. McCormac suddenly said : " We'll stop just before dusk and clear a spot to sleep."

The trail curled in and out of enormous trees with ten feet thick trunks that towered till their tops vanished in the smoky gloom that filled the jungle between the dank earth and the tangle of boughs and foliage and creeper that shut out the sky. The odd sliver of light slanting through looked faded and dusty. McCormac found the sweat soaking him and the air was so hot and heavy that breathing was like feeling vapour seeping into his lungs.

Feeling the gloom was thickening, he stopped and said: " This'll do. Let's get off the track in case someone trips over us in the night."

About twelve feet into the jungle they tore a clear patch in the undergrowth and lay in a huddle on the pulpy earth.

Donaldson said acidly after a while: " Christ, we stink! " Thirst was nagging again. McCormac said they could probably lick some dew off the leaves in the morning and then they would have to suck stones till they came to a stream.

Skinny suddenly screamed and they jerked up in fright. He was thrashing about against the foliage crying, " Snake, I've been bitten! " In the darkness chills swept all of them. A strangled cry broke from Donaldson and he slapped madly at something in the darkness. He was yelling, " It's got me," and then McCormac felt the sharp stab of something in his leg followed by another in the small of his back and then another. He dashed through the undergrowth back to the trail, slapping madly, followed by the others, nearly panicking. Over one of the bites McCormac felt a tiny object moving under his hand. He squeezed it and suddenly knew what it was.

He said in a voice shaky from relief, " It's O.K. They're only ants." Slowly, as he assured them, the heavy breathing gave way to salty curses.

" We'd better sleep up in the trees," McCormac said. " Get up about ten feet and tuck yourself in the fork of a branch and wrap some creepers round you."

The others would not believe it could be done at first, but McCormac got up on a huge branch that was about three feet thick where it joined the trunk ; he wedged himself in that spot, wriggling under some creeper that circled the bough. The bark was spongy and moss-covered, and felt cool. The others tried it then, gingerly and with grunts and curses as they fumbled in the darkness. " Like a lot of ruddy chooks roosting," said Donaldson, surprised that he felt reasonably secure and not unbearably uncomfortable.

As night settled a scream in the jungle nearby made McCormac's skin crawl in terror till he realised what it was. In the frightened silence that followed he said, " It's O.K. Only a monkey, or maybe a little Malayan bear." The night chorus of the jungle was starting; more eerie screeches abruptly split the heavy silence and now and then they heard rustlings in the undergrowth.

That night frayed their nerves badly ; it seemed that it would never end. Now and then one or the other dozed off fitfully and then woke in stiff discomfort, tormented by thirst, or because of another piercing shriek nearby. They were all terrified that krauts might be slithering into them.

Dawn was never so welcome. As it filtered through the foliage they lost most of their fears and clambered stiffly, heavy with fatigue, down to the trail. McCormac went rooting round in the jungle and they heard him cry in a minute, " Come and get it." They found him picking little things like hairy chestnuts off a vine. " Rambutans," he said. He showed them how to split them and then crunch the nuts, which, surprisingly, tasted sweet like a mixture of fruits.

Donaldson found another bush nearby bearing a lot of large berries that he said looked like prickly pear.

" I've never seen them before," McCormac said. He peeled the skin of one and nibbled at the soft pulp inside. " Tastes all right," he said. " Usually if a thing tastes O.K. it's fairly safe." They each ate several of the berries which had an acidy tang and helped them forget their thirst. They all tore slim branches off the bush, peeled the twigs and leaves off to make themselves staves, and started walking along the trail again.

Every half-hour or so they rested for a few minutes, mainly for Roy's sake, though at this stage he was going quite well. Setting off from one of these rests McCormac suddenly jumped and there was a confused flurry as he clubbed his stave on the ground by a trailing creeper. He looked up panting and held up the stave with what looked like a little thong coiled round it. " Kraut," he said, and they looked grimly at it. It was quite dead, more black than gold, and had a tiny bullet head.

That afternoon McCormac stopped and said he could smell burnt sandalwood. He thought it probably meant there was a kampong near, and they went forward very cautiously till they saw a clearing in front with a few atap huts. Two or three natives in loin cloths were wandering about and McCormac suggested they stay clear and watch, in case there were Japanese about. They filtered off the track into the jungle and lay watching the kampong, getting excited when they saw native women drawing water from a wooden trough. Near it was a pile of what McCormac thought were edible roots like yams.

Night came swiftly as usual, and the sky was flecked with thousands of stars that shed a faint light. McCormac led the way, creeping, into the kampong, and they gathered like furtive animals round the water trough, drinking and lifting their heads at any sound. A cooking fire was burning on the other side of the clearing with a few natives around it, but none of them came near the trough. The four grabbed handfuls from the pile of yams and crept through to the trail on the other side of the village. For half a mile McCormac led them along this and then they climbed once more to the low branches of one of the trees, gnawed at the sweet, crisp flesh of the yams, and tried once more to sleep.

In the morning they finished the yams and walked on, with occasional rests, for several hours till Roy started stumbling again and said he was too tired to go on.

" This tree sleeping joke's no ruddy good," Donaldson said. " Let's try and find a spot clear of ants."

Off the trail they tore a clear patch where there seemed to be no ants, laid leaves and ferns over it and sank down thankfully. It was fairly comfortable and they slept. Around dusk they found more berries and rambutans and decided to sleep in the same spot that night. Sleep they did, without trouble from ants, and felt fresher in the morning when they started walking again.

That afternoon they came out of the jungle to a road, a black ribbon of bitumen winding through the trees, just wide enough to thin the tangle overhead so that a misty brightness fanned through the gaps.

Cautiously crossing it McCormac let out a wild cry as he almost put his foot into a trickle of water running in a hollow on the other side. It seemed to be seeping from some rocks and was a little dirty, but they lapped like dogs and sucked with their lips at the tiny, rather slimy rivulets that furrowed the earth under the rocks.

They stayed by the road for three days and nights, clearing

a patch—a sort of nest of leaves and ferns—a few yards in the jungle, drinking water, foraging, eating what berries they could find, resting, sleeping and watching the road while their strength and morale came back. All that time they saw several ox carts pass along the road, half a dozen battered old native lorries and one neat staff car, full of Japanese. That one car decided them to head for the mountains.

On the trail again, away from the sea and rising slightly, the going was worse. The trail was often overgrown ; they had to keep brushing their way through and brambles among the bushes kept tearing across their skin, particularly on the legs. Before the day was over they were all deeply scratched and frightened of the scratches festering in the dirty skin.

All that day they had found no water and very few of the juicier fruits. The hunger that night was nearly as bad as the thirst and the next day was even worse. By noon they were desperate for water after all the sweating, but headed on hoping to find a stream. At nightfall Roy was lightheaded, giving little gasps. McCormac felt his tongue swelling again in a mouth that was dried up and leathery and said he was going to try something he had once read about when he was young.

He took off his shorts, tied one of the legs at the bottom with a piece of creeper, filled it with handfuls of earth and urinated into it. As the liquid filtered through the dirt and the shorts he caught it in the dried gourd of a durian. The others watched him with a fascinated intensity as he sipped a little into his mouth and swallowed it with wry disgust.

" God, it's bitter," he said, but kept sipping till he had finished it.

Skinny said, " I'm game," and did the same himself, and then the others followed suit. They dry-retched a couple of times afterwards, but it seemed to help a little and they slept afterwards.

In the morning Donaldson said, " This is no bloody good. If we don't find water and food it's going to be curtains. Let's get back to the road." The others did not argue. The lure of water would have taken them anywhere.

They found practically no fruit that day except some very small berries that tasted so bitter McCormac said they might be dangerous, and they did not eat them. Rooting around for fruit, however, McCormac came across a rotten tree-trunk with hundreds of little tree bugs crawling over it, quite small and pasty-white. Under McCormac's directions they collected about two hundred of them, wrapped them in a singlet and bashed them against a tree-trunk until they opened up the singlet and found the bugs crushed into a reddish pulp. They were much too hungry to feel squeamishness now and ate most of the pulp, not thinking or caring what it was, only conscious that it was food and tasted a little " high."

That night they slept little, moving on as soon as it was light enough to see, all feeling dizzy but driven on by the prospect of water and taking turns to help Roy. Around noon they came out of the trail on to the road and for an hour lay licking at the water.

Three more days they rested by the road, sleeping in the old " nest." More cunning about food now, they tried nibbling at fern roots and young green bamboo shoots. The taste was raw and earthy, but they did not mind that. McCormac found two or three flying foxes which had apparently killed themselves by hitting trees, and they tore the skins off and picked the raw flesh out with their fingers. It was stringy, but Donaldson said it tasted like old rabbit.

At one time there was a whoop from Donaldson as he was crossing the road. He dived down, grabbing at something, and stood with a little green frog in each hand, grinning all over his dirty bearded face. He skinned them, passed the few slivers of pale white flesh round and they swallowed them raw. An hour later they vomited it up.

Roy's dysentery was bad again, and on the fourth day they started south along the road in the hope of finding another kampong where they might get help. McCormac said there was bound to be the occasional village. A moon at night shed a little light, and he sensibly suggested they walk at night when it was cooler (and safer from Japs) and sleep by day.

They took it easily the first night, covering only about six miles because Roy was shaky, and finding a lot of the juicy " prickly pear " berry. During the next day they slept a few feet off the road in the jungle, and at dusk started walking.

For the first time they saw a clump of coconut palms in what seemed to have once been a cultivated patch but was now thickly covered in undergrowth. Donaldson saw them first and let out an excited bellow. McCormac climbed one as he had often seen the natives do and knocked some of the nuts to the ground. They were green and a little soft, but they bashed them against the trunks until they split, swallowed the rich, sweet " milk " and sucked the pulpy meat. That night they carried some of the nuts with them and ate them at dawn before they slept.

Towards dawn on the fourth night the gloomy funnel of the road opened into a kampong. They stopped on the edge watching the dark shadows of the huts, then followed McCormac off the road, crawling into a clump of bushes on the fringe of the kampong. As the light grew they saw it was a big place and counted over sixty flimsy thatched huts ; about four hundred inhabitants, McCormac guessed. The natives started moving round soon after first light, and it was torment to see the women carrying earthen jars of water and smell food from the cooking fires. Roy's lips were cracked and swollen and he kept doubling up from griping pains, but McCormac would not let them budge. He said stubbornly they had to see first if any Japs were about.

" Even if there aren't," he said, " it'd be crazy to walk in in broad daylight. Maybe they're friendly, maybe not."

They waited in anguish all day, and when it was dark McCormac said, " If I'm not back in an hour, beat it." He crawled out of the bushes into the kampong, walked across the hard-packed earth, passing a couple of natives who took no interest in him in the dark, and stopped at the door of a hut he had marked earlier in the day. Looking inside the doorless frame, he confirmed that it was the village coffee shop and stood a few seconds taking it all in, the mud floor and bamboo tables where three Indonesians in sarongs and bajus (singlets) sat. There was a kerosene tin of coffee over a small flame, shelves of cheap bottles of " pop " and a little wooden counter. Behind the counter lounged an expressionless fat Chinese of about fifty in a baju.

McCormac walked in and instantly the eyes of the Indonesians were staring at his gaunt, filthy body. Going straight up to the counter, he said, " Manna Jippon ? "

The Chinaman's face did not change. He eyed McCormac for a moment and answered in Malay that there were no Japanese in the village.

McCormac said, " I have no food."

" Where are you from ? " the Chinaman countered.

McCormac pointed vaguely north-west.

" There are others ? "

" One is sick with the run-run," McCormac said evasively.

" Wait," said the Chinaman and went out of the door. McCormac waited nervously, and in about three minutes the Chinaman came back. Behind him walked an old man with a thin face and a few white hairs on his head, and McCormac felt a flood of relief as he saw the old man, apparently the headman of the village, was wearing Queen Wilhelmina's medal, a silver badge strung on a chain and hanging almost to his navel. It was a sure sign that the village was friendly to whites.

Half an hour later the four of them were lying comfortably on the rushes of a hut. They had drunk jars of water and eaten a terrifically hot curry that left Donaldson gasping for breath and swilling his mouth out with more water. To Roy's intense embarrassment, a native woman came in with some white powder wrapped in a green leaf, and she firmly rolled him over and injected the powder into his rectum. After that they slept and in the morning Roy's dysentery had gone.

A young Chinese of about twenty came to see them and introduced himself as Nang Sen. He was brisk and friendly, with a mouth full of gold teeth which he constantly showed. The Japs had been through the village some weeks previously, he told them, and raped some of the girls. That was one reason for their friendly reception. He chatted a while of other things and suddenly said, " What are you planning to do ? "

" Stay away from the Jipponese," McCormac said. " We wish to find some troops who may be free still."

" I will be driving a lorry south in a few days," Nang Sen

said. " You can come with me, and perhaps later you can get to Java, where there may be some white troops."

For two days they did little but rest and eat platters of curried rice, sweet boiled roots and green shoots, and by that time a little healthy flesh was visible on their skinny frames. One of the old headman's younger wives brought them jars of water and they washed, feeling much fresher afterwards. The woman dressed their scratches, which were inclined to fester, and took their filthy shorts and singlets away. She boiled them for hours, McCormac discovered, but they were still discoloured with ingrained sweat and grime when she brought them back, though at least they did not smell any more.

On the third day they watched, fascinated, a village wedding, which lasted all day. From cockcrow the bride sat in a chair in the middle of the kampong. She could not have been more than fifteen, though she was fully (and very agreeably) developed, dressed in a simple sarong and a bead-embroidered baju that covered her shoulders. All day she sat silently with her head downcast, looking demurely at the ground while her bridegroom sat beside her receiving guests and gifts and chatting volubly. As the sun disappeared he stood up, lifted her gently to her feet, loosened his sarong and wrapped it loosely around both of them. Under its cover she dropped her own sarong to the ground and they walked together to the hut that had been prepared for them.

A couple of evenings later Nang Sen led them to a battered lorry about twelve years old with hardly a speck of paint left on it. In the back were tins of petrol and some smelly sheets of raw rubber, which they crawled under. The engine rattled and roared, Nang Sen clashed the gears and the lorry jerked into motion.

The lorry bounced along the road all night, and just before dawn Nang Sen ran it off the road behind some bushes in soft, treeless ground that was virtually a swamp. He gave them a little rice and suggested they also pick some fruit, which was growing freely. McCormac came back from his foraging with some dark, shiny green leaves which he said he picked from what he thought was a cinchona bush, about the size of a rhododendron. He handed them round and said,

" Chew them. There's probably quinine in them and we could do with some of that." The leaves were almost unbearably bitter, which seemed to confirm that they might contain quinine. McCormac insisted they keep chewing, and it was a wise precaution because mosquitoes were already buzzing out of the swamp around them. Nang Sen watched their grimaces with his golden-toothed grin and finally handed them some of his betel nut, wrapped in leaves. They chewed at the nut and the sharp taste made it easier to keep chewing, at the same time, the bitter cinchona leaves.

Before they slept Nang Sen pointed out a little green palm in the jungle; it was only a few feet high and he beckoned them over to it. The base was soft and swollen and he jabbed a knife into it; a pale greenish liquid bubbled out and he caught some in a tin bowl. He sipped and offered some to McCormac, and McCormac gingerly sipped and found it was slightly sour but not unpleasant. " Water," Nang Sen said, and added that the palm grew in the more open country, where a man need never die of thirst.

They slept all day and at night rattled again along the road till dawn, when they hid the truck again and slept. Next night was the same except that at dawn they came to a small kampong and had rice and slept in a hut with Nang Sen, who had a cache of petrol hidden in the kampong. McCormac asked Nang Sen exactly what his job was, but Nang Sen only laughed and said he did not mind helping them as he had been fighting the Japanese for years.

They travelled for two more nights, covering hundreds of miles, lying on top of the rubber now, which was considerably softer than the hard floor of the lorry. They passed a couple of Japanese lorries without challenge and jolted along the road without talking much, feeling reasonably relaxed, conscious of an air of unreality about it all but accepting it without question.

One morning Nang Sen slowed and steered the lorry off the road behind some trees and into a sort of ditch. He seemed to know where he was and they trailed after him through rubber trees for half an hour till they came to a kampong and followed him into a hut. He brought in a little Chinese woman who, he said, was his sister ; she was a volatile, bird-like creature and shrilly, though fairly good-humouredly, cursed them in Malayan for being so filthy. First she pushed them outside to wash in a rain tub, then dressed their sores and handed them thin cotton trousers and short smocks in the Chinese style.

For two days they rested, sleeping in rope beds and sniffing the incense from joss sticks burning by a little Buddha in a dark corner of the hut. It was, as Donaldson said, " a damn sight better than smelling ourselves."

About four o'clock one morning the little sister woke them, and they followed her through more rubber trees till at first light they came out to the edge of a wide river. A little sampan was moored there and, prodded by the little sister, they clambered in and she poled them briskly out into the stream. Round a bend in the river McCormac caught sight of a native town, some buildings looming sturdily in the centre over sprawling acres of atap and bamboo huts. The little sister nodded at it and said, " Palembang." The sampan glided by the bones of some bombed and burnt-out wrecks poking forlornly above the water, and the Chinese girl steered it on to the mud at the far side. Almost wordlessly they trailed after her through some secondary jungle and came to a railway line and a goods train of low trucks covered with tarpaulins.

She told them to climb under the tarpaulin, hide under the sheets of rubber inside and wait. " Friends come," she said and turned and walked off. They lay for an hour under the rubber with doubts starting to nibble at their minds. Jabbering voices sounded along the track. A louder voice, obviously Japanese, started shouting and, to McCormac's horror, bodies started scrambling into the trucks. The four lay in silent fright under the rubber while bodies settled themselves around them and continued jabbering. Mercifully the Japanese voice did not seem to be among them. A little later the trucks abruptly jerked and with a rattling and clanking of buffers started to move.

The four lay sweating under the rubber for another half-hour, wondering fearfully what was going to happen, and suddenly someone pulled the rubber sheeting aside and they blinked tensely up at some Javanese grinning down at them.

One of the Javanese said, " You can sit up now. It is safe." Grinning natives handed them each a cigarette and a small parcel of rice cakes wrapped in leaves.

" How did you know we were here ? " McCormac asked after a while, and one of the Javanese said simply, " We were told."

" Who told you ? " McCormac asked.

The Javanese said with a polite smile, " It is not wise to know all." He added that it was the method the natives used to avoid being conscripted for labour by the Japanese.

The trucks rattled along all day, passing through kampongs, jungle and secondary jungle, and the men in the truck slept some of the time on the soft rubber. McCormac judged they were moving south-south-east.

Just before dusk the Javanese woke them. The train was panting up a long rise and the speed was dropping off. The little Javanese who did most of the talking said they must jump off the train there ; he pointed across the jungle and said they must find their way to Oosthaven. One by one the four swung their legs over the side of the trucks, dropped lightly to the earth and ran crouching into the bushes. It was secondary jungle, thick long grass and bushes and the occasional rubber tree.

Together again they ran, still crouching, till they were well away from the railway, made another nest for sleeping that night and in the morning trekked across scrubby country. Several times that day they came across small trees, almost like large bushes, which bore dozens of a little fruit with a soft green skin, vaguely like the " prickly pear " they had eaten further north. McCormac tried one and found a soft stone inside, slightly bitter but not unpleasant. An hour or so later they began to be aware of a sensation that none of them had been in any condition to feel for some time. They had, apparently, swallowed large doses of a potent aphrodisiac, and the symptoms lasted several hours, reaching a peak of uncomfortable and disturbing acuteness.

Skinny seemed to be the worst affected and tortured himself telling some anecdotes of what (if they could be believed) seemed to have been a robust and highly disreputable amorous career. He said later, when the pangs were fading, " Ah well, it shows we're still healthy and capable anyway."

Water was no longer a problem. A lot of the small palms that Nang Sen had shown them were scattered over the country, and when they jabbed a knife in the swollen base the sour, thin liquid gushed and was good to drink. Further on a rather muddy stream meandered through the scrub, and they relaxed and washed and drank for half a day. Roy was still weak and very thin, but McCormac, Donaldson and Skinny carried some sinewy flesh and were beginning to feel fit. Mostly they walked stripped to the waist when the undergrowth was not too high, and all of them were burned a deep grimy brown so that from a distance they could pass as natives. McCormac said, however, that their blue eyes would give them away (all the natives had deep brown eyes).

" We could pass as Eurasians, though," he added. " They can have blue eyes, and if we say we used to work for The Dutch Company [1] we ought to get away with it all right."

In the isolation of the scrubby country it seemed safe to walk by day, but McCormac stopped them often for rests because of Roy. For several days they ate reasonably well, finding berries and fruits, occasional coconuts and young bamboo shoots and roots. McCormac said that at this rate they ought to be able to carry on for years.

At one stage Skinny let out a shout, darted off into the grass by a clump of trees and dived to the ground. He got up in a moment with a little monkey in his hands, squeaking furiously and clawing at him. Toughened as they were they still felt squeamish when he killed it with a knife. McCormac acted as chef, lighting a fire, packing the monkey's body in mud (still with the skin on) and roasting it for hours in the ashes. After that the skin peeled easily away and with their fingers they tore off strips of the flesh, which was pale and sweet. Donaldson only took a couple of bites when he threw

---

[1] The Netherlands East Indies Government was still known to the natives as The Dutch Company

a bit of flesh down, screwed his face up in distaste as he looked at the little body and said, " Hell, this is like cannibalism. I'm not having any more."

Like naughty children the others looked at the monkey, and it was so like a tiny baby that they began to feel sick and ashamed. McCormac covered it with dirt and they left it.

Next day they saw a kampong and walked boldly in among the huts. Some of the natives clustered a little way off and stared curiously, and the headman came out. All the headmen they had met seemed to have the same old prune faces. This one also was wearing Queen Wilhelmina's medal. McCormac, tactfully addressing him as " Tuan," said they were Eurasians escaping from Japanese labour gangs, and a few minutes later they were reclining at ease on rope beds in a hut.

" This Eastern hospitality's pretty good," Skinny said. " I could be happy in this country."

Donaldson commented cynically, " The Law of the East still says they can hand us over to the Japs. They could get a couple of thousand guilders for us."

" I don't think so," McCormac said. " Not while the headman is wearing the Queen's medal."

The headman told them later that at Oosthaven, only twenty miles away, were Japanese who sometimes nosed about the kampongs, so they must remain in the hut and not stay long.

McCormac asked him about the soft green fruit with the bitter stone that had had such a potent effect on them. " Ah," said the headman, " the charm tree," and smiled understandingly. He was either exquisitely hospitable or had a sense of humour, because after dusk they were allowed out briefly to eat curried rice around the communal cooking fire and when they went back to the hut there was a little oil lamp burning there and a plump and not overdressed native girl of obviously mature age lying on one of the beds smiling at them. There was a moment of startled silence and McCormac said, " My God, I've heard of this custom."

" What ? " Skinny asked, goggle-eyed.

" Well, in parts of Sumatra they think a man of mature age

shouldn't sleep alone," McCormac said. "Sometimes a generous headman will donate women."

"Don't the women object?" Skinny wanted to know.

"They'll do anything to get a white tuan," McCormac said, "and even more to marry him." He added a moment later, "I think it's an insult to refuse."

"God, we don't want to insult them," said Skinny quickly. They looked at the girl and she looked at them, eyes moving placidly from one to the other. Donaldson started laughing. He turned and said, "Skinny, I think it'd do you good."

In the morning Skinny was extremely embarrassed. There were no partitions in the hut and the beds were all fairly close together. Donaldson said to him dryly, "You know, I think you were exaggerating with those stories the other day. Why don't you go out and find a charm tree somewhere?"

They moved off along a trail that afternoon with elaborate directions from the headman for reaching a kampong just in from the sea and about two miles from Oosthaven. He advised them to go very carefully even if it took some days, and watch for Japanese in the next kampong before they entered it.

It was on the third morning that Roy's dysentery started again and in the afternoon he started to vomit. By evening he was in a high fever, sweating and shivering, his skin hot to touch. They built a little nest for him under some trees off a fork in the trail and slept there that night, but in the morning Roy was no better.

"He's got malaria, dysentery, the lot," McCormac said. "If he isn't any better by this evening I'm going to try and find that kampong and get help." He stayed by Roy and the other two went foraging for food.

Around noon he heard a hail from the track and was startled to see Skinny approaching with a Chinese-Javanese girl, a dark, pretty creature of about eighteen wearing black silk trousers, a lace baju and an embroidered vest.

"Her name's Li-Tong," said Skinny, who spoke a few words of Malay now. "I found her on the trail and I think she comes from the next kampong."

McCormac spoke to her and she told him she was a daughter

of a brother of the headman and that there were no Japanese in the kampong which was only about two miles away. It was her idea that they should go back with her.

The three men took it in turns to carry Roy pickaback and he was so emaciated that they could have carried him miles. Near the village the girl went ahead so that when they came to it her father and the headman were waiting for them, and, a little apart, the usual crowd of gaping natives.

This time the reception was not quite so friendly, and the reason was fear.

" There are Japanese in Oosthaven and they may hear many things," the headman said.

" They do not worry about Eurasians, Tuan," said McCormac.

" You are Eurasians ? "

" Yes, Tuan," McCormac said.

" We are poor here," the headman murmured. " All young men must work for the Japanese in Oosthaven."

" Then so shall I, Tuan, and pay you my wages," said McCormac. He thought afterwards it must have been the Irish in him that made him say that, but he felt suddenly confident that he could do it. Apparently so did the headman. He nodded and said, " We will give you food and shelter till your friend is better."

McCormac, Donaldson and Skinny were led to a dilapidated bamboo hut and some native women took Roy to another hut. McCormac went over to see him later and found the native women trying to give him some sort of thick herb soup, but the sick man could not keep it down.

In the morning he was barely conscious and muttering restlessly when McCormac walked off with the young men of the village to join the Japanese labour gang. They told him the work was building a road near the water just out of the town and only one stupid Japanese sergeant was in charge.

McCormac saw about a hundred natives already there as they neared the spot, and his nerves started jumping as he saw the Japanese sergeant and walked over to register for work. He bowed and hissed respectfully and as he straightened up the Japanese sergeant, a thick, short man with heavy eyes, noticed his blue eyes. He said, in Malay, with more curiosity than suspicion : " Who are you ? "

" I have escaped from the Dutch Company in the north," McCormac said. " I am trying to reach my family in Bandoeng."

" You have blue eyes ? "

" My father was a German." McCormac had had that story ready for weeks. He had a sudden fright that the Japanese might speak to him in German, but the Japanese probably did not know any German. All he said, quite agreeably, was, " That is a good combination."

From that moment McCormac forgot that he was European and felt and acted completely like a Eurasian. For the next five days he dug earth, carried it in baskets, and cracked rocks with a hammer. Every evening the Japanese sergeant, list-lessly disinterested, handed him 4.50 occupation guilders which McCormac handed to the headman.

It was back-breaking work for a new hand and McCormac said wryly that he was " browned off " slaving all day so that the other two could eat and loaf, though it would have been crazy for Donaldson and Skinny, speaking little but English, to try and deceive the Japanese. Skinny, who looked fairly repulsive with his cropped head, missing teeth, beard and bony frame, spent most of his time with little Li-Tong who seemed to be enchanted by him.

Roy had been getting worse all the time, and there was nothing they could do about it. The native women never left his side, but by the third day he was alternating between coma and delirium and that night he died. Somehow it did not affect the other three very much: death had been close for too long and self-preservation had grown a toughened hide over their emotions. They accepted it and there was little more to it than that. In the morning Donaldson and Skinny helped the natives bury him.

In the evening the headman said to McCormac, sugges-tively: " You will want to be moving on, Tuan."

It was the first time he had called him Tuan and McCormac wondered a little nervously how he had suddenly known they were Europeans. " Can you help us across the Soenda Strait to Java ? " he asked.

The headman looked unenthusiastic. " That would be difficult."

McCormac said: " If we *are* white tuans and the Japanese catch us they may make us talk."

The old man looked suddenly worried and sat quite still, thinking. He said at last: " I think perhaps something might be arranged," and left them.

He was back in the hut in the morning before McCormac was ready to leave with the road gang, and said, " As the Tuan Skinny is to marry his daughter, the father of Li-Tong has arranged that a fisherman will take the two friends across the strait." That is as near to his words as McCormac can remember. He did not take it in for a moment, but looked dumbly at the old man, and then he and Donaldson were staring thunderstruck at Skinny.

Skinny said, embarrassed: " Well . . . I've been doing a bit of a line with Li-Tong and . . . I dunno, I just asked her to marry me. It sort of happened."

Donaldson said: " Well, for Christ's sake . . . ! "

" What's wrong with it," Skinny demanded. " She's pretty nice and it gets you two across the strait anyway."

" Does that mean you're staying here ? " McCormac asked incredulously.

" I can marry her for a while anyway. It'll be safe here. I like the life and when the war's over . . . ". He shrugged.

" Well . . . " and then McCormac was lost for anything to say. At least, he thought, he had found out how the old man knew they were Europeans. He did not know whether to kick Skinny or shake his hand. The old man, he noticed, was politely waiting.

" When can we cross the strait ? " he asked, and the old man said, " To-night."

It was dusk when the small party set off for the water. Skinny came along to say good-bye and Li-Tong and her mother came too. Donaldson kept whistling the wedding march under his breath.

The boat was an old launch, with a mast and sail, and a

small engine. As they were getting in Skinny said, " I can't stay here. I'm coming, too." He turned a little desperately and tried to explain it to Li-Tong in signs and broken Malay. She seemed to understa 1 very quickly, as though she had been expecting it, and started wailing and hanging on to Skinny's arm. There was a scene for several minutes—the girl wailing, Skinny trying to find Malayan words and swearing in English, and the girl's mother talking shrilly. The girl's father spoke sharply to them and they shut up. The old man said to McCormac, " If the Tuan does not stay, the fisherman will not take you."

McCormac translated for Skinny " Looks like you've got to stay anyway," he said, and after a while Skinny growled, " Oh hell ! All right. I'll stay."

The last they saw of him as the launch pitched into the swell was a dim figure in the gloom with the girl standing very near him.

The fisherman was scared of Japanese patrols but they saw nothing. About midnight he put into a small island and left them there, saying something about checking up on some buoys, and when the launch had chugged into the darkness horrible fears grew in them that they had been double-crossed, marooned there to starve. Cursing themselves for being so gullible, they heard the chug-chug of the launch again and a few minutes later the fisherman, by some mystery of navigation, gently grounded the bows on the little beach where he had left them and they splashed aboard again.

It must have been about three o'clock in the morning when the fisherman throttled down and dimly ahead they saw the loom of trees on a shore. The launch nosed gently on to sand and the fisherman told McCormac they were on Java, near a town called Merak, up the coast from Batavia. He told them to wait by the launch and vanished.

An hour later he came out of the trees with another man, a taciturn Javanese ; probably surly at being dragged out of bed, McCormac thought. He and Donaldson shook hands with the fisherman and followed the morose Javanese into the jungle. For two hours they stumbled along a dark jungle trail, moving slowly and keeping close together.

It was getting lighter when they came out of the jungle to some clearer ground and dawn flamed gloriously in the east. In scrubby, secondary jungle they made good time for about three miles till the trail snaked into thicker jungle, and there the Javanese stopped. He waved an arm into the jungle and said, " Friendly soldiers."

" How far ? " McCormac asked.

The Javanese shrugged.

" How can we find them ? "

The native shrugged again as though he did not care. He waved his hand again up the trail, turned and walked off.

" Surly sod," Donaldson said.

" I don't think so," said McCormac. " They're frightened of people knowing too much."

They walked about a mile along the trail into the jungle, found some fruit and lay down to rest, tired out. It was hours later when they were talking about moving off again that a man walked round a bend in the trail only about fifteen yards away. He saw them before they moved. McCormac and Donaldson jumped to their feet ; then saw the man was alone and stood warily and uncertainly, not knowing quite what to expect. The man was young and black-haired and an indeterminate brown, barefoot, but dressed in dirty grey slacks and what had apparently been once a white shirt. He stopped about five feet away and stared expressionlessly. McCormac could not tell whether he was native, Eurasian or what. He could have been anything. They stood several seconds looking at each other and the stranger spoke first. He said · " What are you two fairy-like bastards doing here ? "

They gaped at him, particularly Donaldson, because the stranger had a rich, Australian twang, and was extremely self-possessed.

" Who the hell are you ? " Donaldson asked.

" Who the hell are *you* ? " said the stranger, eyeing them with an odd air of authority. After another silence the stranger added, " If you want help, maybe I can do something. I heard you were around. Where're you from ? "

" Singapore," McCormac said, feeling it was safe to answer.

" I heard there was a big break there," the stranger said.
" Were you among them ? "

" Yes."

" Where are the others ? "

" Dead."

" Except one," put in the cynical Donaldson. " He got a fate worse than death."

" Torture ? "

" Sort of," said Donaldson. " He got married."

For the first time the stranger looked startled. Donaldson explained and the stranger gave a faint grin and remarked, " Jesus, this is a terrible war."

" How did you know we were here ? " asked McCormac.

" I only *ask* questions," the stranger said. " No one round here answers them. Come on, we can talk while we're walking."

He led them along the trail, listening attentively to the account of the past few weeks, and then McCormac could not help asking where they were going.

" I'm taking you to a bloke who's got a sort of a guerrilla show going." The stranger started talking about other things then, laconically and with a dry wit. Neither McCormac nor Donaldson could make him out because he spoke English like an Australian and Javanese like a Javanese. He kept declaiming quaint and often ribald remarks, which, he said, were from Sheridan. (They never did find out who he was, either his name or his nationality. He said he was not Australian but Donaldson was fairly sure he was.)

After about three hours they came to a small clearing in the jungle with about twenty grimy bivouac tents and one larger one. The stranger gave a hail and a tall, blond man came out of the larger tent. He was dressed in Dutch army green and calf boots, with a revolver strapped to his waist. An ugly scar ran from the tip of his left eye to his mouth. The guide said, " A couple from Singapore for you, Mannie." He spoke for a while in what McCormac thought was Dutch, and then turned to the two again, said laconically, " Good luck," and walked off back along the trail.

" I'll take you first," the scarred man said briskly, beckoning

Donaldson into his tent. He interrogated them separately, presumably to see that their stories coincided, and afterwards he said, " You're all right. You can stay with us for a while. You can call me Mansfelt."

He did not tell them much about himself but they gathered that evening that he was Dutch Eurasian and leader of a ragged band of forty-seven guerrillas. Some of them were out foraging at scattered kampongs and the rest were loafing about the clearing, a quiet, not over-clean collection in green shorts and various styles and colours of shirts and bajus. Half were barefoot and the rest wore sandals, except for three Dutch or Eurasians who had calf boots like Mansfelt. The rest seemed to be Javanese. Two of the Javanese did the cooking and they seemed to be short of food because all any of them had that first night was a bowl of rice and some fruit. Mansfelt pointed out a small bivouac tent for McCormac and Donaldson and they crawled into it early, dog-tired, and slept till after dawn.

Some three days after they had joined Mansfelt there was a bustle in the camp and about thirty-five of the guerrillas formed up in an untidy line while Mansfelt inspected them. Half had rifles, one man had a tommy gun and the rest carried swords.

" We are going away for a couple of days," Mansfelt said to McCormac and Donaldson. " You will stay here with the rest." He said, just before he marched the men out into the jungle, " I hope everyone will have rifles when we return."

An elderly Dutchman left behind told McCormac that they were going to raid a small Jap garrison. " They choose only small ones a long way from the camp," he said.

Three mornings later Mansfelt walked into the clearing out of the jungle followed by a straggling line of his men. They all looked tired and dirty, but they seemed to have several more rifles, some bags and food and three teams of two men were carrying ammunition boxes in rope slings. Mansfelt was happy about the ammunition. He said they had lost one man but killed eleven Japanese.

Next morning they broke camp and marched for three days,

mostly south-west, deeper into the country. "We always move a long way after a raid," Mansfelt explained.

That was the pattern of life for weeks until they could hardly remember any other life. Time hung heavily but with a persistent undertone of fear that never quite left them. Mansfelt said there were several other similar bodies and the Japanese hunted them all the time. It was not good, he said, to be caught.

Several times he led his band out on more raids and every time they moved camp soon after. Three or four more men did not come back but Mansfelt claimed the raids had killed over thirty Japanese. Nearly all of his men had rifles now and there were two more tommy guns. McCormac spoke a lot to the quiet little Javanese but Mansfelt told him crisply not to ask too many questions. He gathered that Mansfelt was a Dutch officer and the guerrillas had mostly been in the Netherlands Far East Army. Mansfelt kept fairly aloof from them and lived austerely himself, allowing no liquor in the party.

McCormac and Donaldson were getting restless from doing nothing but Mansfelt would give them no clue as to their future. He kept saying, "Be patient and perhaps something can be done," but the two kept asking him to take them on a raid and finally he did so.

They did not see much. The scouts came back from reconnaissance and led the party for most of one night and all the next day. At dusk they lay off on a hill overlooking a kampong which, Mansfelt said, sheltered a Japanese outpost of about twelve men. About midnight he told McCormac and Donaldson to stay where they were and led the rest of the party away. A quarter of an hour later they heard shots and a lot of shouting, and after another half an hour Mansfelt and his men filtered quietly back through the trees to the hilltop, carrying more ammunition. Mansfelt said with grim pleasure that they had wiped out the Japanese.

For some weeks the party had been working gradually south and the country was fairly open now, with only patches of jungle. Mansfelt said there were very few Japanese in the area.

He woke them one morning, and with him was a stunted,

wizened Javanese. "You are going off with this man," he said. "Do what he tells you and good luck."

"Where are we going?" asked McCormac, but all Mansfelt would say was, "You will find out soon." He brushed aside their thanks for the past weeks and an hour later they were following the guide across country.

In all the days that followed the guide never said more than a dozen words to them. He regarded them dispassionately without being surly, but only grunted whenever McCormac asked a question. They walked silently behind him, affected by the isolation and rarely speaking to each other in the time either; there seemed to be nothing to say and they had lost any feeling of time and, for that matter, any feeling of fear. Reality seemed so remote. For safety and disguise they had taken to wearing loin cloths; at nights they lived like natives in various kampongs, tired and somewhat detached from their surroundings, and by day they walked, until one afternoon they came to a kampong and on the far side of it saw the sea.

The guide talked with the headman—another toothless old man—and the headman steered the two to a hut and told them to rest, refusing to answer any questions except to say, "You will be taken on from here." He would not give any hint as to where.

A woman brought them some rice and about an hour after dusk, as they were settling down to sleep, the headman walked in and said, "It is time to go." They followed him dumbly, exasperated by the mystery; he led them down to the water and they saw a fishing boat bobbing in the light surf of the shallows, with Javanese crewmen holding it steady. The headman pointed to it and said, "Good luck"; they splashed into the water and crawled on board. The boat was about twenty-five feet long, built like a junk, with a single mast, but with an outrigger for stability as it seemed to have a very shallow draft. The crew tumbled in after them and a minute later they were lifting into the swell out into the open sea.

Donaldson said querulously, "Where the hell are we going in this? There can't be any friendly land for a thousand miles."

McCormac asked the little Javanese, but they would not tell him, though he gathered they were off the south coast of Java and heading east.

Apparently they kept fairly close to the land, because as dawn came in the east they saw the junk was nearing the shore, heading for a small kampong bordering the beach and hedged in by thick jungle. They spent the day in a hut there, in their usual state of numb acceptance, and after dusk were taken out again in the junk. Soon after dawn they beached at another kampong and after dusk put out to sea once more. The sea stayed calm and the air was warm; McCormac found there was something hypnotic in the dull progress towards nowhere in particular. They hardly bothered to wonder where they were going now, largely, McCormac thinks, because the idea of arriving somewhere definite was too much to grasp. Life was a vacuum; they were marking time with nothing to do and nothing to worry about. Donaldson said at one stage, " We ought to be able to keep out of the hands of the Japs for years," and that was about as far as their thinking took them.

That cosy thought took a sharp nudge from reality in the morning. The junk was heading into another kampong, as usual, when the Javanese started gabbling excitedly; the man at the steering oar pulled urgently at it and the junk swung about and headed out to sea again. McCormac asked the steersman what had happened and the little Javanese jerked a thumb at the shore and said, " Jipponese! " Fear came back that day, though they had no idea how the Javanese had known that Japanese were in the kampong.

Somewhere about the sixth morning they landed at another kampong; a native led them towards a hut, and as they came up to it a man appeared in the doorway. He was very brown but not Javanese, and, McCormac felt, not Dutch either. He was a little nuggety man in khaki shorts, with black hairs on his shoulders and chest, and in his hand at his side he held a slouch hat. He looked at them steadily and said in an Australian accent, " G'day. Where've you come from ? "

McCormac told him; the man listened, looking keenly at them, and at the end he said, " That's pretty good. Glad to see you've made the grade. A thousand miles through jungle is a long way." He waved them through the door with his hat and they sat on a rope bunk inside.

" What's the form round here?" McCormac asked and could not for a moment believe he had heard properly when the man said, " I'll get in touch with Darwin and we'll get you out of here soon."

" *Darwin!* " Donaldson said. " How? "

" They've got to bring me some supplies, anyway."

" What are you doing here? " asked Donaldson.

" Mucking about," said the man, again deflecting the question. " Most of my mob have already gone—the one's who weren't bumped."

" How long have you been here? "

" Go easy on the questions, mate," the man said. He himself asked some questions about Singapore and then suddenly said, " You'd better get some rest." He called a native and told him to take the two to a hut. As they were going he added, " I'll send some tucker over to you."

The food arrived soon after—tinned corned beef and, of all things, tinned cake that seemed to McCormac incredibly sweet.

A tropical storm swept over the kampong that night and the weather stayed bad for two days. Suddenly faced with a mysterious prospect of getting to Australia, both McCormac and Donaldson developed acute jitters. For weeks they had hardly even thought about getting to civilised and friendly land again ; they had been living in the present, content to be out of Japanese hands and unable to understand that life might begin again. Suddenly the vague dreams had taken shape and they still could not trust in it, being full of terror that at the last moment something would go wrong and the Japanese would get them again. They were nervous and miserable.

On the second night the Australian (who never gave them his name) took them down to the shore to another small fishing boat, which may have been the same junk that had brought them along the coast. He told them to get in but stayed on the shore himself, and as the boat pulled out he yelled, " Lucky bastards. Crack a bottle for me."

The little Javanese crewmen steered the boat straight out

to sea, and after about three-quarters of an hour they threw
out a sea anchor and started to fish. " What's happening ? "
McCormac asked, but all they would say was " Wait." So
they waited, marooned in blackness, puzzled and exasperated
and weary of all the mystery. The hours dragged by as they
rolled in the swell listening to the slap of water against the
hull.

That was the only sound they heard until, seven hours later,
Donaldson cocked his head and said, " What's that ? "
McCormac heard it a moment later, the distant drone of an
aeroplane, and after a few tense seconds they knew it was
getting louder.

The Javanese had heard it and pulled in their lines ; they
sat very still looking up into the darkness. The engines became loud, then faded, returned, sounding over a wide patch,
a disembodied drumming somewhere high in the night. A
pin-prick of light flickered up there. A Javanese in the boat
clicked something and McCormac saw him outlined in a brief
soft glow from the torch he was holding towards the plane,
shielding it with his body from the land. From plane and
torch there were two more quick exchanges, and then the
engine note changed, two long beams flicked on to the sea a
mile away and shrank as the bright white eyes behind them
slid right down to the sea and then flicked off. McCormac
could just hear the gentle idle of the engines.

" Well, he's down in one piece," McCormac said, and
noticed he was sweating.

The Javanese was giving little flicks with the torch and the
quiet rumbling was coming nearer. A dark, hulking monster
moved in the blackness towards them and then the little boat
nudged against the hull. A door in the monster snapped open
and framed in dim light stood a man in shorts. A voice said,
" Come on, make it snappy! "

McCormac said urgently, " Hello. Are you taking us
back ? "

" Who's that ? " said the startled voice.

After that it was confused. McCormac vaguely remembers
some more words and stumbling, and then he was in the belly
of the Catalina with Donaldson and a couple of young

Australian Air Force men were staring at their beards and loin cloths. Others were passing boxes out through the hatch into the fishing boat, and then the door was shut. It was fast and almost completely wordless apart from a little muttering and grunting. The engines roared suddenly, they were bumping over the swell, and then the bumping stopped and they felt a smooth vibration and gentle swaying.

They gave a jerky account of what had happened to them ; it was difficult to talk in the plane, and McCormac found he could hardly be bothered to try. He remembers that he stirred after a while and asked what the date was, and one of the Australians said, " Tuesday the sixteenth." " The sixteenth of what ? " asked McCormac, and the Australian looked startled and said, " September. What did you think it was ? " September ! That was five months since the break from Pasir Panjang. McCormac thought dully for a few moments and said, " I didn't know. The papers haven't been delivered very regularly in the jungle lately." The Australian brought out a bottle of whisky and said, " We ought to parade you jokers through Darwin."

After that they slept nearly all the twelve hours till they landed at Darwin and found—as many returning prisoners have found—that they did not feel happy at all, only light-headed and confused and queer. It was over, that was all, but just for the moment there was nothing in its place ; they could not get hold of life again.

They began to think sensibly again about forty-eight hours later, and it was then that the postponed grief about Pat hit McCormac because then it became part of his life again. In faint hope he kept asking about the *Wakefield*, but they came back and said no one knew what had happened to her, and that made it rather obvious. No survivors.

A month later in Ceylon, on his way back to England, he was still confused. It is strange what an experience can do to you. He still felt outside ordinary life and had become rather solitary. In the R.A.F. mess at Kogala he picked up an overseas copy of the *Daily Mail*, and on the front page was a picture of Pat. She was holding a baby in her arms, and the little story with the picture said that she was calling the baby

Dawn because she was born at dawn as the troopship from Singapore was nearing England.

.　　.　　.　　.　　.

In late 1945 McCormac, with a very good grip on life, was back in Singapore as a squadron leader on Mountbatten's staff. He went to the War Crimes Court one day, and even now he cannot describe the shock he had when he recognised the first Japanese who was told to stand up. It was Teruchi, and McCormac saw him sentenced to death for a long list of atrocities.

He went to Mountbatten and said, " Sir, may I have the sword of the first of the Japanese sentenced to-day ? "

" Why ? " Mountbatten demanded.

McCormac pointed to the scars near his eye and his mouth. " He gave me these with that sword, sir." He told Mountbatten briefly about it and Mountbatten said briskly, " Right. It's yours."

McCormac uses it now to hack at the brambles in his garden at Welling, in Kent. Pat hates the sight of it, Dawn could not care less, but the two young boys think it is magnificent.

McCormac was decorated with the D.C.M. and commissioned after the escape and worked then on teaching other airmen the ways of escape in the jungle. Glad to get back to Singapore when it fell, he found that the place still held menace for him; he was riding in a car beside Lord Mountbatten one day when a malcontent's bullet smashed through the glass and passed through McCormac's hand. They said at the time that the sniper must have aimed at him—the penalty of resembling Mountbatten in appearance. He left the Air Force in 1948 and goes now each day from his suburban home to the Midland Bank in the heart of the City of London. The change could not be greater and there are times when McCormac is nostalgic for the excitement of Singapore.

ISLAND OF RESISTANCE

*Robert Anthony (" Steve ") Carson was born on May 6, 1923.
All the time he was at Coventry Technical College he wanted to
fly, but his parents would not let him join the R.A.F., so he went
as an apprentice engineer to Morris Motors and was young
enough to regard the outbreak of war somewhat as a heaven-sent
chance to learn to fly. However, under age and in a reserved
job, the way was still barred, so he took to Civil Defence ambulance driving as a sideline and as soon as he was old enough eased
himself out of his reserved job and into the R.A.F. He trained
as a fighter pilot at Cranwell, was commissioned, joined No. 222
(Spitfire) Squadron—part of the 2nd Tactical Air Force—and
went with them, in the Invasion, to fight in Europe.*

On September 29, 1944, Robert Carson was shot down at an
awkward moment. He had made two runs over the convoy
on the Dutch road, seen his shells slamming into the truck-
loads of panicky German soldiers and was running in for the
third time when the engine banged frighteningly, something
shot out of the flat, mullet-head cowling in front and the
Spitfire shuddered violently as the engine seized.

An axiom among fighter pilots says that troops are always
eager to meet the man who has been strafing them. Carson
swept about a hundred feet over their heads, speed dropping
as he used it to claim a little height, trying to stretch his glide
as far as he could, though any high performance fighter glides
dead-stick like a brick. He swung left towards a field,
snapped his flaps down and held her off till she squashed and
slid noisily to a stop. Unclipping, he swung out of the cockpit
and, looking back, saw the soldiers fanning fast off the road
towards him half a mile back. Cursing his clumsy flying
boots, he ran like hell the other way. At that time Carson was
just twenty-one, compact and nimble, with large, capable
hands.

He tore through a hedge, across two fields and dead ahead

saw a canal about twenty-five feet wide barring his path. Without breaking step or faltering he took off in full run on wings of fear and landed in the middle, going right under because it was deep. The shock of the cold water brought him out of the panic and he half swam, half floundered to the far side, pulled himself on to the bank and was running again. The country was dead flat, like so much of Holland ; no cover anywhere.

Ten minutes later he stumbled almost to his knees, feeling he could run no more. The breath sawed hard in his throat and his heart was pounding in his ears. Looking back fearfully he did not see a single German soldier and understood why when a Spitfire rose steeply over the fields, pulling round in a climbing turn at the same moment as the crackle of its distant cannon fire reached him. He wondered which of his friends it was, and, because he had once been straffed himself, felt almost sympathy for the vengeful pursuers caught in the open fields and cringing into the grass as they waited for it.

Half walking, half jogging, he passed some farm workers, who stared open-mouthed, and later saw three farmhouses ahead. They all looked the same ; making a quick decision he walked cautiously round the back of the middle one, and a florid, middle-aged man came out in farm clothes, looking startled at the battledress and flying boots. Quick-witted, the farmer grasped the situation instantly, grabbed Carson by the arm and hustled him into a barn by the house. In stumbling English and with gestures he made the boy understand that he was to burrow under the hay if he heard Germans, and then turned and ran out of the barn. In a minute he slipped quietly back through the door carrying over his arm a good brown tweed suit, and as he helped Carson off with his battledress and into the suit he managed to make him understand that he would like the suit back after the war. Carson, who knew a few German words, gathered that it was his Sunday best. The farmer pulled some of the hay aside then and underneath Carson saw a sten gun and a couple of automatics. The farmer handed him a 7 mm. automatic. " Allies," the farmer said, grinning, making signs to indicate that the guns had been dropped from the air. Suddenly solemn again he told Carson he was lucky to have chosen this farm. The ones on either side belonged to Dutch Nazis. On a map he pointed with a thick forefinger to show that the spot was about a hundred kilometres from the Canadian troops.

After dusk he led Carson over fields to a house in a nearby village called Krimpen, on the banks of the Lek River, and outside the back door Carson met Dirk, the hearty, burly ship repairer. Dirk took him down to the river where he had his ships and on a barge moored there Carson relaxed in a bunk with some bread and cheese and passed a peaceful night.

Dirk told him in the morning that he would arrange to get him a Dutch identity card. In the evening he came back a little flustered and said the Germans were searching the village. Taking the boy by the arm and talking loudly to him in incomprehensible Dutch, he led him out into the main street, past a disciplined little troop of the searching German soldiers (Carson blushing like a schoolgirl and feeling very guilty) to a schoolteacher's house which the Germans had already searched. Chris, the schoolteacher, was a smiling, obliging, blond man who sheltered Carson for four days till a man came one evening, spoke briefly to Chris, and after he went Chris handed Carson a neat piece of folded green cardboard.

" Rub this in your hands till it looks worn," he said. " It is your new identity card. You are Piet Smit, land worker, and I will call you Piet. Get used to it."

Carson looked at it and said in wonder : " It really looks real."

" It is real," Chris said, " except for the signature. We get the cards from the official stocks. Now . . . we will arrange for you to go north where you will find more food and fewer Germans."

" *Away* from the front ? "

" Yes. You will shelter in a house. It will not be exciting. There is a curfew at seven, the Germans start shooting after it, so your nights will be dull for a young man, but you must wait till the armies catch up with you."

Carson said : " Sorry. Not me. I'm no good at that. I want to have a go at getting through the lines."

" Do not be foolish," Chris said severely, the schoolmaster coming out in him. " You will be caught. Or killed in the battle. Or both. You should do as we say."

" Look, Chris," Carson said, " I do appreciate all you've done but I'd go silly sitting on my bottom all day. Other people have got through the lines. Why shouldn't I ? "

" You hear only of the lucky ones who get through," Chris explained. " Not the unlucky ones. There are more of them."

" I was always lucky," Carson insisted.

After half an hour's argument Carson was still stubborn so Chris, slightly ruffled, brought out of a downstairs closet a battered old bicycle without tyres. " It is the best I can do for you," he said, and added tersely, " I hope it brings you luck because that is what you are going to need."

In the morning Chris went out and came back in about half an hour with a sinewy, extremely competent-looking girl of about twenty. She was pushing a bicycle and Chris introduced her as Griselda. " She will guide you south to a house," he said.

Griselda smiled briefly. She was apparently ready to go and five minutes later Carson rode off about a hundred yards behind her, the battered rims of his bicycle wheels clattering over the cobbles so that he thought everyone must be staring at him.

Coming up to the ferry over the Lek he saw a German soldier on board collecting the fares and felt his heartbeats quicken with fear. Chris had briefed him well : Carson handed the German the correct money (it was the first German he had dealt with) and the soldier muttered something at him, but Carson was pretending to look at his front wheel and the German moved off. Two more Germans searched some of the passengers as they got off on the far side but Carson, sweating, landed unmolested. He saw a line of Red Cross lorries waiting on the road ; at least they were white, with red crosses painted on the sides. All of them were packed with obviously healthy and well-armed German soldiers.

For nearly six hours that day he rode a hundred yards behind Griselda, who seemed to be tireless. About six-thirty they went through a winding village called Bleskgraaf, and when Carson came out on the other side he could not see the girl. He rode back through the village but there was no sign of her and he started worrying about the curfew. It was so close to curfew time that he guessed this was the village where he was supposed to spend the night. But where ?

He rode back through the village again ; still no sign of Griselda but a doctor's plate caught his eye outside a house and the name on it was Inglese. It seemed an unmistakable omen ; walking round to the back of the house he knocked.

The doctor himself came to the door, a bony, stooped, elderly man. Carson said in stumbling German, " Ich bin Englische Fliegeroffizier," and the doctor said quickly in thick English, " Come inside at once." It never even crossed his mind that Carson might be a disguised German trying to trap Dutch Resistance people. Dutchmen were usually wary of them (with plenty of reason), but the doctor said later he did not think a German could ever have an accent like Carson's.

Shortly after curfew time Carson was sitting down to dinner with the doctor ; five minutes later the maid rushed in trembling and said there were two German soldiers at the door. Carson dived out of the French windows into the back garden and hid among some rhubarb. The doctor called him in half an hour later and said the Germans were only making a routine check and now he had been searched it was safer than ever.

Next day the doctor brought an eager youth and a girl in and told Carson they would guide him to an address in the town of Dordrecht. It was the system as before, Carson riding his rattletrap old bike behind the two guides. A German check post gave him a bad fright on the way, stopping him and asking for his papers. He pulled out his identity card, the German looked casually at it, handed it back, and Carson rode on.

In Dordrecht they took him into a grey stone house in a garden back from the road, showed him into a room, smiled and walked out. Across the room, watching him closely, sat a silent young man ; short and thick-set with fair, close-cropped hair. The man merely gazed, tight-lipped, saying nothing and Carson sat in another chair. A quarter of an hour passed ; the man had not opened his mouth and Carson felt the silent tension getting unbearable. He was fidgety, wondering what sort of test this was and then he heard the other man say something explosively under his breath. It sounded like " Goddam," and Carson said :

" I say, do you speak English ? "

" I sure as hell do," said Lootenant Grover P. Parker, of California, who had been shot down two days before, been captured, escaped that morning from the Dordrecht lock-up and been picked up by the Dutch.

The tension broke and they each burst into a torrent of words. A few minutes later an English-speaking Dutchman came into the room and apologised for being so long. (They realised later he had probably been listening, waiting for them to talk naturally to each other so he would know whether either was a German " plant ".) He said he was going to send them to a place called the Biesbosch, an area of thickly overgrown marsh in the fork where the Waal flowed into the Maas River. There was a well-armed Organisation there, he added, and the Germans were usually frightened to go into it.

Another fair young Dutchman came in the morning and led them for several miles across quiet country till they came out on the Maas River at a spot where a skiff was moored. Across on the far shore they saw a tangle of thick reeds about seven feet high, and here and there a tree. " Biesbosch," the Dutchman said briefly. He rowed them across to a rotted landing stage and led the way along a narrow, beaten path that was almost a funnel where the thick, dry-green reeds crowded in on both sides, curving over their heads. Stagnant canals choked with weeds and reeds kept cutting through the path and they crossed them on narrow planks.

The path sharply spread out into a small clearing and in a canal running along one side of it a man sat in a canoe. " Ach, der Kommandant," the guide said half to himself, half to Carson.

He gave a hail and the man paddled to the bank and climbed out. The guide spoke in Dutch and the Kommandant solemnly shook their hands and said in English with a stiff accent, " How do you do ?" He was about forty, fair and sharp-featured with sunken cheeks, wore a thick, crew-neck sweater and had a big automatic pistol stuck in the waistband of his pants. It was a keen face, Carson thought, but " hooded," curiously empty of active expression. He found in the times that followed that the Kommandant seldom let a flicker of emotion show. The main thing for the moment was that he spoke English. He said, " If you will always do as I say you can stay with us. I am afraid it is not comfortable."

The guide turned back and they followed the Kommandant along more winding paths for a quarter of an hour till Carson became aware of the long low shape of a barge lying surprisingly in the reeds. The Kommandant led them on to the deck over a plank and Carson saw that it was moored in another choked canal. She was an old and dirty barge with only a little faded, peeling paint on her.

Looking curiously around they followed the Kommandant along the rusty deck to a cabin at the rear, and as he put his head in the door Carson caught the sweaty smell of bodies. A dozen or so men were lounging inside, some on bunks, a couple at a table, dressed mostly in singlets and pants, and all of them looking unshaven and dirty. With a shock he saw a young woman lying on a bunk ; she looked heavy and sluttish.

The Kommandant called one of the men and a big, broad-shouldered young man of about twenty-four swung off a bunk and came over. " This is Jan," the Kommandant said. " He will take care of you." Jan put out his hand and said in a deep voice and very good English, " I do hope you do not mind sharing a bunk."

They found he had been quite a cultured student until the Germans had interrupted his studies ; since then he had become a ruthless young man, though to Carson and Parker he was always friendly and cheerful. Like most of the Dutch they had encountered, he was fair-haired.

Jan introduced the others, but they seemed a graceless lot

and all Carson and Parker got were a few grunts. Even the girl was unfriendly. They dined that evening on bread and potatoes, and most of the potatoes were pitted and bad. Carson was oppressed by the smell, the surly carelessness and the general fœtid atmosphere of the Biesbosch. He asked Jan how soon they could move on towards the Allied lines, but Jan said that the country further on was thick with Germans and check points and that the Germans were taking savage measures with anyone they caught.

" Stay here and wait until they reach us," he said. " It will not be long now." He added wryly, " We have been waiting a long time and it is worth waiting a little more."

He found them a top bunk and Carson and Parker crammed into it together, though they had little sleep because the girl and another man were in the bunk below behaving with absolutely no inhibitions whatsoever.

In the morning Jan took them off the barge for a walk and led them deep into the middle of the Biesbosch, where they came out of the narrow paths to a peaceful clearing with a canal running through it and a pretty stone bridge arching over the canal. It was warm and sunny and they stopped to rest on the bridge. Jan was saying, " You know we are doing more than just waiting here. There is another barge . . ." He stopped as Carson let out an alarmed little cry. He was looking past Jan's shoulder, and Parker and Jan swung round and saw two German soldiers walking out of the reeds into the clearing. One had a rifle slung over his shoulder, the other wore a pistol holster on his belt. They headed straight for the bridge.

Jan mumbled, hardly moving his lips, " Do not look aggressive. I will do the talking." Carson put his hand in his coat pocket, gripped the butt of his pistol and thumbed the safety catch to " Fire." Parker, he thought, would undoubtedly be doing the same.

He saw that the soldier with the holster wore the skull and crossbones of a Panzer division on his cap. Under it was a thin face and sharp eyes. The other German was younger and looked rather seedy. They walked on the bridge and stopped in front of Jan, looking wary but not truculent. The man with the skull and crossbones badge spoke. Carson got the bare gist of some question about a nearby farm. Jan answered him in German, and while they talked the two Germans kept watching the three of them.

The older man must have become aware of the atmosphere. He stuck his thumbs in his belt ; his fingers lay over the holster flap and Carson saw him surreptitiously pulling the flap loose from the brass stud. Parker apparently saw it too, because he suddenly drew his own pistol and yelled, " Hande hoch! " The younger German gave a little cry of shock, jerked his rifle off his shoulder and it went off point-blank, the bullet passing between Carson and Parker. Then he was running and it all happened very fast.

Carson had his pistol out ; he fired and the running German fell on his face and started screaming. Parker was shooting jerkily, his face expressionless. His first bullet hit the other German in the stomach, the second one went through the side of the neck as the German spun round and the third one went through his left hand ; then the German went down.

The man Carson had shot was moving on the ground like a weak crab, and Carson thought vaguely, " This isn't like the movies at all. He should be dead."

Parker's man was making a lot of noise and then he stopped yelling as Parker went up to him and moaned, " Bruder, Bruder, nicht schiessen."

Jan said in a worried voice, " I hope there are no other Germans near. We had better go."

" We can't leave these poor devils here," Carson said. He had picked up the dropped rifle, and Parker took the pistol out of the other man's holster. The two wounded had quietened down and were gasping.

A violent rustling sounded through the reeds, growing louder ; Carson's scalp crawled with fear and then some of the Dutchmen from the barge burst into the clearing. The Kommandant was with them and looked dispassionately at the two Germans.

" There will probably be trouble," he said. He spoke quietly, with a detached solemnity. Two of his band picked up the wounded men pickaback and the Kommandant led them all down a new trail.

"What's going to happen? Where're we going?" Carson asked Jan, and Jan grinned. "To the prison camp. You'll see," he said mysteriously.

After about ten minutes the Kommandant turned and vanished off the track into the reeds. The others followed him, and not till he reached the spot did Carson see the big black barge moored virtually alongside the track. It was perhaps bigger than the other barge and lay in a canal which ran about four feet behind the reeds ; it was invisible unless you pushed a foot or two into the reeds at the place where the plank led on to the deck. He stepped across the plank and saw the Dutchmen lowering the wounded men into a hatchway ; walking over, he looked into the hatch and the smell that came up nearly made him sick. In the square of light, dirty faces were looking up.

"German deserters," Jan said. "We have thirty down there now." He added, grinning, "We had to persuade some of them to desert."

A couple of the Dutchmen slipped down the hatch into the hold, commandeered some of the Germans' shirts and spent half an hour dressing the wounds of the two wounded. Both were conscious and the man Carson had shot was quite cheerful. The other one, hit three times, seemed too weak to talk.

Carson had heard some growling among the Germans below, and when the Dutch came up they said the Germans were angry about the shootings, particularly when they heard that a couple of Allied airmen were responsible. Apparently they did not care particularly about the two men who were shot, but merely regarded the shooting as setting a disturbing new precedent in their cloistered life.

The Kommandant said to Carson and Parker : "The Germans in the village across the Maas will have heard the shots, and when they miss the two men I think they will send soldiers to search. We are going to disperse for a day or two, but as you are really responsible you must stay on the barge and guard them."

Neither Carson nor Parker found the idea appealing.

" What if the Germans below start a fuss ? " Carson asked.
" If we have to send a couple of bullets down to keep them
quiet, it'll draw any searchers pretty fast."

" I do not think these Germans will make trouble," the
Kommandant said, with a faint smile. " They are safer here
with us than with their own people. I assure you they know
that."

When the Dutch had gone Carson and Parker sat in the
wheelhouse of the barge with rifles, taking it in turn to watch
the hatch. They had to leave part of the hatch open so the
Germans could get some air in the foul space below, but they
seemed a dispirited lot with no fight left in them. One
German stuck his head out of the hatch and tried to pull himself out on to the deck, but Parker pointed the hollow end of
his rifle at him, clicked the bolt and aimed with such a
methodical air that the German abruptly dropped back into
the hold.

The day passed quietly, but about an hour after dusk the
German patrol came over. Carson saw the reflections of
several lights bobbing over the reeds in the direction of the
Maas, and a little later they heard the German shouts. For
a long time they watched the lights flickering over the reeds,
and gradually the lights were working nearer to them and the
shouts getting louder.

Parker kept saying, " They'll never find us here," but
Carson thought his voice sounded a little too carefully con-
trolled. He could hear his own heart thudding. The lights
came within about two hundred yards of them and then, to
his enormous relief, they seemed to be receding again and the
shouts became fainter.

In the morning two Dutchmen brushed across the gang-
plank carrying some buckets of boiled potatoes, which they
shared out impartially among the prisoners below. Only the
Kommandant and Jan were left aboard the other barge, they
reported ; the rest were hiding in farmhouses for miles
around.

Carson and Parker did not leave the prison barge until, two
mornings later, the Dutch arrived with more food, and one of
them took Carson and Parker over to the other barge, where

they found the Organisation reassembling. The two last members arrived just after Carson, and walking in front of them with their hands clasped on their heads were two men in farm clothes. The men behind were sticking heavy pistols into the ribs of their captives and said grimly that they were Dutch Nazis.

Carson, for the first time, saw the Kommandant let his feelings show ; talking to the captives his voice was biting and angry, and at the end he turned away with a disgusted wave of the hand and said, " Take them to the other barge."

Several Dutchmen prodded their compatriot Nazis down the trail at pistol point, and Carson and Parker trailed after them. The leaders had just vanished out of Carson's sight round a bend in the trail when a pistol suddenly cracked several times. Carson ran round the bend and saw the two Dutch Nazis lying on the track, quite dead.

One of the guards said, with a grim smile, " They tried to run for it." Carson never found out whether that was the truth or not. They buried them in the reeds just off the track. Two of the Dutch, Carson noted, had been carrying trenching tools.

The man he had shot a few days earlier by the little bridge, and who had seemed to be recovering quite well, took a turn for the worse ; his belly started to swell and he was running a high fever. They brought him up out of the hold and put him in the wheelhouse, but there was little else they could do for him. He was in a lot of pain, but they could get no doctor or drugs and he became delirious, getting obviously weaker, and then sank into a coma. In the morning he was dead. They filled his pockets with heavy stones, and one of the Germans in the hold, who had been a headquarters clerk, was brought up to speak a burial service as they dropped his body in the canal among the reeds.

For two or three weeks the days passed with little incident. Carson and Parker did several nights' guard duty on the prison barge, and at other times they stayed on the first barge. The Organisation had brought in several more German deserters and now there were over forty of them crammed into the stinking hold. Some of them had been getting restless, complaining loudly about the food and conditions. All they got was a few grubby boiled potatoes a day and sometimes some bread. For drinking they threw a bucket over the side and drew up the water that looked cloudy and tasted muddy and was probably responsible for the dysentery some of the prisoners had. The Kommandant let them up on deck in batches for an hour a day for air and exercise and told them curtly that no country infested by Germans ever had enough food. His attitude to them, Carson thought, was like that of a reformatory teacher dealing with dead-end kids.

The Organisation itself had little more food than the Germans. They had to get it black market from surrounding farms and some of the farmers, terrified of being caught supplying them, did not always co-operate enthusiastically. Carson was hungry all the time. Now and then they had the luxury of a little sugar to sprinkle on the bread and Carson came to think that black bread and sugar was better than any cake he had ever tasted. Parker, on the other hand, was harder to please. Every time they gave him a little sugar on his bread he used to say, " Goddam, I hate sugar," and wolf it down.

One day a Dutchman brought in a German officer, an unpleasant, stuffy young man who had deserted his troops but still regarded himself as an important personage, entitled to special respect and privileges. On the way to the barge he had made the mistake of informing the Dutch guard that he (the guard) was lacking in manners and breeding, and when they got to the hatch the guard propelled him into the depths with a shrewdly placed foot.

In a minute the officer was screaming through the hatch that a German officer should never have to live with the troops, particularly in such conditions. He demanded special treatment.

Carson, whose shoes had been falling apart, called him up on deck, took his magnificent shiny top-boots and sent him below again, feeling tempted to speed him on his way with one of his new boots.

Parker said, " Goddam, that guy reminds me of some Cambridge University characters I met once."

One morning one of the Dutch came back from a food expedition and said that advancing British troops had reached Tilburg and Breda—about twenty-five miles from the Biesbosch. Carson, who had been getting more and more restless, thought that was near enough to try an all-or-nothing dash for the lines. Both he and Parker had long tired of the novelty of holding an enclave of German prisoners on German-held territory. Sick of being half-starved and hunted and covered in lice like everyone else, Carson told the Kommandant he and Parker were going to make a dash for it, and the Kommandant said simply : " We need you here. Now that your troops are getting near we can do some things to help them."

German activity was increasing in the area, he explained, and German patrols becoming more common in the Biesbosch. In his unemotional way he suggested that they make the district unhealthy for the Germans by laying some ambushes. He was a strange and compelling personality, the Kommandant. It was not that he begged them to stay. He merely said that there was useful work to do and they stayed.

Jan was immediately keen on the ambush idea and he teamed up with Carson and Parker to make one of the " task forces."

They picked a spot in the reeds opposite the village across the Maas and hid there and watched. On the second morning an old Dutch duck catcher who lived in the Biesbosch panted up to them in their hiding spot and said that two German soldiers were looting his house. They went back with him, told him to keep in the background, and cautiously walked out of the path across the clearing towards the house. The Dutchman's wife came to the window and signalled violently and they stopped, trying to make out what she meant, when a German soldier came out of the door with a rifle. He yelled at them to walk ahead with their hands up, but the three pretended not to understand, turned and were walking away when they heard the click of the rifle bolt very clearly and the shots started as they broke into a run. Carson heard the zip-zip of a couple of bullets and then he and Parker and Jan dived into the reeds, to fall into a canal just behind. Both

Germans were running down towards them now, firing into the reeds. The three tried to move further away, but every time they moved the reeds rattled and shook on top, giving them away.

The Germans were panting and tramping just behind the reeds, and then the shots started again, zipping through the reeds and tearing white furrows on the water. Sinking their bodies in the stagnant shallows, Carson and the other two watched the reeds, keeping their pistol hands above water, waiting for the chance of a shot. Slowly they squirmed back and back until they were across the canal.

An occasional shot still came through the reeds, but the Germans were shooting blindly as they walked cautiously along the bank, listening, and the nearest bullet slashed through the reeds a good thirty yards away. After a while Carson slowly hauled himself through the reeds on the other side of the canal, and the other two crawled after him. They ran down the paths to try and intercept the two Germans on their way back to the village but the Germans must have taken some other path because they did not see them.

A day or two later they had better luck. Watching across the river from the spy nest in the reeds they saw four German soldiers get in a skiff and start rowing across the Maas to the Biesbosch. The three of them ran and hid in the reeds by a trail leading up from the river but the Germans chose a different path, and then began a fantastic five hours as the three men blindly tried to shadow the Germans, running along trails, splashing across streams and dykes, trying to head them off, most of the time having only a dim idea of where the Germans were and all the time taking the risk of running slap into them along one of the narrow trails that funnelled through the marshes. Once or twice they sighted them crossing cleared patches of the marshes but never in time to head them off.

Carson was thinking of going back to the skiff to get them on the way back at the water's edge (though it would be in sight of the troops across the river) when the four Germans emerged from the reeds some distance off, strolled across a clearing and entered a small hut. Carson saw, without joy, that the soldiers were heavily armed. Among them they had a light machine gun, two tommy guns and a rifle. Carson, Jan and Parker only had pistols.

A broken hay-rick stood near the hut and the three hid on top of it, waiting for the Germans to come out. As dusk fell they saw one of the Germans in the hut going from window to window, and it became clear that he was a sentry and that the Germans would not leave the hut that night. With a sentry it was too risky to rush the hut, so they settled to sleep in the hay and wait for the morning.

Jan, who had been a guerrilla and fugitive for three years, was awake at first light and woke the other two. They watched the Germans moving inside the hut. Jan thought that they were too exposed and isolated on the hay-rick for an ambush in broad daylight, and suggested they go back along the trail that the soldiers would probably follow to the skiff. Backing quietly away, keeping the rick between them and the house, they came to a spot where the ground rose a little away from the trail. On the rise, barely five yards from the track, clustered a thicket of shrubs. It was the ideal spot and they settled behind the shrubs and waited.

It was about an hour later that the soldiers came down the track in single file, the front man carrying one of the dangerous tommy guns. Jan whispered : " I'll take the front man." Parker said : " I'll shoot for a double in the middle."

Carson got a bead through the leaves on the last man about twenty yards back and took up the first pull on the trigger. There was a loud bang beside him as Jan fired and then Carson fired. Parker was standing up firing, head above the shrubs, shooting methodically. On the trail a paralysed fraction of a moment snapped in a flurry of chaos and panic. The front man was staggering, the second one fell instantly, the third bounded into the reeds on the other side of the track and the last man dropped his machine gun and hared off back the way he had come. Carson, furious at having missed, was standing up firing like Parker at the running man, pistol banging like a series of backfires till there was only a click, and the last man also vanished in the reeds.

Carson slid another clip into the butt and Jan and Parker,

keeping under cover, fired systematically into the reeds where the third man had jumped. Soon there was a frightened cry in the reeds, " Kamerad ! Kamerad ! "

Jan yelled for him to come out with his hands up and a moment later the reeds rattled and shook and the German stepped hesitantly on to the track. He was trembling uncontrollably with shock and fright and the tears were running down his face. He looked dumbly at them and at the two soldiers lying on the ground. He did not seem able to talk.

" We got to get the other one," Parker said. " If he gets back and talks that'll be a bad deal."

They walked carefully along the track to the spot where the fourth man had disappeared, prodding the other German in front with their pistols as some sort of a shield. Jan called out in German telling the missing man to come out and surrender, but there was no answer, and after a while they pushed gingerly into the reeds to smoke him out. Carson felt his flesh creep, hoping the missing man did not have a pistol. They searched for several minutes and were about to give it up when Parker called, " Here he is." Carson pushed through the reeds and saw the soldier lying half under water at the edge of a ditch. He had a bullet in the base of his neck and was quite dead.

They went back then with the prisoner to the spot of the ambush where the others were lying. One of them died as they got there, but the other was still alive and conscious, blood gushing out of a bad wound in his chest. Jan said, " It's too far to carry him back to the barge. He wouldn't live anyway."

" What the devil can we do then ? " Carson asked.

" Make him kaput," Jan said.

" Oh God, no."

" I'll do it," said Jan. " Don't watch."

He walked quickly up to the wounded man who watched him pathetically and dumbly. Carson turned away as Jan swiftly knelt. The gun banged once and Carson felt he was going to be sick.

Jan said quietly, " Forgive me."

They took the surviving German and the guns back to the barge.

Carson, Parker and Jan went on several more sorties during the next confused days, but there was no more killing, for which Carson was glad. They intercepted a few more Germans, but, backed by moral force of their new tommy guns, they let rip from the reeds with short bursts over the enemy heads and the soldiers dropped their weapons instantly and gladly surrendered. They took them back to the barge. Other Dutchmen of the Organisation brought in more prisoners and by the end of October they counted seventy demoralised Germans grumbling and scratching at lice in the stinking hold.

The deep thumps of heavy guns were coming across the Maas now and at night they saw the glow of fires. Every day the guns sounded louder and every night the fires were nearer. On October 4 they found themselves on the barge in the middle of an artillery duel, shells screeching over them like shrill thunder from the British guns across the river and the Germans behind the Biesbosch. One of the Dutchmen came back from a reconnaissance and said that the Germans had pulled out of the village across the river and that the British were very close to it. Carson had a few words with Parker and then they went to the Kommandant and Carson told him they were going to try a dash across the river just before dawn.

This time the Kommandant nodded. " That is the best," he said solemnly. " You must tell them that we are here and I will send one of my men with you."

He surprised Carson then by revealing that they could start the engine of the barge and that if Carson could send an " all clear " message back by the Dutchman, they could steer the barge out of the canal into the river and across.

An hour before dawn Carson, Parker and a Dutchman moved down the trail to the river, got into a skiff at the old landing and quietly paddled across the river, not daring to talk even in whispers because sound carries so clearly in the stillness just before dawn.

They landed a few hundred yards from the village and as

the grey light came Carson climbed a willow to try and see
what was happening in the village. In a minute a loud explosion sent up a mushroom of dirt a hundred yards away and
then there was another, and then another, rather closer.
Carson caught the flashes a couple of miles beyond the village
and realised they had been spotted by a British battery. He
almost fell out of the tree and they scrambled into cover along
the river bank, the Dutchman holding his bleeding hand
where he had been hit by a shell splinter.

Crawling towards the village they saw no movement at all.
It was silent and seemed deserted, and they crawled under
cover to the corner of a house on the outskirts and settled
down to watch.

Half an hour later a man darted from behind a house,
crossed the street and vanished into a doorway. A minute
later he flitted out of the doorway and vanished behind
another house, and Carson, heart jumping into his throat,
saw that the man was in British battledress.

They watched the soldier work his way down the street,
fascinated by the quick, nervous dashes into cover, praying
that no snipers were left in the village. No sound or movement came from the houses and when the soldier darted into
view again about fifty yards away Carson saw the N.C.O.'s
chevrons on his sleeve and yelled, " Hey, sergeant!"

The soldier was instantly out of sight in a doorway. Carson
yelled again, " We're Allied Air Force officers escaping. The
Germans have pushed off out of here."

There was a brief silence, and then the soldier's voice came :
" Come out with your hands up. Walk in the middle of the
road."

" Well, for Christ's sake don't shoot," Carson yelled.
" Here we come."

They walked up the middle of the road with their hands up
and Parker said : " Goddam. I dodge the Jerries all this
time and then get captured by the British."

    .   .   .   .   .

An hour later they were telling a lieutenant-colonel of the
Rifle Brigade what they knew of the German movements and

the situation in the Biesbosch. A little after dusk the Dutchman went back across the river and towards midnight they heard the chugging of the barge's engine. It grew louder and louder and after about half an hour the barge moved slowly out of the darkness and grounded on the friendly shore. The Kommandant jumped over the bows and waded ashore, allowing his face to wrinkle into a wide smile as they took him to see the colonel, but the happiest of all seemed to be the seventy Germans in the hold.

Carson got back to 222 Squadron so quickly that the Biesbosch was still full of Germans, and he flew over and shot them up. He was awarded the Military Cross for his evasion. After the war he married a Coventry girl, stayed in the R.A.F. with a permanent commission, became a test pilot for a while and then a flying instructor. Transferring to jets, he went to Germany in 1948 as a flight commander in No. 67 (Vampire) Squadron. Later he returned to England to become an instructor on Meteors. His wife is a sailplane pilot and they have one son.

THE WOMEN WHO TOOK A HAND

Indestructible is the word for James Dowd. He is short, wiry and spirited, and as tough and resilient as a piece of gristle. Born in Greenock, Scotland, on June 25, 1922, he went to St. Lawrence's, St. Mary's and St. Columba's schools and joined the R.A.F. as a boy entrant in 1939. As soon as war broke out he volunteered for flying and on his eighteenth birthday, in 1940 (just after Dunkirk), started training as a wireless operator-air gunner. When he graduated he did a full tour of bomber operations on No. 83 Squadron. After a rest he went back for more and on March 13, 1942, was shot down on the first trip of his second tour.

WHILE statesmen rally the nations, generals rally the soldiers, and soldiers heroically slaughter each other, some half the populations concerned are usually uninflamed by the battle cries. They are called women, and in the face of the epic drama of war they go on preferring dull things like gossip, small children, the price of bread, and men. They seem to think that a man is only a man and not a noble Roman or a barbarous Goth, according to his identification card. The third time he escaped Sergeant James Dowd took advantage of this female treason.

He was a Friday the thirteenth victim; on that day in March, 1942, the Manchester in which he was a gunner had come down in flames on the way to Cologne. The hard-bitten, wiry little Scot had bailed out, and then been bailed up by a farmer with a shotgun. A couple of weeks later he was looking out of the barbed wire of the R.A.F. compound at all the other ugly huts in the big camp at Lamsdorf in Eastern Germany, about forty miles south-east of Breslau, where the old Polish border ran down to meet Czechoslovakia. Within twenty-four hours he had learned that it was very hard to escape from the compound but simple to escape from the working parties which were sent out into the country. However, the Germans knew that too and did not allow R.A.F. aircrew out on working parties.

Dowd allowed for that by changing places with an Army private who had to go out on working parties but did not like to work. Dowd took his name, his uniform and his place in the working party which the Germans took by train to some wired barracks thirty miles away. When they got there Dowd found that his job was draining sewage ditches ; it was an added incentive not to linger, and at dusk on the day of his arrival he wrapped his coat round the bars of a window in the prison hut to muffle the sound, bashed at them till they bent a little, wriggled through and ran into the night.

For twelve days he walked towards Switzerland, eating potatoes and turnips from the fields and sleeping under bushes. Some suspicious Germans walked over him one morning, and back at Lamsdorf he did a spell of solitary confinement on bread and water for escaping.

After his sentence was over they let him out for a few days and then took him back to the cells again as extra punishment for changing places with the soldier. In the first hour he changed cells with another soldier and was so appallingly brazen about it that the Germans did not notice. It was very sporting of the soldier, because he had to do Dowd's fourteen days and Dowd only had to serve his four days. He came out and went on another working party to a paper mill, worked dutifully for a week or so, then stole a bicycle and pedalled away.

Escaping on wheels seemed so much easier and quicker than walking, and then he came to a roundabout and innocently steered left around it instead of right. It looked so obvious to the two police who were resting by it. This time he got twenty-eight days' solitary, and when he came out Kissell, the compound Unteroffizier, watched him closely.

After the Dieppe raid the Germans took reprisals and Dowd, like the hundreds of other prisoners, spent three months with handcuffs on. Then winter was on them. Winter is the season for thinking, not escaping. Dowd did a lot of thinking, and much of it was around the bitter lesson he had learned that escaping from the cage and the guards is only half the battle. The other half is in getting out of enemy-held territory. He thought a great deal about that angle of it.

When the spring came he complained of being ill through the bad food (and the lack of it) and they put him in the prison hospital. A Private Strachan was admitted to the hospital at the same time. Strachan said he did not mind a temporary promotion to R.A.F. sergeant, so when they got undressed in the ward Dowd got into Strachan's bed and Strachan got into his.

He spent a fortnight being treated for Strachan's lumbago, studying German (which he was picking up fast) and talking to an Australian sergeant pilot called Reed, who had escaped and been caught at Stettin trying to board a Swedish ship.

" The best way to get there is to let the Jerry railways take you," Reed said. " It's a piece of cake if you get some civvy clothes and some German money and papers."

Dowd learned from Reed about the port area of Stettin, and when he walked out of the hospital in Strachan's battledress he persuaded one of the amateur artists in the camp to design him some forged papers saying he was a Belgian electrical mechanic travelling to a new job at Stettin. By a little gentle bribery he acquired two hundred German marks, and the day before his twenty-first birthday he went out with some British soldiers to a sawmill at the grey old town of Grottkau, about twenty miles west of Lamsdorf.

At night, after work, three German soldiers of the elderly garrison type locked them in part of a hut next to the sawmill, but after a week Dowd and the others had trained them to be tolerant to the point of submissiveness. It was quite easy. The guards wanted peace and quietness. The prisoners said they would give them peace and quietness if they did what they were told. Otherwise they would give them hell. Both sides knew that if the guards could not adequately control their prisoners they would be sent to the Russian front. By the end of the week the bars on the window of the prisoners' room could be (and were) lifted out at will.

Grottkau was a normal German wartime town, occupied by women of various types and ages and by a few men who qualified either for short pants or long beards. The young men were away fighting for Hitler, except, of course, for the British prisoners. For the women it was the old story of supply and demand, with emphasis on demand.

Most nights the prisoners felt distaste for their drab barrack, removed the bars and went for walks in the less frequented lanes of the town, finding that some of the girls, conscious of being women first and German second, were quite friendly. A jaunty Scottish corporal known as Buster got along very well with a young wife whose husband was away and who lived alone in a house near the sawmill. He told her how comfortless it was in the barrack hut, and she, blooming with sympathy, insisted he sleep in her house nearly every night; which he did, returning just before dawn, checking to see that all the others were back and replacing the iron bar for the sake of appearances. He said she worried that he was working too hard in the sawmill and fed him in the evenings to keep up his strength. The Germans provided the death penalty for these sort of contacts, but the carefree Buster said it was the way he had always wanted to die.

Dowd had caught the eye of a girl called Anna, whose father owned a share of the sawmill. She was blonde, about twenty-two, with a fresh-faced prettiness. In the evenings she used to meet Dowd by a stream outside the town, where they could talk safely ; it was not healthy for a German girl to be seen with an enemy prisoner.

From the day he had arrived Dowd had been hoarding all the non-perishable food he could lay his hands on, trading his cigarettes for things like chocolate, porridge and biscuits. About his third week at Grottkau he told Anna he was going to escape and wanted her help. At first she was terrified, but Dowd kept persuading her and after a couple of days she rather timidly agreed to get him some civilian clothes.

He knew that Buster had already escaped a couple of times and, as Buster knew so much about the local life, asked him if he would like to make the break with him. " I've got some marks," Dowd pointed out, " so we can go by train."

" They check all the fast trains," Buster said, " and I've got no papers."

" We'll do it in stages by slow train."

" All right," Buster sighed. " It's a pity, in a way, to leave Grottkau."

A few nights later Anna came down to the stream hugging a parcel under her arm and handed it to Dowd as though it were hot. He opened it and found an old lounge suit coat, a tie, some civilian shoes and the sort of ski-ing cap that Northern Europeans often wear.

" My father does not wear them now," Anna said.

He persuaded a Pole who worked in the sawmill to bring some brown dye from the town and dyed his shirt and battle-dress trousers. The Pole, who had been a tailor, stitched turn-ups on the trousers, and then, two nights before they planned to go, Buster disappeared. He crawled back through the window the next night and woke Dowd. " I'm staying with my girl for a couple of days," he said. " Just having a last fling. See you outside the railway station six o'clock to-morrow night."

All the next day—August 29, 1943—Dowd felt the old exhilaration seeping through him. The guard locked them in at five-thirty and Dowd stripped off his prison battledress and carefully put on his new civilian outfit. It was still daylight outside, but this was Sunday—deliberately planned—and the timber yard was empty. At five forty-five he took out the bar, slipped out into the yard, dodged warily among the timber stacks, climbed nimbly over the back fence and walked along the street, pulling his cap fairly low over his eyes.

At the station he found Buster and a weeping woman beside him. Buster looked almost dapper in a felt hat, flannel bags and a coat that fitted reasonably well.

" Let's go," he said. " I've got the tickets to Brieg."

The woman lifted her face, trying to smile, and Buster bent and kissed her gently. Walking away from her to the platform he said laconically, " You know, this is the first time I've been really literally in a husband's shoes. I'm in his coat and pants too."

The train came in on time ; they climbed aboard and cheerfully watched the houses of Grottkau slide out of view behind.

Brieg was a town on the line to Breslau. They were there in an hour and had to wait several hours for a train to Breslau. Eating some of their biscuits, Dowd could see that Buster was fidgety.

" I don't like this Breslau junket," Buster said restively after a while. " It'll be stiff with coppers and I don't want any more jankers."

" Well, you can't go back now," Dowd said tersely. There was a brief silence and Buster said, " Look, I know a woman at Oderburg. She's Czech and she helped me once before. I think I'll try and stay with her for a while again. Maybe she can get me some papers." It looked as though he had made up his mind ; almost as though he had been planning it all the time. He kept saying he could walk to the place and seemed in a hurry to go.

" All right," Dowd said. " Don't overdo it. See you after the war."

Buster grinned, shook hands, waved cheerfully and then Dowd was waiting alone on the platform. The train was a long time coming, and when it hissed and panted into the platform he stepped quickly aboard, saw instantly that it seemed to be full of soldiers and stood in the corridor looking stolidly out of the window.

He felt relieved when it started to move, but it occurred to him as it slid out that the platform was still full of people, and he wondered why they had not boarded the train. He edged his eyes to the left and right along the corridor and saw they were all men and all in uniform. Oh, God ! A troop train.

And then there was a girl in a uniform staring at him and coming down the corridor. She stopped directly in front of him and demanded : " What are you doing on an army train ? " He guessed it was a railway uniform and that she was some kind of conductress.

He mumbled in his bad German that he was a Belgian worker and did not realise this was a troop train.

She said in a business-like way that it was a " Schnellzug " (express) and he must pay a surcharge of two marks. He paid it, she gave him a receipt and just before she turned away she shook a finger at him and said, " You had better look out."

A white lamb in a herd of black sheep, he turned to try and look unconcernedly out of the window, acutely aware of an S.S. man in a black uniform scowling at him a bare two yards away. A corporal of the railway police appeared at the end of the carriage, silver breastplate hanging impressively like a new moon on the chain round his neck. He came along the rocking corridor with the jerky side-to-side motion, fending himself off the sides with each elbow. Dowd saw his eyes spot him and the brows contract in anger. The man was towering over him and demanding to know who he was and what he was doing in the train.

He was a foreign worker, Dowd was stumbling to say ; he didn't know it was a troop train ; his stomach felt like water and he was thinking grimly, " Here we go again."

Beside him a Luftwaffe Oberfeldwebel (flight sergeant), who had heard Dowd trying to explain to the girl, started telling the corporal with a tolerant air that the trespasser was a Belgian who had made a mistake and had paid the extra fare. The corporal quietened down, his voice dropped to a grumble, he snorted at Dowd and stalked on.

At half-past eleven the train steamed into Breslau. Dowd thankfully got out, walked into the booking hall, saw there was a train leaving for Frankfurt-on-Oder at midnight, bought a ticket and half an hour later was on his way. Now it seemed to be going smoothly ; he ate some of his sandwiches (bully beef and fried egg—the egg by courtesy of Anna) and dozed on and off till they came to Frankfurt-on-Oder at half-past six.

In the station lavatory he washed and shaved, feeling much better afterwards, and an hour later boarded another local train for Eberswalde, thirty miles north-east of Berlin. Again there were no checks on the train, and he was feeling so confident now that at Eberswalde he took his first chance and boarded the express for Stettin. They were rolling fast through the countryside when a policeman in a green uniform came into the compartment, and he cursed himself for taking the chance. The man muttered something he did not catch and held out his hand. Dowd handed over his papers and the policeman hardly looked at them. It was a most per-

functory glance ; he handed them back and walked on.
Twenty-three hours after climbing out of the barrack hut
window Dowd was walking out of Stettin Station into the
streets.

He walked for a long time, for the first time feeling uncertain ; now he was here he did not know what to do next.
There was an old painted sign in front that said " Bier," and
it was like a beacon ; the reaction was automatic. He passed
under the sign and through the doors. Breasting the zinc
bar he looked affectionately at his first beer for sixteen
months, took a sip, scowled critically at it, lit a cigarette,
pulled thoughtfully at his beer and began to feel a little more
relaxed.

Someone was speaking to him ; he turned and looked
warily at the weedy youth by his side asking for a light. He
struck a match for him and the youth started talking about the
war. Dowd could hardly make out what he was saying. He
answered in grunts for a while and, getting a sudden idea,
turned and said :

" You are not German ? "

The youth said apologetically, no, he was Polish.

" Ich bin Schwedischer Marine," Dowd said, and added
that he had missed his ship and wanted to find some other
Swedish sailors.

" Swedish sailors ? " the young man said. " There were
always some at the —— " ; he said some word that Dowd
did not understand. He shook his head. What was that
place ?

The Pole repeated the word and Dowd shook his head
again.

The Pole grinned, leaned close and made unmistakable
gestures. He made his meaning very clear.

" Bordel ? " Dowd said.

The Pole nodded delightedly. " Für Ausländer," he said.
For foreigners ! Dowd felt his heart kick.

" Kein Deutsche ? " It was almost too much to hope for.

" Kein Deutsche," the Pole grinned. No Germans !

Dowd wanted to know where it was and the Pole said he
would gladly show him. They went into the street, around

several corners, and in Kleineoderstrasse the Pole stopped in front of a grubby grey house.

Dowd followed him through the door and looked, fascinated, at the mob in the big front room. There were about thirty men of all types and sizes and ages, mostly roughly dressed, and he counted ten girls. The place was hot and smoky and a lot of the people were drinking. Some of the men were sitting on benches round the walls and some of the girls were sitting on their knees ; others were standing up talking to men, and he noticed that the girls seemed more at ease. He thought some of them looked quite pretty ; they were fully dressed—at least on the surface—and talking as though they were at a cocktail party. The hum of conversation rose discordantly all round, the clash of different tongues and bursts of laughter.

The Pole said they were Polish and Ukrainian girls. He walked over to talk to a scruffy man in a grubby white coat; probably a waiter, Dowd thought. Two big blond men in a corner were arguing ; he guessed they were Swedes, but they seemed drunk and he did not want to get mixed up with drunks. A fat old woman by a door in the far wall was scowling at them. A girl walked across the room holding a man by the hand, and as they went through the far door the fat woman nodded a brief mechanical smile at the man.

Dowd moved about self-consciously, listening to conversations, trying to pick out Swedes, but apart from the two drunks he could not find any. He bought a beer off the man in the white coat and, after enduring it all for an hour, he went out of the front door to get some air.

Three men were standing by the step of the door, two young ones glaring at a big fair one. The shorter of the young ones said angrily, " You —— Swedish bastard," and Dowd stopped dead and looked in unbelief.

He had spoken in English !

He was about twenty, looked so obviously English, an escaper like himself, and Dowd was suddenly tingling with gladness. The Swede, mumbling incoherently, quite drunk, waved his arm vaguely and disgustedly and lurched down the street.

Dowd walked over to the two young men and without preamble said urgently, " Look, what's the score blokes ? "

They gaped at him.

" It's all right," Dowd said. " I'm R.A.F. I've escaped. You're English, aren't you ? "

" No, Dutch," the shorter man said, and there was a taut silence. The short one broke it, saying quickly, " Don't talk here. Come on." (English, as it happened, was the only language the two had had in common with the Swede.)

They walked along the street away from the brothel and when no one was near the short man—youth really—said quietly : " What are you trying to do ? "

" Get on a Swedish ship," Dowd said. He told them where he had come from and that now he was uncertain of what to do.

" You cannot stay in the street," the short one said. " You must have shelter for the night. You should come and sleep with us now."

As they walked he said his name was Johnny. The tall one was Dirk, but it was Johnny who did all the talking. They took him up to their room in a boarding house. There were two beds in the room and Johnny insisted there was enough room in his bed for Dowd to share it.

In the morning Johnny said he would take a day off from work (he was forced labour, he explained) and take Dowd round the harbour on the little launch that still did pleasure trips.

" We will see the Swedish ships," he said. They went all round the Freihaven and saw two Swedish ships loading. Johnny agreed that the best thing would be to try and contact some of the crew ashore. He gave Dowd a little Swedish seamen's union badge to wear in his cap—refusing to say where he had got it—took him to a café where they could have off-ration food, soup, red cabbage and potatoes, and an hour before dusk Johnny led the way back to the brothel.

Dowd thought it was very quiet when they went in. He saw as many people there as the previous night but the gaiety seemed to have gone and the talk was not so spontaneous. The madame was scowling over by the far door. He wandered

about the room with Johnny listening for Swedish voices.
There was a bustle by the front door and the room went very
still. Three men in raincoats and felt hats were standing there.
Johnny was suddenly pale. He whispered, " Gestapo! "

He and Dowd were by the far door. Dowd turned and
walked past the madame, opened the door and as he went
through a dark girl came off the stairs to walk into the room.
He smiled at her and pointed upstairs. She smiled back,
turned and led the way. At the top she opened a door ; he
followed her in, closed the door and as she turned to him he
said in German, " You are not a German girl ? "

It must have been obvious from his accent that he was a
foreigner himself. She made a face and said, No, she was
Polish, and Dowd took the plunge.

" I'm an English flyer," he whispered. " I must hide for a
little while."

The girl went very white and her mouth opened. She
looked as though she were going to scream. Dowd clenched
his fist, feeling he would hit her if she did—hard. A little
sound came out of her and she was trembling.

" No," she said. " No. You must go. Please go. Please."

Dowd was talking, pleading, begging, and then they both
heard the feet on the stairs and he shut up abruptly. They
were both utterly still. The girl abruptly pointed under the
bed. He moved quickly across the room and crawled under it.
The bed creaked as the girl sat on it. He saw her ankles by
his eyes and his heart was going hard. A door opened down
the corridor and he heard voices. More footsteps. The
handle of the door rattled and clicked and he knew it was
opening. A man's voice sounded in the opening.

" Have you any customers ? "

He must be keeping his face behind the door. The girl said :
" No. It is a bad night." The man laughed agreeably and
said, " We should alter that." He seemed to linger behind
the door and then he must have made up his mind. The door
shut and his footsteps died away outside.

Dowd gave him a few seconds and wriggled out. He
whispered in his inadequate German, " Danke Schön,
Fräulein. Danke Schön. Sie ist sehr gut."

She smiled at him rather pathetically.

" I must wait till they go," he breathed, and sat beside her on the bed—after a little silence they began to talk. He learned her name was Maria and she was nineteen. She was dark-haired with pale skin and quite pretty. Her people had a farm near Lodz and the Germans said they could keep it if she came to Stettin to work.

" The rotten swine," Dowd commented, and she shrugged.

" I do not have to sleep with Germans," she said. " That is something."

Feeling the friendship was on a firm basis of mutual sympathy, Dowd asked her if she could put him in touch with some Swedish sailors, and she was terrified again. She kept saying, " They would kill me if they found out," and after a while he knew it was no good keeping on at her. They were both silent and he thought how unreal it was that he should be sitting in the room of a Polish prostitute at Stettin. It was a pleasant enough room, with a carpet and frilly curtains, and he said tritely, " Do you like it here ? "

She shrugged again. " It is a good house. Some of the men are kind. Not always. There was a fight here to-night. That is why the Gestapo came."

Not quite knowing what to say he muttered, " I'm sorry I have no money to give you for what you have done."

She smiled and said that a girl did not always have to have money, and he saw with interest that she was being ambiguous —and provocative.

Some time later she went downstairs and came back to say that the Gestapo had gone. Dowd said he must go, too, and then she surprised him. She would try and find some Swedish sailors, she said, and added : " If you can come back to-morrow night I may have some news."

He thanked her warmly, feeling that words were inadequate, and went quietly down the stairs, wondering about women. The big room was nearly empty ; he walked straight out into the street and there was Johnny waiting with another man a few yards away. He felt lightheaded with relief : they turned and walked down the street with him.

" I did not see them take you out so I thought I would

wait," Johnny said. He introduced the other man as a Dutch friend who would take him to his dormitory in a foreign workers' camp. By a barbed wire enclosure down by the docks, Johnny left them.

In the barrack hut inside the guarded wire Dowd slept in an empty bunk and in the morning he found that three Germans had slept in the hut, too, on air raid duty. They were eyeing him suspiciously as a stranger in the hut but went out without comment.

Two green-uniformed police walked into the hut five minutes later and asked for the stranger. There was no escaping them. The workers had to point him out and he stood there helplessly. They stopped in front of him and one said, " What are you doing here ? "

" Ich bin Schwedischer Marine," Dowd said and indicated Johnny's badge in his cap. He was trying to explain that he had lost his way back to his ship. The policeman looked at the badge and apparently they knew it. " Ach so," one of them said. He shrugged and they both turned and walked out.

Dowd scuttled out of the camp as soon as he could and spent the day walking around the harbour and sitting on a seat on the Haaken Terrasse, looking over the water.

An hour before dusk he went back to the brothel. The girl Maria was in the big room and walked straight over to him and shook hands with a worried smile. There was no news, she said ; she had seen no Swedes. He could see she was badly frightened and took her upstairs to talk to her. They sat on the bed and he asked her to keep on trying, but the madame and the other girls had apparently been talking to her, telling her she was crazy to take such risks. She kept shaking her head and looking as though she were going to cry. He knew after a while that it was useless, left her there and went downstairs.

No one in the big room looked to be Swedish and for the first time he was getting a hopeless feeling. Now he was on his own and there was the immediate problem of where to spend the night. He would not last long in the streets after midnight. There was only one thing to do ; he went out of the house and started walking. It was half an hour before he came to open country on the outskirts of the city and crawled into a copse.

A cold dawn woke him early and he walked back into the town, calling at the railway station to freshen up with a wash in the lavatories. In a café by the waterfront he had some soup, coffee and bread. As he came out he saw three men approaching and recognised on their caps the Swedish sailors' badge. Wheeling, he walked alongside and said, " Sind sie Schwede ? "

The man nearest looked at him blankly, so Dowd muttered cautiously in English : " Are you Swedish ? "

" Yes," the man said, surprised, also in English, and then, suspiciously, " Who are you ? "

" What are the chances of getting on to a Swedish ship ? " Dowd asked.

" You're English ? "

" I'm not German."

" English ? "

" I'm Scottish," Dowd said, as though it mattered. The men were eyeing him without friendliness. " Can you help me get on to a Swedish ship ? "

" No, it is not possible," one of the men said. He shook his head impatiently. " The ships are guarded." Quite obviously they did not want to have anything to do with him. One of them said, " Give yourself up," and they turned away and left him there.

Furious, he crossed the Oder over the Hansebruecke. Anchored in the river lay a little steamer with a Danish flag painted on her side ; he read her name, *Margarita*, and wondered if she would be moving into a wharf somewhere. Taking the ferry across the Freihaven, he walked along the docks and in a few minutes found what he was looking for—a small auxiliary sailing ship with the Swedish flag on the jack over the taffrail, moored by a quay. Walking casually up and down the tall wire fence that cut off the quay, he memorised the lay-out of the quay and the buildings and when he felt he would know it blindfold went back to the town and spent the afternoon in a cinema.

It was dusk when he took the ferry over the Freihaven again and waited in the shadows watching the quay. It seemed deserted. He walked quickly up to the fence, pulled himself nimbly up and over and headed for the little Swedish ship. He was walking alongside the ship, saw thankfully that there was no guard on the gangway and was reaching out his hand for the handrope of the gangway when a German dock policeman walked round the corner of the dock-shed about ten yards away, saw him, and let out a hail.

The familiar, cold, sick feeling swept through him. Thinking fast, he staggered, rolled his head drunkenly and lifted it to peer at the policeman, swaying slightly. The policeman was striding towards him ; Christ, he thought, I've had it. I'll kick him in the stomach. He saw the pistol holster on the man's belt and changed his mind. Bluff it through. The policeman said : " Ausweis bitte mein Herr ! "

Fumbling in his pockets, playing for time, Dowd had an idea ; he said in his bad German, slurring his words, " I have twenty passes." He pulled out a full packet of twenty cigarettes and held them out to the policeman and the policeman (who was rationed to three a day) took the packet.

" What are you doing here ? " he asked.

He was a Swedish sailor, Dowd said thickly. This was his ship, the *Margarita*.

" You have drunk too much," the policeman said. " This is not the *Margarita*." He grabbed Dowd's arm and said, " Komm."

Carefully stumbling, Dowd walked with him along the quay and the policeman, still holding his arm firmly, guided him through a door. Three soldiers in the room looked up and he knew it was a guardhouse. They were staring at him, and he stared blearily back, bracing himself to try and bluff.

The policeman was pushing him across the room to an open door. He steered Dowd through and Dowd incredulously found himself in the street outside.

" Try that way for the *Margarita*," the guard said, pointing along the street. Dowd felt his arm released. He had the wit to mumble, " Danke Schön. Danke Schön," and weaved along the street, hardly believing. He badly wanted to hurry, but he waited till he came to a corner, turned it and ran. It occurred to him after a while—and the thought made him shudder—that the cigarettes he had given the policeman were a packet of English Gold Flakes from his last parcel in the prison camp. He kept on running.

Without much trouble he found his way back to the ferry shed and waited there a long time, but no ferry came. He was alone there, so he lay on the bench and slept.

Hours later he woke with someone shaking his shoulder, opened his eyes and saw an old workman looking down at him.

" The ferry is about to leave," the workman said, and Dowd saw that it was dawn. He went back in the ferry, washed in the public lavatory and after breakfast found he had only thirty marks left. All morning he walked up and down the Haaken Terrasse looking for Swedish sailors, but did not see a single one. It was the same in the afternoon, and around six o'clock he went despondently to a tavern to think it over. There seemed to be only one thing to do. He walked out and headed for the ferry. It was do or die this time. Find a Swedish ship and board her or . . . he didn't know what.

Halfway across the Hansebruecke a tall young man in a group walking the other way stopped, turned to him and asked in faulty German where they could find a good tavern. Dowd's eyes were staring at his lapel. Stuck in it was a badge of the Danish flag.

He pointed at the badge and asked, " Däne ? "

" Ja."

" Do you speak English ? "

The young man's eyebrows shot up. He said uncertainly, " Yes. I speak some English a little."

" I'm Royal Air Force." Dowd spoke fast. " I've escaped. I want to get on a boat for Sweden. Do you know of a boat ? "

The young man was staring at him. His mouth split into a grin and the grin abruptly vanished. He jerked his head across the bridge and said, " Come with us."

Dowd walked back over the bridge with him. The other four trailed behind. " Let us go to a tavern," the Dane said, and they walked in a stiff silence.

" In here," Dowd said. He led them into the tavern he had left only two minutes before. There were not many people in it and he and the young men stood silently in an isolated group by the bar while the man behind it set up the beers.

When he had gone the Dane muttered in what was presumably his own tongue to the other men, and they looked at Dowd in amazement. The first man turned back to him and said, " How do we know you are what you say you are ? "

Dowd reached into his pocket and brought out his last packet of Gold Flakes. He showed it surreptitiously under the bar and the Dane smiled, nodded and said, " Good." He lifted his beer in salute, grinned again and said, " Skol ! "

Dowd asked a moment later, " Are you from a ship ? "

" I am the bosun of the *Margarita*," the Dane said.

" Can you get me on her ? "

The Dane was grinning all over his face with excitement. " We are sailing in the morning," he declared. " You come with us."

Sheer exhilaration swept through Dowd. He lifted his glass and said, " Skol." The Dane turned and talked to the others, and they grinned and nodded their heads. One of them said, " German bastards ! " (It turned out to be virtually the only English he knew.)

The tall Dane looked suddenly serious. " We are not going to Sweden," he explained. " We go to Riga, but you do not worry. We get you to Sweden."

" All right," Dowd said, " that's good enough." It was a small let-down but it did not worry him. He was getting on a ship with friends and leaving Germany for the Baltic.

The Dane said his name was Hans and all the others were Danes from the crew of the *Margarita*. They shook Dowd's hand warmly and he thought how different they were from the Swedes. They were all in their twenties and the brisk, decisive Hans, who seemed to be the leader, said that some day they would all like to get away from the Germans and join the British Navy.

They did not stay long in the tavern. Hans bought a bottle of schnapps and led them outside. By some stone steps leading down into the water by the bridge Hans stopped and Dowd saw the dim lines of the ship with her riding lights less than a hundred yards away in the stream. Hans bellowed at

her and in a couple of minutes a rowing boat headed in to
the steps. A middle-aged Danish seaman was the only occu-
pant and they all went down into her. Hans told the oarsman
about Dowd, and the seaman looked gloomily at Dowd and
muttered something. Hans handed him the bottle of
schnapps.

" He says the German guard is on board," he explained.
" I tell him to go up first with the schnapps for the guard."

At the ship the oarsman went first up the short Jacob's
ladder that hung over the low well-deck. He must have taken
the German into the galley or somewhere, because Hans put
his head over the rail, nodded quickly and Dowd went up on
to the deck and followed Hans quickly into the fo'c'sle.

" Easy, eh ! " Hans said.

Dowd slept in a spare bunk and was woken in the morning
by Hans shaking him and whispering in his ear, " You must
hide. The Germans are searching the ship." Hans helped
him squeeze under a bunk in a dark corner of the fo'c'sle ;
there were only about nine inches clearance and he could just
make it, lying with his white face to the bulkhead. Something metallic was dumped on the floor by the bed and a
nauseating smell came to him. He heard the others go out
of the fo'c'sle and lay there alone, cramped and fearful and
sickened by the smell.

A German voice spoke outside and heavy footsteps clumped
into the fo'c'sle. Dowd was trying to breathe noiselessly
through his mouth. The footsteps were moving about,
scraping on the floor. He almost stopped breathing as they
stopped by the bunk, and then, down by the floor, almost
by his head in the narrow space he heard a voice say, " Ach,
Schweinerei ! "

The boots were moving again and he heard them go out of
the door.

He was there twenty more minutes, gagging at the stench,
before more footsteps sounded in the fo'c'sle and he heard
Hans's voice telling him to come out. He got his feet out and
stuck, and Hans dragged him the rest of the way.

Some of the young sailors stood round smiling with relief,
and when he had relaxed a little Dowd asked Hans what on

earth it was that he had put with him under the bunk. Hans went into the washroom and came out grinning with a chamber pot.

" I thought it would make the German not so thorough," he said.

Everyone seemed happy about it, and it occurred to Dowd that the search had been a very near thing ; he guessed what would have happened to Hans and the others if the German had found him and was amazed at the casual courage they had shown. Trying to find words to thank them, he became aware that the ship was trembling, looked out of a porthole and saw the old buildings of Stettin slowly moving back. A great peace and joy filled him.

The cook brought him bacon and eggs, white bread and butter and coffee, and after the months of black bread and potatoes he thought he had never tasted anything so wonderful.

Hans told him he must not go out of the fo'c'sle. None of the officers, he said, knew that Dowd was on board and it was better that they should not know, so Dowd sat by a porthole all morning watching the low banks of the river gliding past. The river widened into the estuary at Swinemunde and the ship was pitching gently as it headed past the cluster of docks into the grey Baltic. It was the loveliest view of Germany he had ever had.

She plodded placidly north and Dowd resigned himself to irksome days in the fo'c'sle. The *Margarita* was less than two thousand tons, a dirty little tramp, thirty years old, with a woodbine smoke-stack amidships. She had only a crew of twelve, and Hans said the five officers among them never came into the fo'c'sle.

Away to starboard the dark line of the German coast lay on the rim of the water, but to port stretched only open sea. Dowd asked Hans if he could get to Sweden, and Hans thought that the best way was to go with them back to Denmark after Riga and get help there from the Danish Resistance. The idea was disturbing. Denmark was full of Germans.

The seamen were all friendly except for the middle-aged

one, who was taciturn with everyone. The cook, fat and bald like so many sea-cooks, wore incongruously a pair of horn-rimmed glasses and brought Dowd's meals to the fo'c'sle. The food was welcome as a break from boredom as much as for anything else. At night Hans took him on deck for air and exercise, but he stayed in the well-deck shadows, ready to slip into the fo'c'sle if any officer came near. Hans warned him : " If the captain hears you are on board he will hand you over to the Germans. He is pro-British but has a wife and family, and if the Germans catch him with people like you his family will all stop breathing."

When Hans was on watch Dowd tried to talk in broken German with some of the young sailors, but their German was worse than his, so most of the time he lay in a bunk.

On the third day they steamed into Riga, tied up at a wharf just outside the city, and the winches rattled and clattered all day swinging baskets of stone chips out of the holds. Hans said he thought the stone was for making runways in Russia. He was unhappy that his work helped the Nazi war effort and talked again, wistfully, of his own desires to get away from the Germans and fight them.

Unloading was slow and the *Margarita's* hold seemed to carry a lot of stone, because they lay for six days at the wharf, and all the time Dowd lurked restlessly in the fo'c'sle. He was worrying now ; it was impossible to stop thinking about the risks ahead, and thinking made them grow in his mind. On the sixth day Hans said they were leaving that evening and the relief was enormous.

It was nearly dusk when Hans rushed into the fo'c'sle again and said tersely, " We are being scarched again."

Dowd dived under the bunk and Hans threw a blanket underneath to cover him up. From somewhere Hans got hold of the mephitic chamber pot and dumped it by the bunk. Dowd was facing out this time and could not turn over. He started to gag and lifted the blanket a shade to get air. One eye, pressed close to the deck, could see across the floor under a fold of the blanket. He was sweating with fear and the stifling atmosphere.

Footsteps clumped into the fo'c'sle and the eye under the

blanket saw jackboots walking across the floor on the far side. The man snuffed distastefully as he caught the smell, and then his head appeared as he leaned a hand on the floor and looked under the far bunks. The head vanished as he straightened, the boots scraped as he turned and walked across the fo'c'sle. Dowd heard the boots clump along the near bunks and saw them stop less than three feet from his eye. The boots bent at the toes, a hand rested palm down on the floor and Dowd briefly glimpsed a metal cap badge and a ridge of cheekbone. Instantly they were gone and in the paralysed moment he heard the man spit his breath out disgustedly. The boots were clumping again and then the fo'c'sle was quiet. Dowd lay limp and motionless for a long time till Hans came.

They were at sea an hour later, bound for Copenhagen.

In the morning Dowd said tentatively to Hans : " Could we take over the ship—knock the officers out somehow—and run her into Sweden ? "

Hans said, shocked : " That is piracy," though a little later he added, " I would like to, but the families of the officers in Denmark would stop breathing."

The next morning Dowd said : " Couldn't we pinch a ship's boat at night and make for Sweden ? "

Hans started to shake his head indulgently and then he stopped and said slowly, as though he were thinking aloud : " If we come to the minefield near the Öresund at night we must anchor for the pilot through the channel. It is close to Sweden. We could row there . . . if we can steal a boat without being stopped."

Dowd was instantly excited but Hans warned him that they could only do it if they stopped by the minefield at night.

After his watch in the evening he hurried into the fo'c'sle, went up to Dowd in his bunk, eyes shining, whispered that they would probably reach the minefield the following night and that the four young sailors—the ones who had been with him in Stettin—were coming with them. Dowd was electrified.

Hans said he would stage a practice boat drill—the captain would be delighted to see him so conscientious—and when they had the boat in the water Dowd could slip out of the fo'c'sle, slide down the falls to them and they would be lost in the darkness in ten seconds. Dowd did not sleep thinking about it. In the morning the sailors stowed their kitbags surreptitiously in a small covered boat lashed on chocks beside the well-deck hatch and the day dragged interminably.

At dusk the anchor rattled down near a marker beacon on a tiny white tower rising out of the sea where the minefield started. The beacon flashed on as the night deepened, and, looking out of a fo'c'sle porthole, Dowd was dismayed to see how it lit the sea for a long way round them. Hans came in cursing. " We cannot go," he groaned with frustration. " It is too light. It is impossible now."

Dowd, in torment, pleaded : " We can surely to God make a dash for it."

" We can't," Hans said. " They have rifles up on the bridge. They would have to try and stop us."

Dowd felt like banging his head against the bulkhead.

They were sitting despairingly in the fo'c'sle when the ship's siren blew long and huskily.

" Air raid," Hans said and ran out on deck. Dowd followed to the door. He caught a faint drone somewhere in the over-cast and then everything was suddenly dark.

Hans was saying in a fierce, exultant whisper, " I thought that might happen," and it was only then Dowd noticed that the beacon had been switched off.

" Get ready and wait," Hans snapped, and ran across the hatch, hailing the young sailors for boat drill. In a few seconds they came clattering along the deck to the little covered boat and briskly started tearing the canvas and lashings off. Hans swung a derrick in position—there were no davits for this boat—and then they were heaving on the handwinch. The boat rose jerkily under the creaking block, swung over the side and sank out of sight under the rail. The sailors were sliding down the rope. Hans turned and called urgently, " Come on ! " Dowd ran to the rail, slithered down the rope and Hans came fast after him. Someone slipped the hook and the strong tide was sweeping them fast down the side of the hull. The bridge floated silently past; he saw the dark, high stern looming and then they were gliding noiselessly into the cavern of night. The ship merged with the darkness and they must have been a hundred yards past it when a querulous hail reached them, a disembodied voice calling vainly from another world. It could not have been more than three minutes since the siren had gone.

Hans said something in Danish and the young sailors unshipped the oars, laid them in the rowlocks and pulled. Hans had the tiller ropes, his face to the sky, steering by the stars.

" I think about eight miles to go," he murmured.

Far across the water Dowd could see dim lights ; they were too low to be stars and he knew it was Sweden. Suddenly he wanted to go mad and scream and cheer.

No one spoke ; sound travels over night water and German patrol boats covered the Baltic. The oars splashed gently, water rippled quietly at the bows and there was no other sound.

They had been going for an hour when they heard voices and oars somewhere ahead and the sailors stopped rowing. They sat motionless, drifting, hardly breathing, and Dowd found he was trembling. The voices were indistinct, but getting louder. He guessed they must be about a hundred yards away and then they slowly faded. When they could hear them no more the sailors dipped the oars again in the water and the tension relaxed.

It must have been much more than eight miles because the sky was paling when Dowd saw the grey loom of Sweden about a mile ahead. Growing light showed a rocky coast with wooded hills rising behind, and Hans, who seemed to know where he was, turned the boat towards a headland.

" We are inside the limit," he said. " They cannot get us now."

It was a little too much to grasp. Dowd felt he should be elated but found he was drained of intense feeling. He could not help thinking of the *Margarita* stranded out there in the world of the Germans with five seething officers, one sailor and a cook and the rest of the crew gone with an elusive stowaway to join the British Navy. It was so preposterous that he started to giggle. He told the others and they all started laughing in an overwrought way.

Round the headland the breakwater of a little port jutted into the water and behind it a town sloped in a huddle on the hillside. " Ah good ! " Hans said. " It is Limhamn."

The little boat glided into shelter, along by the stone piers of the seafront, past the little white yachts with the Swedish pennants. A Swedish soldier waved and grinned from the walls and pointed to some stone steps. They pulled into the steps and clambered out on to Sweden.

A man stood at the top of the steps with a Customs badge in his cap. Who were they, he wanted to know, and Hans told him.

" From Germany ? "

" Yes."

The man beamed, patted Dowd on the back and said, " Come in, boys."

They followed with their suitcases into the little Customs house where the man, loyal to the traditions of his service, went through their bags and found three bottles of schnapps.

" You must pay duty on these," he said, and Dowd realised at last that he was back in the free world.

Dowd flew back to England locked in the bomb-bay of a Mosquito plane—a common method of returning from Sweden in those days. He was commissioned, and at the end of the war returned to Germany to help round-up Allied prisoners and look after them. Then he flew all over the Far East in Transport Command. In December, 1946, he left the Air Force, but a year of quiet civilian life was enough; in November, 1947, he joined up once more and now is a signals technician, happy only when he is flying. He has remained a bachelor.

THE MAN WHO WOULD NOT DIE

Anthony Snell was typical of the young " R.A.F. type " of good family, good school, etc.—tall, elegant and with that slightly absurd, very English, deprecating dry humour. Born on March 19, 1922, he was educated at Cheltenham College. Always interested in music and the theatre, he left school on the outbreak of war, aged seventeen, to tour troop camps with a concert party. As soon as he was eighteen he volunteered for R.A.F. aircrew and trained as a fighter pilot in U.S.A., where he spent his leaves hitch-hiking all over the country (at one stage covering 1,400 miles in three days, a jaunt which ended with him being arrested near the Mexican border as a suspected drug smuggler). Returning to England, he flew with No. 242 (Spitfire) Squadron over England, France, Gibraltar, Algeria, Tunisia and Malta. He had just turned twenty-one when the squadron went to Malta.

At the time Malta was taking its beating two unusually pretty sisters lived near the aerodrome at Takali. One was dark and the other was a rare Maltese blonde, and both were warmly, if light-heartedly, pursued by more than half the fighter pilots on the aerodrome—till the middle of 1943. After that the pilots called them the Jinx Sisters and stayed away, because the two girls had thirteen pilots " confirmed." The thirteen were not smitten by Cupid's arrows. Every boy the girls seemed to favour was shot down a week or two later. It was only coincidence, but a consistent and unhealthy one ; two girls and the kisses of death.

The day before the invasion of Sicily, Tony Snell asked the blonde one to dance with him at a little café at Rabat, near the aerodrome. When the fiddles and the accordeon finished mangling the number and they came off the tiled floor, one of the other pilots on 242 Squadron, Jack Lowther, a rugged, fair-moustached Australian, said to Snell, " You've had it now, Tony."

Snell made a rude gesture and said, " Boloney, old boy.

I'm seeing her to-morrow night." He was carefree and confident, twenty-one and nearly a caricature of the English
officer fighter pilot : tall and a little gangly, good school, a
lean, well-boned face, sensitive mouth, " operational " moustache, and the lock of hair falling over his forehead that
irritates tidy men and attracts all women.

In the morning he tumbled out of bed at three o'clock to fly
on the dawn show over the invasion (and was fired on in the
half-light—with terrifying accuracy—by the Royal Navy). A
quick lunch and he took off for the fighting again. The
Sicilian bays were messy with landing craft and the hills
were smudged with feathers of smoke from fires. That's all
you ever see from ten thousand feet. Four Me. 109s sliced
out of some cloud down towards the beaches and the 242
Squadron Spitfires wheeled after them. Snell got a quick
squirt at one and saw him smoke and pull up into the cloud
again. Several pneumatic drills abruptly started hammering
into the armour plate behind the cockpit ; he had the paralysing shock of knowing it was happening to him, and as he
reefed her into a tight turn saw four more 109s shooting past
and curving above.

The next five minutes were confused and busy, a mixture
of coolness, sick fright and steep turns ; he twisted out of the
way of one and another was diving on him. That kept
happening ; his engine was smoking all the time, and then
there was fire in the smoke, the flames fluttering to ribbons
behind the cockpit. He was two hundred feet over the rocky
ground, saw a little green field, snapped his flaps down, cut
switches, fishtailed dangerously, looking behind and in front,
and then she ground her belly on the field and skidded a
hundred yards in a trail of boiling brown dust. He ran in the
drifting dust to a little stone building about thirty yards away
and barged through a rough wooden door.

The hut was full of hay, and the shells of the strafing
fighters started banging outside and cracking against the walls.
He saw a stone trough in the hut and dived into it. Engines
kept roaring low over the roof in waves, punctuated by the
cannon shells exploding on and around the hut ; then the
engines faded and a swarthy, unshaven little man with a

big moustache crawled out of the hay and looked blankly at Snell, who was lifting his head warily out of the trough. Snell poked his head outside the hut and saw the blazing wreck of his Spitfire. A little dazedly he watched the flames move down the fuselage and devour his insignia " S " (for Snell) on the side. Cannon shells in the magazines started exploding. He felt the peasant tugging at his sleeve, turned and talked to him in French, but the peasant only stared speechlessly, so he took his Mae West off, pulled his survival kit out of the pocket in it, opened it, handed a banknote out of his money to the peasant and put a finger to his lips.

The little man looked at the note, let out a startled cry and ran yelling from the hut. Snell followed him, cursing, and saw other peasants running towards them from the fields. Obviously Italians. There was an orchard on the other side of the hut, and a moment later Snell, running hard, vanished into it.

He ran and walked for half an hour across scrubby, stony ground, veering into olive groves for cover, heading south all the time, hoping to glimpse the sea. Well ahead he could hear the grumbling rumble of the battle round the beaches. He must be about ten miles from the landings and, if he were careful enough and the invaders moved fast enough, he should link up with them in a few hours. The main thing was to dodge enemy troops.

Moving cautiously through undergrowth towards a hill-top to orientate himself he saw huts and tents a bare two hundred yards away on a shoulder of a hill and Italian soldiers walking around. Sinking into a clump of bushes he waited for two hours till darkness cloaked the land and then moved carefully round the other side of the hill, tip-toeing over the rocky patches.

The moon edging over the horizon betrayed a sharp movement against the skyline a bare fifteen yards in front—the helmet and shoulders of a soldier. Snell froze on the spot with a dreadful access of shock. The outline was still ; he thought it was probably a sentry and crept back quietly, worrying about sentries on all the hills. The safest way south seemed to be along the valley, though even down in the gloom he might still be visible to the sentry. He saw a stick on the ground about three feet long, picked it up and started to hobble down the valley like an old man, hoping any sentry who saw him would mistake him for a peasant. There was no hail from the hill.

For two hours he moved like that down the valley, crouching to cross the clear patches, and then saw ahead a small hut with a large tree beside it. Two dark shapes bobbed up in a crouching position on the other side of the tree, and from them came two bright orange flashes and loud bangs.

Automatically he was thinking, " Those cheap Eytie rifles," and then he had dropped to the ground and was rolling to one side, pulling out his .45 pistol. There was another flash from the dark shapes ; he fired three times at the flash and he was on his feet running, crouching, to the other side of the hut.

From that far side of the hut more flashes and bangs came; Snell fired twice, dropped to the ground, and for a few moments everything was silent. He had one round left and knew he was out in the open against two parties under cover. Thought and action came almost together : he yelled " Kamerad," and then, in his best French, " J'suis ami. J'suis ami. J'suis Français de Vichy. Ne tirez pas ! "

Someone was muttering and a voice said in French, " Qui va ! "

" Ami. Ami Français de l'armée Vichy," Snell shouted, heart thudding. " Ne tirez pas. J'suis seul." He put his arms above his head and stood up so they would see the arms first. He was taut with fright, but no one fired and he walked forward slowly, lowering his arms and, as casually as he could, tucking his pistol back in its holster. Shadows closed about him and he saw there were about eight Italian soldiers. He talked fast ; he was a friend of Italy and fighting with them, and thanked " le bon Dieu " that they had cleared up the misunderstanding before anyone had been hurt.

The Italians seemed as frightened as he, and one of them said he was sorry about the firing. Snell noted, gratefully, that they spoke worse French than he did. One of them asked if he was thirsty and, being very thirsty, Snell said,

" Mais oui. J'ai bien soif." The little soldier passed him a bottle of wine and he took a long swig. He asked where he could find " l'ennemi " and a great chattering broke out. No one seemed to know ; the chattering was confusing and, feeling that he was losing track of the conversation, Snell said decisively, " Eh bien. Je les chercherai," waved his hand at them, said " Merci beaucoup et bonsoir," turned and walked away.

He felt he was cringing, waiting for a bullet, but the Italians must have been either too innocent or too confused, because nothing happened and soon, out of their sight in the darkness, he found a path leading south, reloaded his pistol and walked on.

From his survival map he knew that somewhere ahead lay a road near the coast. The firing was louder now than in the afternoon and sometimes he saw a sharp glow in the sky, but always some way off. He came to tank tracks that churned up the stony ground, and then beyond them saw the road, a flat, dimly shiny surface under the moon. Gingerly he walked over it and nearly jumped out of his skin as a deep voice in the darkness said, " Halt! " It came from ahead and two dim shapes loomed about ten yards in front. The voice said something like " Hoch Hande," and he started lifting his hands above his head, hiding the automatic in his right hand.

In a moment he was talking French again, trying the same old trick, and heard something tinkling along the ground towards him. Instinctively he jumped aside and ducked, and a moment later the grenade went off a few feet from him with a great flash and shattering noise. He was running back across the road. Two shots banged behind and then two more grenades, but he was across the road now and dived into some long grass, raising his pistol and watching for the sentries. They went to earth too ; there were no more shots, no sounds at all, and he silently wormed backwards, ran crouching in the other direction and turned south-east to flank the sentries.

Now the sounds of battle were spreading round him in a wide arc ; no tight embrace, but somehow enveloping. He was near. Ragged bursts of firing jolted his nerves ; no flashes but untidy patterns of staccato noises, menacing and unpredictable in the darkness. Quick bursts, intermittent thumps and jarring cracks, the restless, thundery orchestration of war closing in. From some anonymous source, perhaps only a mile away, a stream of tracer shells came floating across the sky like a string of fiery pearls. Near, very near, now. He was not alone, but shared the darkness with others—enemy troops, or perhaps already a friendly forward patrol. The luminous hands of his watch showed it was 3 a.m.—just twenty-four hours since he had crawled out of bed to start invasion day. So much to happen in twenty-four hours. Too much to take in, but let comprehension await deliverance.

Much nearer, to the north a machine-gun started firing southwards and barely two hundred yards from him, in a small coppice, another machine-gun answered it, firing north. A thrill shot through him—the gun firing north must be Allied, from the soldiers pouring up from the beaches. Deliverance. The link again with life and friends. That much at least he could comprehend and thank God for it.

The firing stopped and a couple of twigs snapped in the coppice. He crawled towards the sound and had only covered a hundred yards when he saw the dim shape of an aeroplane on his right, and beyond it some tents. God, this must be the airfield—the last thing he had heard at briefing before take-off was that the Allies had captured an airfield. He crawled towards the tents and saw two sentries under a tree about twenty yards away. One moved slightly and the moonlight glinted on his helmet. An American helmet ! A wonderful exhilaration tingled through him and he softly called " Desert Rats "—the password of the day.

No answer. The answer should have been " Kill Italians," but he could not see the sentries any more. Suddenly wary, he retreated till he came across some cases obviously containing equipment, could not make out any markings on them, but from the size of them and the solid nature he was certain they were American crates. He crawled towards the coppice again and once more called, " Desert Rats ! " Again no answer, and then he could wait no longer ; he stood boldly up and called again.

Out of the gloom two shadows came and he could see the machine pistols pointing at him. One of them was talking in a strange, harsh tongue and Snell knew he had joined the sad band of those who have mistaken coal-scuttle helmets for American ones. He tried talking in French again but they did not understand. Both of them were abrupt and surly and with a machine pistol prodding his back Snell marched in front of them across the airfield. A German officer joined them out of the darkness and they stopped and started to search him.

It was rather a farce. He kept taking things out of his pockets on the pretext of turning them out to help them, and then transferring most of the things in his hands to pockets already searched, and in that way saved his silk map (by blowing his nose on it), compass and some lira notes, but they found enough to know he was an enemy. They walked on and came to a wooden hut. Some one flashed a torch on him and asked his name, rank and number. The officer went away and Snell stood waiting with the guards by the hut, bitterly angry with himself.

A quarter of a mile away on the airfield a Bofors started banging and he saw the clips of tracer curling down flat and low towards what one of the guards said was a beach. Machine-guns started flickering and rattling on the beach answering the Bofors, and in the flashes (not so far away) he glimpsed shadowy figures running and, more vaguely behind them, dark monsters he knew were landing barges. An indescribable moment. How near to friends and how fast, he knew, they planned to advance ! The airfield was probably encircled already and by morning he would be free. In forty-eight hours he would be back on the squadron with a wonderful line to shoot.

The officer came out of the hut, talked to the two guards in German and turned to Snell, saying in English, " You are now prisoner." How very unimaginatively German to proclaim the obvious : making it official, Snell supposed tolerantly, before the situation reversed itself. The German said, " Keep your hands up," and motioned him to start walking. Snell walked and they came close beside and behind him. They had gone about a hundred yards when the officer said, " Halt." Snell turned inquiringly ; no building was near,

James Dowd, as a sergeant (wireless operator-air gunner) on No. 83 Squadron, Scampton, in February, 1942, just before he was shot down.

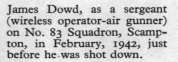

Dowd in Rhodesia in 1949, when he was doing a training course there after going back into the R.A.F.

Tony Snell, in 1945, after the second operation on his arms.

Anthony Snell after leaving the R.A.F. and becoming an actor.

(Left)

Charles McCormac in Singapore, November 20th, 1941—just before the Japanese invasion that turned life into a nightmare.

(Below)

Charles McCormac at his desk in the Midland Bank, February, 1952.

Robert (Steve) Carson on the wing of his Spitfire shortly before he
was shot down.

Carson, as an instructor on Meteors, February, 1952.

Cyril Rofe, taken just after he reached freedom in the uniform the Russians gave him.

Rofe, taken in 1951, wearing the tie of the R.A.F. Escaping Society. (The jagged line in the tie, just visible, symbolises barbed wire.)

Harry Wheeler about to climb into the cockpit of his Typhoon for his first operational trip after his escape.

Harry Wheeler Engineer, 1952.

John King, taken on the day
he returned to his squadron,
and before he had time to
shave.

King, photographed in 1951,
adjutant and navigator on a
jet night fighter squadron.

Group Captain Whitley showing Mr. Churchill round Linton-on-Ouse in 1942.

The photograph of John Whitley taken in the basement of the Bon Marché in Paris for his fake identity card.

John Whitley, as an Air Vice-Marshal in Germany in 1951.

they were standing on open ground. The officer said :
" Kneel down ! "

" What ? " Snell was puzzled. The three Germans were
hanging back about three yards.

" Kneel down." The officer said it louder.

" What for ? What are you doing ? " Snell said, confused.
He was watching them and starting to bend his knees a little,
more in an awkward crouch than a kneel. A soft blue light
shone on him from a baby torch and he saw the three gun
barrels pointing at him.

In blind instinct and sheer horror he dived aside and in the
same instant the guns banged deafeningly. He saw bright
flashes and felt a terrible blow in the right shoulder, went
down for a moment, jumped up running like mad, horribly
shocked. More ragged bangs, a great flash lit the night with
an explosion just behind him. He felt other thuds in his
body ; he was running over stones and little rocks, tripping
and sobbing, down on his knees and up again and the banging
kept on. Dear God, they'd turned the heavy gun on him.
More shocking explosions at his heels. It was horror, and
then he tripped and crashed down between two rocks ; his
right arm seemed to vanish into a hole in the ground and he
could not move. He tried but could not move ; he just lay
dizzily in the cranny and when he tried to lift his body his
muscles were watery. There were a couple more bangs far
off ; he heard the bullets ping on the rocks and whine into
the distance and he lay there feeling nothing except a confused
awareness deep in his head. It started to clear and he lay
there waiting for them to come up and finish him off, but they
did not come. A queerly distorted voice in the distance,
and then silence.

After a while he realised that it had actually happened and
that he was dying. Stupidly he began to worry that he would
not be able to see the blonde at Rabat. Maybe Lowther
would explain to her.

Feeling was coming back ; no pain but a pumping in his
shoulder like an artery. It would be over in a few minutes
and he would not have to worry.

One day at school he had sprained his ankle playing rugger

and had tried to play on. A master had said audibly, " That boy's got guts." He remembered now. It was not guts to lie down and die. He thought vaguely about that for a while and it seemed that for self-respect he must make one more effort. He tried to move and found his left arm was fairly effective, pushed it against the ground and forced himself into a sitting position, back resting against a rock. In the moonlight he could see bullet holes in his left forearm and a lot of blood. His right shoulder seemed to be in a mess, what he could see of it, and he thought his arm was nearly off. He thought, " Oh Christ, I'll be one-armed," and immediately after thought, " Oh hell, it doesn't matter being one-armed if you're dead."

With his left arm he pulled his shirt over his head and clumsily twisted it tightly round his shoulder. Somehow he struggled to his feet, standing straddle-legged, and then everything went round and round and black. It cleared and he was sitting on the rock. Some stubborn instinct took him. The North Star was shining clearly and in the other direction, south, where the landings were, he saw a rock, pushed himself to his feet and stumbled towards it, blacking out as he reached it, and sank on to it. As the mists cleared he saw another rock and lurched towards it. Vaguely he remembers doing that again and again, getting weaker and with the black-outs coming more easily. Dawn was lighting the sky and he knew he could not go on much longer. Trying to hold on to his strength he saw some soldiers moving about forty yards away, but could not tell whether they were British or German. With a last effort he got to his feet again, took a few steps and fell on his face.

Someone was rolling him over and dimly he saw men moving and bending over him. They were Germans ; he saw that, too, but was almost past caring. One of them brought a stretcher ; they lifted him on to it and carried him for a while. When they put him down an officer was leaning over him and he saw it was the officer who had led the execution party a few hours before. The officer was saying : " The commander has ordered you to be shot. What is your last request ? "

Snell thought, despairingly, "Oh Jesus!" He said faintly : "Why are you shooting me?"

"For spying on the aerodrome."

"I'm a British flying officer shot down yesterday. Why can't you look at the things you took off me?"

"The commander says you are a spy."

"I want to see the commander. That is my last request."

The officer said, "Wait here," as though Snell might get up and run away. Three German soldiers with rifles slung over their shoulders walked up and stood awkwardly near him, looking the other way. The execution squad!

The officer came back. He said, "Were you from Malta?"

"Yes."

"What is your squadron number?"

Snell rolled his head over the other way on the stretcher and said faintly after a few seconds : "I won't tell you that. You know I won't."

The German gave a tight and not unkindly smile. He said, "All right. You will go to a hospital." He took out a cigarette, put it in Snell's mouth and lit it, but Snell could not draw on it. He was utterly limp and could not feel anything, though there was a tired, rather irrelevant awareness that it had been a long, long day.

Later they loaded him into a truck and he had a bumpy and hellish ride to a German field hospital up towards Catania ; when he got there he could no longer move his head or arms. They gave him a blood transfusion and spent a long time discovering, probing and dressing the following wounds :

One bullet between the fingers of the right hand.

Two bullets in the right shoulder.

Two bullets through the left arm.

One bullet graze on the left hip.

One bullet and part of one chipping the spine and coming to rest near it.

Fifteen pieces of grenade in the body and legs, one piece severing the radial nerve of the left wrist.

For some days he lay in a stupor, and when they stopped pumping the drugs into him he had a lot of pain but could also feel the strength coming back into him. He started to think about escape several days before the doctor told him he was not going to die.

They took him to Messina, lying in an open truck under a scorching sun, and loaded him on to a hospital ship in a bed next to an English officer who had a bullet in his head and kept shouting, " Bring up the tanks, bring up the tanks," until he died.

A week later Snell was in a prison hospital in Lucca, ten miles from Pisa. Being young he mended fast and in a few weeks was able to get out of bed. He started escape training immediately, walking about the ward at first and then taking to tramping round the prison garden, increasing the distance each day, so he would be ready if a chance came. From his Red Cross invalid parcels he started hoarding chocolate, soup cubes and Horlicks' tablets, and also old bandages and ointments.

A few days after the Allies invaded Italy, in September, there was a flurry at the hospital and the orderlies went round grinning and saying that Allied troops had landed nearby ; there was going to be an Armistice and by the following morning they would be safe. That night they held a thanks-giving service and were too excited to sleep much, but in the morning it was the Germans who arrived.

A week later the new masters loaded all the prisoners on to a hospital train for Germany and as they rattled past Bologna, Snell, though his right arm was still in a sling, teamed up with a British Army major named Peter Lewis to jump from the carriage window. He and Lewis had always quarrelled violently in hospital but now they were in adjoining bunks and decided to forget their differences. Lewis was a good tough type ; he had a big moustache, an M.C. and three wounds from the Sicily landing where he was captured.

The train was panting up a hill ; two army officers started quarrelling with a guard at the end of the carriage, the man in the bottom bunk yanked the window down and Snell lowered his feet through the window. His feet found a ledge ; for a moment he hung on, then jumped, rolled over on the stony ground beside the line, picked himself up and ran into some bushes just off the track. The train clanked into the night and Snell, in the moments of aloneness by the rails, felt the tides of new emotions, a sense of vulnerability, exposed and defenceless, blending with the knowledge that fear and crisis lay ahead but not, perhaps, life.

He began to whistle " Lili Marlene." In a few seconds he heard " Lili Marlene " being whistled softly up the line, walked towards it and a moment later saw Lewis. They shook hands and grinned breathlessly, both of them shaking all over, and both bruised, though their wounds luckily had not burst. They cut away from the railway lines across fields for about a mile till they found a little copse, pushed into the middle, scraped themselves hip-holes and lay down to sleep.

In a few minutes they were shivering with cold. They only had battledress and huddled together to try and keep warm, but the cold spread right through them and they shivered miserably and sleeplessly all night. At dawn they started walking to get warm, heading south by the sun and wondering how far they would have to go before they reached the Allied armies. Like all the others at that time they thought that the Allies were fanning fast through Italy from a dozen landings on the coast.

Peasants in the fields kept looking up from their hoeing or picking and staring curiously after them, making them feel conspicuous and nervous, and then they came to a ditch that was deep and too wide to jump. They looked up and down but there was no sign of a bridge and they were wondering, a little helplessly, what to do about it when a peasant approached with a longish stick over his shoulders, and they faded out of sight behind a hedge.

The peasant came to the ditch, put one end of his stick in the water and pole-vaulted across. Snell and Lewis tore a tough, dry branch off the hedge, trimmed it and in turn vaulted across the ditch, finding it easy.

In the warmth of noon they flopped wearily on the grass and slept. At dusk they were moving on and saw a clump of farm buildings. Snell could see no telephone wires; he tossed a coin to see who would take the chance and the coin chose him. Lewis hid in some bushes and Snell walked up to the farm.

A dark, stocky little man, unshaven and about forty, came out of the house as he approached and said instantly, " Inglese ? " Snell eyed him warily during the moment of final decision, then nodded and pointed to his mouth, asking for food. The little man looked ridiculously pleased. He held out his hand and then beckoned Snell through the door. Snell said, " Amigo. Amigo! " pointing to the bushes where he had left Lewis. The farmer grinned ; Snell went back and got Lewis and when they got to the farmhouse, the farmer, grinning still, handed them a bottle of vino. Later his wife produced bread and salami and a horde of dirty children stood at their elbows and sniffed and gaped while they ate.

All the family seemed friendly. Snell asked where they were and the farmer said they were in the Po Valley, near Mantova. Later he switched on the radio, fiddled with the knobs and turned with a flourish and a triumphant beam as the prim, dispassionate voice of a B.B.C. announcer sounded in the room. They listened to the news, rather tensely to the part dealing with Italy, and learned bitterly that the Allied armies were struggling hundreds of miles south.

" What do we do now ? " Lewis said. " Stick around here and see what the form is, or push off south and try our luck ? "

" I'll ask the farmer," Snell said.

The little man was not encouraging. They could stay the night in the hayloft but would have to leave early because a German patrol sometimes came round. He drew his finger across his throat and said that he and his family would be executed if the Germans knew he had helped them. There were Fascists in the district who could not be trusted.

" Well, it's southward ho," Snell said.

After the farmer had left them in the hayloft, Lewis said, rather worried : " I can't believe all these people are on the level. I've got a horrible idea they'll bring the Germans to wake us up in the morning. They've been fighting us for three years and it doesn't make sense that they'd suddenly risk their lives for us."

" We'll have to take a chance," Snell said. " If this farmer's all right we'll probably know there are others we can trust, too. Anyway. I'm too flaked out for a midnight flit."

The farmer woke them soon after dawn. He did not bring the Germans but he *did* bring them each a peaked cap, a tattered old coat and some patched trousers and the two Englishmen were amazed and rather touched. Clothes were scarce and dear in Italy and he was not a rich farmer.

Lewis found the rats had stolen his socks in the night, so the farmer went and brought him socks too.

They put the old clothes on over their battledress so that if they were caught they could show that they were not spies. The farmer's wife gave them a huge breakfast and some food to carry and they walked south, following power lines across the fields that the farmer said led towards Rome.

About 10 a.m. the rain came, heavy and prolonged, catching them in the open and soaking them before they could find shelter, so they decided to walk on, wet as they were. Squelching along a slushy road through the drizzle they heard a honking behind them and a staff car full of Germans rushed past. The Germans barely spared them a glance and after he had got over the shock, Snell said, " You know, we're just a couple of Eytie peasants now. This trip's going to be a piece of cake."

A farm cart slowly overtook them and the old peasant driver turned in his seat and said, " Want a lift, Tommy ? "

They looked at him in fright and dived through the hedge into the fields.

" How the hell did he know ? " Snell asked, worried. " We're going to be up the creek if the Germans can pick us as easily."

Not long after, three little urchins ran up, tugged at their coats and started shouting, " Inglese, Inglese ! "

Snell turned and hissed at them, " Go away, you little beasts," but they took no notice except possibly to shout louder, and Snell and Lewis did not shake them off for nearly a mile.

Dismayed, they faced the fact that they were dangerously conspicuous and for some days skulked along the big ditches of the Po Valley, raiding vineyards for grapes and working warily south, hiding or detouring for miles to avoid people. Soon they knew that physical weakness was overtaking both of them—there was no hiding from partially healed wounds and hunger—and one afternoon Snell took a chance and spoke to a bald-headed, wrinkled old farmer in a field, asking shelter for the night. The old man knew instantly, as usual, that they were English, and took them into a loft with two beds, blankets and even sheets.

In the morning Snell's right shoulder was hurting badly and he felt feverish. He asked the farmer if they could stay a few days to rest, but the man shook his bald head nervously, and said he was too frightened of the Germans. Lewis's wounds were swelling too and it was becoming uncomfortably clear they would have to rest somewhere for a while.

The farmer said, compassionately, that they would have to move by lunch time. As unshaven faces might betray them he sent for the village barber, a likeable voluble little monkey of a man who cycled up to the farm and gave them both shave, shampoo and haircut.

They were wearily getting ready to move off when a grubby small boy scuttled into the loft, handed Snell a folded piece of paper and scuttled out again. Snell opened it and read, scrawled in English :

" *Stay where you are. You are among friends. To-night you will be taken to a safe place.*"

For a minute or two they could not believe it.

" How the hell did they know we were here ? " Lewis wanted to know.

" I dunno," Snell said. " I'm beginning to think we underrated the Eyties."

They showed the note to the farmer and said they must stay, and a little fearfully he let them.

A little after dusk two men of the local Underground rode up on bicycles. They had black hats over their eyes, wore black cloaks and acted like a couple of histrionic pimpernels, squeezing the last drop of dramatic pleasure out of the intrigue. One of them was the monkey-faced little barber of the morning.

Snell and Lewis perched themselves on the handlebars and were cycled uncomfortably several miles to a farmhouse on the outskirts of a village called Fabrico, where they were greeted at the door by a tall, solemn Italian who said he was local leader of the Underground.

" I did not know there was an organised Underground in Italy," Snell remarked frankly, and the Italian smiled wryly and said, " We have been preparing for these days for a long time."

One of the Italians in the house was a trained nurse. She dressed their wounds and they ate magnificently of black-market food (including pre-war quality fruit cake). The Italian leader wrinkled his nose a little at their peasant clothes, and on the second day he produced for each of them a smart lounge suit, overcoat, shoes, felt hat, shirts and ties, under-clothes and a wad of lira.

" My God," Lewis said, eyeing himself approvingly in a full-length mirror, " we're gentlemen again! "

Next morning they walked at a discreet distance behind two Italian guides to the railway station, followed them into a cattle truck and pretended to read Italian newspapers for several hours till the train reached Modena, where they followed the guides out of the truck till they saw another man in front bending down tying his shoelace. Snell lit a cigarette to let him know they had seen him, and they trailed after him through a maze of little streets till the new guide knocked on the door of a house. As they caught up with him a grill in the door opened, the guide gave a password, and a moment later they were all inside. A dark, thick-set Italian of about thirty-five, with a pleasant, smiling face, shook their hands and said in atrocious English, " I am very glad to meet you. Enter and have some coffee." He introduced himself as Mario Lugli. Later they learned that he was the man who had formed and led the Underground in Modena.

They stayed there five weeks, eating black-market food, reading English novels and magazines and listening to the B.B.C. Other escapees, they learned, were living in other flats run by the Undergound in Modena, and sometimes they visited these other flats and had tea-parties and played bridge.

They met several of Mario's Italian helpers—Don Monari, the young priest ; Anderlini, the shopkeeper ; Anna, the dark, pretty young girl of twenty who risked her life to try to frank the fake identity cards at the Town Hall; Tino, the barber who trimmed their moustaches to a debonair Italian thinness; Guiseppe Grossi, the dentist who attended to Lewis's teeth, and others.

One day Mario asked Snell if he would survey a possible airfield for the landing of supplies down in the waist of Italy. He warned frankly that it would be dangerous.

In the morning Snell walked out into Modena Cathedral and knelt in a pew. A man padded up and knelt beside him, tugged at his sleeve, and Snell followed him out and they got on a bus and travelled on it for six hours.

In the mountains to the south they left the bus and spent the night in a peasant's cottage. The guide warned that Fascists who infested the area had gouged out the eyes of some escapers they had caught to try and make them talk. He gave Snell an automatic pistol and said the idea was to shoot first and ask questions afterwards.

After two days in the cottage waiting for fog to clear they climbed four thousand feet to a plateau under the summit of Mt. Cimone, one of the highest peaks in the Apennines. Snell found the plateau was too small for a landing ground but would be suitable for dropping supplies. They took the bus back to Modena and he compiled maps and reports on the area. One of the copies he sewed into the lining of his small ski-ing cap in case the others went astray; Mario watched him doing it and said warningly, " If they catch you, they will find that and shoot you as a spy," but Snell rashly took no heed of the advice, saying that if caught he could drop the cap and disown it as it was really too small for him.

Two days later the Germans raided one of the Underground's flats and caught several escapers. It was a fair assumption that the Gestapo would handle them and that under torture they might give away the other places, so Il Capitano hustled Snell and Lewis to a new flat that the Underground had not used before. A motherly woman lived there with her son, Luigi, a gay young man with an olive-oily skin, glistening teeth and a rubbery smile. He had been in the Italian Navy and been four times torpedoed by the British, but bore no grudge ; in fact, after a couple of nights, he said he was going to take them to the local cinema but arrived home too late from work to do so. It was just as well—they heard in the morning that, when the lights went up after the show, German soldiers were standing at all the exits and took all the young men and put them on a train for Germany an hour later.

Luigi was engaged to an extremely pretty girl, who visited them a couple of times. To Snell's disgust, Luigi only saw her about twice a week—on all the other nights he used to go and see other girls, and told lurid stories of what he did with them. On these extra-curricular nights his mother used to wait up for him, and when he came smugly in the door would scream three words at him in Italian—" You great pig !" It did not worry Luigi but gave her great satisfaction.

Yet Luigi was not impervious to worry. He came home subdued one night and told Snell dolorously that his fiancée was going to have a baby and that he was the father. He was desperate to know what to do.

" Why, that's easy," Snell said. " Marry her. She's your fiancée and she's a wonderful girl."

" Marry her ! " Luigi wailed, the agony throbbing in his voice. " No, no. Not that."

His mother, wickedly satisfied, hounded him night and day after that to marry the girl, while Luigi sulked and grew haggard. The atmosphere in the flat was awkward. Mario took Snell and Lewis out one day to have their photographs taken, and next morning woke them early in bed, handed them identity cards with their photographs on and said, " To-night you go to Switzerland." They were to be the first to try the new route just surveyed by Don Monari, the shy young priest. Anna, they discovered later, had been within two seconds of being caught when, at her third attempt, she had sneaked behind a German's back at the Town Hall to put the official stamp on their identity cards.

Two guides led the way to Modena station that evening, and when the train came in it was like the wartime trains in England, crammed and in almost total darkness. The four of them squeezed in. Snell was carrying a small case with his and Lewis's spare food and clothes and swung the case up on to a rack. It would not stay on, so he gave it a hard shove and it knocked another case off the other side of the rack on to a sleeping Italian's head. There was a shriek and a frenzied torrent of Italian. Snell tried to back away into the unyielding mass of bodies wedged in the corridor, but one of the guides saved him by taking the blame and apologising humbly.

The uproar died down, the train rattled on and they managed to light cigarettes to calm their nerves. Lewis caught an unpleasant smell of burning cloth and noticed with dismay that his cigarette had set light to the coat of the man next to him. He dropped his cigarette, trod on it and tried to edge away just as the man noticed his smouldering coat. He started beating at it, yelling shrilly in Italian. Luckily, the quick-witted guide who had taken the blame before was also smoking ; he leaned forward and took the blame again and, after a while, peace came once more to the carriage.

It was a tedious trip ; they left the train at Milan early in the morning and went into the buffet for a drink. Suddenly Lewis spun round, gulped his drink and hurried outside. Snell and the two guides followed and found him sitting on a seat, rather pale.

" What the devil's wrong ? " Snell asked irritably.

Lewis gulped and said, " I suddenly saw I was standing next to the Italian officer who took me off Sicily in his landing craft to a hospital ship."

" Oh, my God ! " Snell said. " Did he . . .? "

" No. Don't think so. I was covered in bandages then. It just gave me a shock, that's all."

They were all nervy now ; the light confidence they had acquired in the past few weeks had abruptly evaporated and Snell and Lewis felt naked and guilty, conscious of the ease with which Italians before had known that they were English.

Just before dawn a prosperous looking man spoke to one of their guides, who smiled and greeted him warmly and, a moment later, introduced him to Snell and Lewis as their mentor for the next stage. The new guide did not waste time ; he already had their tickets and led Snell and Lewis into one of a string of cattle trucks at another platform.

The train moved off soon after, and an hour later a ticket

collector came into the truck and asked for tickets. Lewis handed over his ; the conductor looked at it and shot a sharp question at Lewis, who looked back blankly, having no idea what it was all about. The ticket collector repeated his question and Lewis knew that everyone in the truck was looking intently at him. Hesitantly he pointed to the scar on the side of his face, made some unintelligible mumbling noises and, to his enormous relief, the guide took charge of the situation, saying to the conductor, pointing at Lewis, " He is deaf and dumb from the bombing."

The conductor, instantly sympathetic, explained that Lewis had given up the wrong part of his ticket. The guide took the correct stub from Lewis, gave it to the conductor and then, with a touch of genius, pretended to tell Lewis what was wrong in mock deaf and dumb language.

Snell whispered to Lewis a little later, " I must say this organisation has got some pretty clueful guides." Lewis was about to agree with great warmth when he suddenly re-membered he was deaf and dumb and pretended not to hear. He did not think he could stand another crisis.

The train puttered slowly across the countryside and in the late afternoon jerked to a stop at a tiny hamlet west of Turin. A fair-haired boy of about sixteen walked along the line of trucks, recognised the guide, grinned and beckoned, and as he dropped to the ground out of the truck Snell saw the Alps towering rugged and snow-capped almost overhead.

The boy pointed at them and said, " Svizzera, dieci kilometri." It was a considerable thrill.

Most of the villagers, he explained, made their living by smuggling goods over the frontier. " Goods " included refugees and escapers. The boy led them to a pigsty, saying that it was a good spot to hide till dusk, and so Snell and Lewis chewed bread and cheese sitting philosophically beside a large sow, which coldly ignored them.

At night the boy came back and took them to a cottage, and they were just sitting down to some food with some smuggler peasants when the door opened and in walked a ruthless-looking man in the gaudy uniform of a Fascist guard. Snell stared, paralysed, feeling numb at first and then sick as he realised that on the brink of freedom they were trapped. He remembered the map sewn in his cap and thought desperately he must lose it or hide it—if he had time. Or try and disown it.

The guard saw him, saw he was shaken, and said, " Do not worry. I work for the Underground. It is my duty to see that the frontier guards will not be active in this sector to-night."

Everyone thought it was such a wonderful joke (particularly Snell and Lewis) that they decided to have a party. The smugglers produced a wicker-bound fiasco of raw farm chianti and the drinking and singing started. Snell and Lewis were the star turns with " Tipperary," " Pack up your troubles " and one or two rather fruity R.A.F. songs.

After four hours of that they thought they had better get some rest for the climb ahead, but it seemed that they had no sooner put their heads down than one of the smugglers woke them and said the frontier was clear. They must start climbing.

Outside the air was cold and reviving, and in the thin light of a half moon they followed two of the smugglers up steep stony trails. As they got higher the trails grew steeper ; they were sweating freely and their heavy breathing steamed thickly in the frosty air. Two hours dragged by and they stopped exhausted, lying on the ground to rest till the cold made them shiver. Lewis kept asking the guides how much further they had to go, and the guides said that they would see the frontier round the next bend, but when they moved off again every corner they turned showed another path, steeper and just as endless.

Lewis's back wound started to throb, sending a sharp pain through him with every step. They had to stop more and more often for rests, and Lewis said he was feeling dizzy. They came to snow, first a few patches and then a wide carpet that got thicker and thicker as they stumbled upward, endlessly upward. Lewis kept flopping on the snow and pressing his face against its coldness. He ate some handfuls of it to try and freshen himself, though the guides frowned and said it was bad for him.

Snell was getting groggy now, but the guides said there was still another half-hour of climbing in front of them. Lewis was suddenly lying on the snow muttering something about having " had it." He felt he could not move any more, and did not want to move in any case ; he could close his eyes and fall asleep and not wake up again, and wanted to do that desperately, not caring about not waking up again. Snell was standing over him prodding him with his feet, almost kicking him and pulling ineffectually at his coat. The guides came back and between the three of them they got Lewis on his feet once more. Snell took his hand and tried to pull him, and the guides pushed from behind, and they stumbled up through the snow like drunken men until, as dawn was breaking, one of the guides pointed to small, undramatic red and white posts and said, " Switzerland! "

Snell and Lewis stared wordlessly, and then Snell grabbed Lewis's hand, shook it, slapped him on the back, grabbed the guides' hands and with the last strength he had pumped them up and down like a madman.

Two hours later, still on their feet, but only just, Snell and Lewis, on their own now, came to a white Swiss farmhouse on a hillside over a village. They knocked and a plump and placid Swiss housewife opened the door. Snell said in French, feeling a little like a pioneer who has swum back across the Styx, " We are English escapers from Italy."

He will never forget the answer.

" Oh, really," said the woman who had never known war, " You're the first two we've had to-day."

In Switzerland, under British care, Snell had both arms operated on to repair some of the deep-seated damage from his wounds, and after a long convalescence was repatriated to England on the liberation of France. He was decorated with the D.S.O. for his escape (and his activities during it). Before the war was over he was fit enough to insist on flying again; he joined No. 504, the first Meteor squadron, and became one of the first of the few to fly and become operational on jets. After the war he went back to hospital for further major operations on both arms (*he still suffers from the effects of his wounds*). *The R.A.F. then flew him to Italy to thank and repay partisans for the help they had given to escaping British prisoners. In Modena he found again Mario Lugli, whose name will never be forgotten locally; the Germans had caught him just after Snell and Lewis had left. They tortured him for a long time but he would not talk. Then they were going to shoot him, but he feigned insanity till they threw him out of the gaol in disgust (he immediately went off to the hills and joined another partisan band). Snell found Lugli busy organising a Boys' Town to look after orphans, especially orphans of Resistance fighters who had lost their lives. He was dedicating the home to the memory of Don Monari, the priest. The Germans had caught Don Monari also; stripped him, lashed him with barbed wire to the front of a lorry and driven him over the mountains. He was never heard of again. It was the Fascists who had caught the shopkeeper Anderlini. They tortured him for some days and when he still refused to betray the others, shot him against a wall near Modena. The girl Anna, Snell found in bed with a new-born baby, and a proud young husband standing by. He felt that such aid and thanks as he could give them were strikingly inadequate.*

Back in England, Snell left the R.A.F. to become an actor and has worked since with several repertory companies and theatre clubs and in touring plays, including a year with the very successful Worm's Eye View. *He has also worked in television and films, playing a wide range of roles from eighteen-year-olds to eighty-year-olds. He has also become godfather to Lewis's younger son, Nicholas. Still a bachelor, Snell likes playing the piano by ear and composing music; also owning and driving fast sports cars, the latest being a Lagonda Special.*

MIRACLE IN THE DESERT

Born in Blandford, Dorset, on July 19, 1922, John King went to Blandford Grammar School until 1938, then left to work in a local government office. Early in 1939, wanting more than a sheltered desk, he volunteered for the Fleet Air Arm but was still waiting for call-up at the outbreak of war, so he joined the R.A.F. instead and trained as an observer in Canada. By 1942 he was flying with No. 104 (Bomber) Squadron in the Western Desert.

JOHN KING handed his watch to the adjutant just before the Wellington P for Peter hauled herself off the hard-packed Kabrit sand and set course over the Canal for Tobruk. It was the first time he had left his watch behind; he felt silly trying to explain why and the adjutant had laughed indulgently and said that a lot of people felt like that before their thirteenth trip.

At two thousand feet under a thin moon they could see the line where pale sand rimmed the sea and it was like looking at a big map. South of Sidi Barrani One-Eyed-Joe the searchlight woke up and waved his long white finger round the black sky in the same spot as usual; he had never found anyone yet but when they saw One-Eyed-Joe they always knew where they were. King murmured, " Thanks Jerry " and checked his pin-point on his map. Five minutes before e.t.a. he left his map table and crawled down to the bomb-sight.

It was just as he yelled " Bombs gone " that P for Peter shuddered as something thumped her and Wills was jinking and diving as they ran for the far darkness. In three minutes the searchlights had given them up and the flashes of the flak were a long way back. King had given Wills his course home and was arguing with Jackson, the second pilot, about the coffee thermos when the smooth note of the port engine started breaking up into roughness and sharp bangs. Wills said something about over-heating. The bangs got louder, shaking the plane like a rolling mill, and when the temperature ran right off the clock Wills cut the engine and feathered before it seized.

Then the other engine was overheating. He throttled back to ease her and the altimeter needle started to slide slowly round the wrong way. He throttled on and the engine started running rough. Once more he throttled back—the engine cleared and the altimeter needle started sliding back again. They threw out the guns, the ammunition trays, the bomb-sight and anything else loose they could find and the needle kept unwinding.

" Can't make it, blokes," Wills said over the intercom.

He ran in from the sea over the desert and they were so low that King could see the rocks of the coast. He said, " Watch the escarpment, Willy. It's about a thousand feet high round here."

" O.K.," Wills said and turned east inside the escarpment towards Alamein. In a few minutes he saw the Libyan wire slide under the wing about five hundred feet below. " We're in Egypt anyway," he said. Hartley, the wireless operator, was tapping out a position message to base.

Wills said, " Take up crash positions," and King crawled on to the " dead man's bed," took a grip on a stowage bracket on the bulkhead and hung on grimly.

It seemed a long time before the jolt came—not a very heavy jolt—there was a grinding and rending and then every-thing was still and quiet and King smelled the thick roughness of dust in his nostrils.

Through a tear in the side of the fuselage he saw a glare near the port engine, yelled " Fire," grabbed an extinguisher, smashed open the emergency escape panel and jumped out. Bodies came tumbling after and he said, standing by the wing, " It's all right. You left the landing light on, Willy." Ahead of the plane the glare lit a sheet of flat sand spotted with stumpy camel-thorn bushes and in the backwash of the light he saw that the Wellington had her buckled nose well down and her tail slanting into the air. He said, " Who's here? Are we all O.K.? "

A scream came from the tail and they swung round in fright and saw a shape twisting on the ground. King yelled,

"It's Jock," and ran up to it with the others. Barr, the durable little Scottish rear gunner, was rolling over on to his knees and they knew in a while from the salty language that he was not badly hurt. He had turned his turret to the beam and stepped out of the doors, discovering only as he fell that the tail was hoisted about eight feet off the ground. They hauled him to his feet and he was all right in a minute.

Wills switched off the tell-tale landing light and the six of them stood uncertainly in the black silence of the desert. Someone said, "Where are we, Johnny, d'you know?" King climbed back to his map table and came out with his astro-sextant and a torch. His hand was shaking so much he had to rest the sextant on the wing, took his sight and plotted it from his tables.

"According to me we're just south of the coast between Sollum and Buq-Buq," he said. "That puts us about three hundred miles from the bomb line at Alamein. If we can get that far we can probably do a quick scuttle by night into the Quattara Depression and outflank the line."

"I'm not walking that before breakfast," Jackson announced. Facetiously he yelled : "Taxi! Taxi!"

"That's about our only chance," Barr said. "We'll have to knock off some Jerry transport and drive back. Which way's the road?"

Wills thought they had passed over the road shortly before the crash so they should be between the road and the escarpment.

"Fair enough," King said. "We'll have to wait till dawn to see what the form is so we might as well relax."

"Good show," murmured the blithe Jackson. "Let's get stuck into some grub and coffee."

They ate some of their sandwiches and lay on the sand, resting their heads on parachute packs. None of them was relaxed enough to sleep, though it was warm and peaceful and a million stars glowed softly over their heads.

"Good thing it's summer," Jackson said, but Barr grunted —"You won't think so at noon to-morrow."

At dawn they saw the bald escarpment rising off the desert about two miles south. To the north, about a mile away, they could make out the thin black line of the bitumen road, the only road that traversed the twelve hundred miles of sand between Alexandria and Tripoli. The road was bare—no sign of a car or truck for miles—and they knew that for the time being they were fairly safe where they were. Wrecked aircraft were common in the desert and no lonely truck rolling along the desert road was likely to turn off and bounce over the camel-thorn to have a look at another one.

The road was so bare of cover it would be risky trying to stop a car by day. They decided to walk to the road at nightfall and when a truck or car came along by itself one man would step into the road as though thumbing a lift. When the driver pulled up, not dreaming that way out here the hitch-hiker was an enemy, the others would jump forward with the revolvers.

" No shooting unless we have to," King said. " They can play at that, too, and we're out on a limb here."

Looking over his maps that morning he found there was a waterhole marked about a mile back towards the escarpment from where he judged them to be. He and Wills walked out to find it, and tramped for hours without seeing a sign of it. Back at the plane Hartley and the carefree Jackson were sleeping peacefully and Barr was watching the road. Two trucks and two cars had gone by, he reported, and there had been many miles between them.

At dusk they walked to the road. King waited by the side, Jackson and Hartley spread out a hundred yards on each side of him to whistle if a suitable car approached (they would not risk covered trucks) and Wills, Ted the front gunner, and Barr waited behind King. Barr was handling his revolver in a very businesslike way.

It was a long and frustrating wait. Several times the headlights came gleaming along the road and King tensed himself, but no whistle came and the lights went speeding past. A couple of them were cars, obviously just the kind they were waiting for. He walked irritatedly along to both Jackson and Hartley but they both swore they had whistled. He told them to come nearer so he could hear.

Next time the headlights neared he heard the whistle all right but by that time the car was shooting past. He walked down and chivvied Jackson again but Jackson said he could not whistle any sooner because he could not tell in the glare of the headlights whether a vehicle was suitable till it was passing him. On the long straight road the vehicles were all rolling fast.

The night seemed endless, the longest King could remember. A few more cars and lorries passed before they could move and as dawn glowed in the east he called the others and they walked despondently back to the aircraft. They ate some bully and biscuits, got a little sleep, and around noon tough little Barr got to his feet and said briskly : " What about another crack at the road ? "

King demurred : " It's not worth it by day, Jock. Not enough cover . . . not unless we have to. We'll try it again to-night."

" There're some rocks up along the road. They're good enough cover," Barr insisted. " Let's have a go. We'll never bloodywell do it by night."

It was a spirited argument but in the end King and Wills over-ruled him, and went off towards the escarpment to look for the waterhole again. It was no good ; they walked for miles, saw only sand, stones and camel-thorn, and walked dispiritedly back to the plane. They were staggered to find it deserted ; called out and looked into the torn fuselage but the others were gone.

" Either the Jerries have been or they've gone off to the road," Wills said grimly.

" They wouldn't try the road on their own," King said. " Jock might be that crazy but the others aren't." He added a moment later, " If it was the Jerries they might be coming back for us."

They walked round the plane trying to see if there were any vehicle tracks and it was King who saw the German car in a dust cloud moving towards them across the desert from the road. He yelled to Wills: " Into the plane, quick," and they ran for it, crawled through the hatch and hid down near the tail.

The noise of an engine came up to the plane ; they heard tyres on the stony ground, and then the engine stopped.

King was trembling. If they had not been seen running for the plane he thought they had an even chance of getting away with it.

Footsteps grated on the sand and a voice just outside the fuselage by the tail, almost next to his ear, said : " Where the hell are Johnny and Willy ! They ought've been back by this."

Startled relief ran through him like an electric current and he yelled, " Jock ! Jock ! We're in here."

He crawled excitedly up the fuselage, stuck his head out of the hatch and saw a Volkswagen in Afrika Korps camouflage by the wing. Barr, Jackson, Ted and Hartley were grinning smugly with revolvers in their hands and beside the Volkswagen stood a sheepish German officer and two German soldiers.

" What d'you think of her ? " Barr grinned.

" How did you get her ? "

" On the road. Piece of cake." He told them how they had hidden behind the rocks and how he had walked out to thumb a lift. It had gone perfectly. The car had pulled up, he had shoved his revolver under their noses and the others came out and did the same. The officer was a doctor, Barr added, and spoke a little English.

They were the first Germans King had seen in the war and he looked at them fascinated. All of them wore drill slacks like himself, canvas boots and little peaked caps like ski-ing caps, and he had to admit they did not look bad types at all. Frightened he was going to be shot, the doctor was eager to be friendly and kept saying that they were not to worry about him because he accepted the situation. He seemed genuinely sorry that no one was wounded and in need of his services.

King was delighted to find that the car had ration bags, jerrycans of water and petrol and a spade ; also a couple of empty jerrycans which Wills filled with petrol from the smashed bomber's tanks. They transferred what food they had left, a landing compass, the sextant, and a few other things.

" Now what'll we do with the Jerries ? " Barr asked.

The doctor looked worried.

" We can't shoot 'em," Jackson said. " Take their boots."

The doctor looked relieved and bent to his laces.

Barr got behind the wheel and the other five squeezed aboard, King beside Barr, two on the back seat and two sitting on the back over the seat. Barr hoped pessimistically that the springs would hold. He fiddled experimentally with the gears for a while, said, " Here we go," and the Volkswagen jerked forward. They left the doctor and the other two Germans standing by the wing and Jackson said cheerfully after a while, " I'll bet that bastard isn't smiling now. If he ever catches up with us he'll operate on us and we'll never be the same again."

Barr drove east, parallel to the road but well over towards the escarpment. King had the map on his knee looking for detail to pin-point their position. The sand was flat and smooth for a while, apart from the camel-thorn, but then they stopped on the lip of a wadi that cut down from the escarpment and Barr looked dismayed at the steep, stony depth of it. He steered the Volkswagen along beside the wadi and in less than half a mile came to a spot where the banks were broken where army engineers had cut a rough road down into it and across. Easing the car down he revved up the other side and then, nervous of the springs under the heavy load, kept her moving across the sand at about twelve miles an hour, trying to steer between the clumps of camel-thorn.

King was trying to work out how they should go about outflanking the bomb-line. About forty miles from the coast the Alamein Line stopped at the Quattara Depression, a plain of endless sand dunes, soft, drifting and trackless. Cars could not drive there ; men could not fight there. It was a barren No Man's land, watched only from the air. He suggested they should leave the car on the edge of the Depression about five miles behind the line and try a fast night walk around the flank. The others said, " Good show. Good show," and were cheerfully singing a rude song as they bounced over the desert when they came to a single strand of barbed wire running on posts across the sand in front of them. A board hung on one of the posts ; Barr drove towards it and they saw on it a roughly painted skull and crossbones and the words, " Achtung. Minen."

He turned and drove along the wire looking for the end of

the minefield and had gone several hundred yards with no end
in sight when King jerked his head to one side and shouted,
" Stop.　Stop! For God's sake pull up, Jock."

Barr, startled, braked the car.　King, pointing down at the
sand, said, " Look at that, will you! "

The others saw the little flat, circular thing half hidden
under the sand ; it looked like grey painted metal and was
about six inches across.

Wills said in a stricken voice.　" We're on the wrong side
of the fence.　*This* is the minefield."

For a while there was silence and no one moved.

" There's another one over there," Barr said, pointing on
the other side, ahead of the car.

King wondered aloud how many more there were still
covered by the sand.　They all wondered that, and guessed
that most of the mines were still uncovered.

" Well, we can't spend the rest of our lives here," Barr
grunted. " Better stick in the car."　The wire strand was
about four yards away ; he swung the wheel, let out his clutch
and, revving hard, they plunged towards the wire and burst
through.

On the other side they stopped and King got out and walked
gingerly over to one of the signboards.　It said " Achtung.
Minen " on both sides and he walked back and said disgustedly, " What a clottish bloody thing to do."

At dusk he estimated that they had done about forty miles.
That night it grew cold and they wrapped themselves in
parachute silk and slept huddled together.

In the morning they came to a couple more wadis but found
tracks broken across them as before.　The desert was more
broken now with low ridges running down like spines from
the escarpment to the sea.　The car kept going up over the
ridges and down into the hollows and Jackson said he was
going to be seasick any moment.

Pulling over one of the ridges they almost ran into the
middle of a group of men squatting on the sand.　Barr braked
sharply and they saw with relief that the men were Arabs—
six of them, with three camels on their haunches nearby.
Nearly all the desert Senussi were friendly.

" Ask 'em if they've seen any Jerries around," King suggested. " Maybe they can tell us where we are, too."

The Arabs gazed without particular interest. King jumped down and an old Arab with a short, grizzled beard got off his haunches. " Saida," King said, and the old Arab nodded gravely and intoned " Saida." King could see a flea crawling on his neck above the dirty gelabia and, keeping his distance, held out the map and tried to ask in sign language where they were. The old man looked at the map blankly. King, Wills and Barr in turn tried to ask if any Germans or Italians were about but the old man continued to look blank. Some of the other Arabs came and stood around and Jackson said curiously, " Look, half these types seem to have lost their left hands."

Only then King noticed the dirty bandages round the wrists and remembered someone telling him that Arabs punished cut-throats and robbers by chopping off a hand. He told the others and Barr said, " Come on. No future in these customers. Let's get going." They got back in the car, keeping their hands near their revolvers, and drove off.

That day was a scorcher and the desert shimmered in heat-haze so that at times sheets of it seemed to lift and float eerily above the sand, retreating before them as they drove on, and then dissolving. Disembodied peaks lifted over the ridges of the escarpment, changing shape weirdly as the car moved along. Several times King would have sworn he saw little lakes shining on the sand ahead ; they looked so real but they always vanished as the car came near.

In the early afternoon a vague cluster of buildings shimmered to the north and King estimated that if it was not another mirage it was probably Mersa Matruh. Barr swung the car south to skirt the Stuka landing grounds at Bagush.

Here the escarpment ran deep inland, much lower, and turning east at the foot of it the car ran into a rough patch where the tyres scrabbled over thousands of sharp little stones. A sharp bang came from one of the front tyres and Barr braked quickly ; their first puncture. The Volkswagen had a good tool kit and they were on their way again in half an hour. Five minutes later the other front tyre went. This time the repair was done faster but they did not like the look of the tyres. All of them were worn and the canvas was showing on both of the front ones.

At dusk King took a sight and estimated that they were between Matruh and Fuka and about ten miles south of the coast. That night it was so cold that he lay awake for hours, shivering, and in the early hours of the morning, when morale is lowest, began feeling that they would never make it. So far they had not seen a single enemy and he wondered how long their luck would hold. From now on they would be running into dangerous areas.

In the morning they kept running across more stony patches, and by noon, when they stopped for bully beef and biscuits, they had had three more punctures. Shortly after moving off again they had another one, and this time there was a great rent in the tube. Barr threw it away and packed parachute silk inside the tyre instead. It was better than running on the rim, but only just.

Somewhere south-east of Fuka they stopped at dusk and rostered each man to take a turn as sentry through the night. Around midnight the man who was to have woken King for his turn fell asleep instead, and in the morning they were shaken to find a set of heavy tyre marks ten yards from them. King was positive they had not been there the previous night.

The other front tyre blew out that morning and they had to pack this one, too, with parachute silk. As they moved off again Jackson said cheerfully, " Well, at least we can't get any more punctures in front," but Barr growled that it was the springs they had to worry about now. The car was juddering badly ; he dropped to about eight miles an hour to nurse her along and had a hard time steering between the worst ruts in the stony ground. The day's run was less than fifty miles, King estimating when it was dark enough for a sight that they were somewhere south of Daba, the German fighter base. (They all knew Daba. The squadron had been based there a few weeks earlier—before the retreat to Alamein.)

In the morning they had gone about two miles when one of the front springs snapped with a sharp crack. They got out and had a look, but all Barr could do was put the car into low gear and keep her moving at walking speed, flinching all the time as the front of the car thumped hard on the axle. Grinding up a long slope to a ridge there was another crack and the bonnet flopped on the sand between the splayed wheels, and they knew that the axle had gone.

" She's had it this time," grunted King, looking at the snapped metal. " Looks as though we walk the rest of the way." He spread his map on his knee and put his finger on the spot where he guessed they were. " About twenty, twenty-five miles to the bomb-line," he said, " and about fifteen miles from the coast." He ran his finger diagonally down to the end of the blue-pencilled bomb-line and added : " And a damn long way from the Quattara Depression."

" We've had the Depression," Wills put in grimly.

" Why ? " Barr demanded.

" Because it's about sixty miles down into the Depression and round into our blokes' lines," Wills said. " If we have to walk, we've got to do it in one night. If we get stuck out on the bundoo on our own by day down near the lines we'll get picked up for certain."

" What about walking through the German lines? " Hartley wanted to know.

" It's been done before," King said.

" Maybe they'll be asleep," suggested Jackson, the optimist.

" Maybe they won't," said Barr. " And what about the minefields on the other side if we do get through the Jerries ? "

" We're going to have to risk those whichever way we go," said King. " That's been done before too."

It was too hot and too risky to walk by day—that was clear. They sat by the car to wait for the cover and the coolness of night. King and Barr walked to the top of the ridge and dropped flat on the ground when they got there. Two miles away six tanks were trundling north across the sand, dragging thick trails of dust. They watched them vanish, not so sorry now that the axle had broken, because if they had carried on they would have been roughly where the tanks passed.

Back at the car, they decided to leave everything behind but water-bottles. It was not going to be easy walking over desert in flying boots. The ration bag was still nearly half full and they hacked open the bully-beef tins and gorged themselves.

The moment the sun vanished they started walking, climbing to the top of the ridge and seeing miles of bare desert ahead. King was carrying his landing compass ; he took a bearing due east, the shortest way to the line, and they walked briskly down the other side. It was dark in ten minutes, but King kept them on track by the luminous dial of the compass. Around their feet the pale sand was fairly visible, but after a few yards it merged into the blackness.

For the first hour and a half it was fairly easy going. The sand was flat and not too soft, and when they felt they had made about five miles they rested for ten minutes, taking off their fur-lined boots to let their hot feet cool.

At the end of the next hour Barr and Hartley were beginning to limp, and they rested again. King asked anxiously if the two thought they could make it, and Barr grunted, " We've damn well got to make it . . . we've only got to-night to make it in."

They had been walking again for about fifteen minutes when someone said sharply, " Look at that! " The darkness a few miles ahead was suddenly flickering with sharp flashes, and many seconds later the dull thump of the guns reached them. " That's it," Wills said soberly. They stopped and looked at the flashes for a while, and King felt nervous excitement tingling through him. He said, " Well, we know where we are."

Barr commented dryly, " They don't look very sleepy."

" What are they—ours or theirs ? " Jackson wondered.

" If they're ours we'd be pretty well in the front line now," King considered. " They must be Jerry."

" I dunno," muttered Barr. " You can't see ten yards in this darkness. We could be right in the middle of the Jerry line now."

" If they were ours we'd be in the middle of a lot of thumping big shell bursts," Wills remarked sensibly. " They're Jerry. Come on, let's get weaving."

They moved ahead again, keeping close together and looking warily around them, particularly ahead, but the night was thick and silent. Barr's feet were hurting him a lot ; he kept fairly quiet about it, but even in the gloom they could see he was limping painfully. He tried taking his boots off and walking in his bare feet, but the ground was stony and that was even worse. Wills had a knife on him, so Barr slit the heels of his boots where they rubbed him most, and after that found he could walk a little more easily.

Little by little the muffled rumbling of the guns hardened into heavier, more explicit explosions, and the flashes were getting nearer. Occasionally a flare splashed into brilliant light low in the sky and they knew that that was where the line was. King was steering by the stars now, keeping Altair on his right, Polaris on his left and walking at right angles between them. Without warning the flashes and thumps of the guns stopped and the front was dark and silent.

After another hour they saw a dark shape ahead and to one side and sank silently to the sand. Barr crawled a little closer to it and identified it as the covered top of a truck parked in a dug-out pen, with the sand heaped along the sides as cover from bombing. The detoured around it and headed on, but now they were going very slowly and no one was even whispering.

They passed two or three more trucks and in the back of one saw the glowing end of a cigarette. A little later voices were mumbling off to the right. King found he was walking with his shoulders hunched, flicking his eyes about furtively. His mouth was dry, and he recognised that symptom and the shivery feeling all through him as the way he felt before take-off on a raid, though this was worse. He felt like a blind man walking near a precipice. They were either in or very near the line now. Perhaps only a mile away were British troops, but in between, almost certainly, lay a minefield . . . a thick one. He had been putting off thinking about the mines, but it had to catch up with you in the end. He did not know whether he was more frightened of the Germans or the minefields.

In front of them the line of a low ridge cut against the sky that was a shade less black than the ground. They were moving up the slope when King sank to the ground with a gentle " Hsss." Then the others saw the two dark shapes on the ridge that looked like men. Quietly they moved off at an angle and as they reached the ridge found a haversack and some pieces of metal equipment.

With a shattering noise a motor bike started up about fifty yards behind them and moved off somewhere.

Barr whispered, " Look, let's walk as though we belonged here. They won't dream we're British." He had his revolver in his hand.

" All right," King muttered. " Come on." He took his own revolver out and they walked down the slope.

They passed another truck parked in a pit-shelter, then another and another. A tent loomed out of the darkness, then two more, and in one of them a man was snoring. Veering slightly, they walked boldly on. Apart from the soft crunch of their boots on the sand the desert was eerily silent.

Abruptly a sharp voice shouted about ten yards away and King's nerves jumped. They sank down and froze. The voice shouted again, obviously at them, and King thought he caught the word " Halt ! "

He said incredulously, thrilled, hardly believing they had come to the British lines, " Are you English ? "

A bright orange flash and a bang came from the direction of the voice, and they lay flat and terrified. There was another flash and bang.

For a few seconds it was silent, and then all around they heard movement and the mutter of voices.

King aimed at the spot where the shots had come from. Barr, doing the same, was whispering, " Let's dive for cover." King was drawing his legs up, bracing himself to jump and run, when he saw dark shapes all round and knew they were trapped.

One of the crew shouted in a strained voice, " For God's sake, stop shooting. We're British."

A crisp voice came out of the darkness, " Hoch Hande."

It was too quick and confusing to remember feeling. They had their hands up, and as the dark shapes moved nearer they stood up, dropping their revolvers on the sand. A hooded torch shone briefly on them and they heard German voices.

Men were prodding them in the back and they walked about a hundred yards till they stumbled into a hole in the sand like a very wide slit trench. They sat in it with shadowy figures around them. A soldier arrived who spoke some halting English and they told him they were shot-down airmen. The soldier went away and they waited, shivering, huddled together for hours till the sun came and they saw they were in an area pitted with slit trenches. Two German soldiers were guarding them ; others were walking casually about nearby, but a hundred yards to the east some soldiers were crouching to keep under the ridge.

King asked one where the Tommies were, and the man pointed east and said, " Halb kilometre."

" Less than half a mile," King translated bitterly. " We damn near made it."

The German who spoke English came back and told them amiably that the soldier who had first hailed them in the night had thought they were German and was warning them that they were heading for the minefield a hundred metres ahead. He said confidently that they would all have been blown up.

Another German brought them tinned meat and biscuits, and about nine o'clock a truck with an Italian driver and soldiers pulled up and the Germans pushed them over the tailboard. The truck rolled north across the sand and fifteen minutes later swung west along the coast road. Out of the back they could see a ridge held by British troops, and silently watched it grow smaller.

It was only a quarter of an hour later that the truck turned off the road by a barbed-wire enclosure, and as the Italians were nudging them through the gate King knew he had been there before. It was beside one of the Daba landing grounds, and a few hundred yards away he recognised the spot where the squadron mess tent had been. They looked at it through the barbed wire, muttering pungently.

The cage was a square of hot sand surrounded by thick barbed wire. About twenty British soldiers were already in it, looking dead-beat. Most had been trapped in the retreat and many had dysentery and sores. About noon an Italian threw them a little tinned meat and some biscuits, but it was water they wanted more than anything.

Hours later another Italian came with jerrycans of water, but when he saw the airmen he started screaming at them and would give them nothing to drink. An army lieutenant in the cage who spoke a little Italian translated : " He says he's been straffed by the R.A.F. and no water for you. You'd better have some of ours."

The night was bitterly cold again, but by ten in the morning the sun was blazing hot. At noon they were given a little water but no food.

An enormous lorry pulled up by the gate and the guards screamed at the crew of P for Peter to come out. At rifle point they climbed over the tailboard, and the army lieutenant and an army sergeant were put in with them. Four nondescript Italian soldiers climbed in and they were rolling fast along the road westwards again. There was little traffic on the road ; a convoy of lorries shot past from the other direction, one or two Volkswagens and, strangely enough, several captured jeeps. It was annoying to see the Germans driving them.

Barr grunted, " This is no damn good. We've got to do something fast or we've had it," and that started the escape talk. They edged away from the guards, who were squatting by the tailboard, and tried to talk naturally, breaking into rather false laughter now and then to hide the conspiracy, though none of the guards seemed to understand English and in any case the screaming of the tyres over the bitumen drowned their voices.

It took something less than a minute to decide that the obvious course was to rush the guards, capture the truck and head south-east over the desert once more for the Quattara Depression. The best time would probably be when the lorry pulled off the road for the night.

" What if they stop at some camp ? " Barr demanded. " Let's jump 'em now."

" We're not likely to find any camp along here," the lieutenant said. " If we go for 'em now we'll probably have to shoot it out with the driver and guard in front. We can't get at them from here."

" I'm game." Barr was eager.

" It's not as simple as that," the lieutenant said. " There's something in the rules of war that, if you're captured and use violence to escape, they can shoot you or something if they get you again. I'd say there's a fair chance we'll be caught again, so if we have to use rough stuff let's keep shooting out of it. It might save our skins."

Barr rather reluctantly agreed. King said seriously, " If anyone wants to pull out of this thing he'd better say so now."

No one said anything. They sat fairly silently while the lorry bowled fast and noisily along the road, hour after hour. They must have been doing over forty miles an hour, King thought, and he found that the waiting, rolling farther and farther away from the lines, frayed his nerves. The road seemed deserted—that was reassuring—but the sun was getting low and they must be nearly two hundred miles from the line now. He started worrying about if and when, and especially where, the lorry would stop for the night, and had almost convinced himself gloomily that they were carrying on to some camp when the lorry started slowing and turned and stopped about fifteen yards into the desert.

Everyone got out and two of the guards stood over the prisoners with rifles while the others put their guns down and lit a petrol fire on the sand. King and the lieutenant lounged by the side of the truck trying to seem listless. Even Barr was contriving to look timid and defeated. One of the soldiers after a while slung his rifle over his shoulder and, like a sheep, the other did the same. The drivers and the other two guards left some food cooking on the fire and wandered back to the lorry.

The army sergeant, a thick-jawed old sweat, had been edging craftily nearer the two guards with rifles. One of the guards put a cigarette in his mouth and offered one to the other man. He lit a match, and as the other leaned towards it the army sergeant jumped and yelled " Now." He grabbed the shoulders of the man with the match, slung him to the ground and the quiet scene exploded into action. King had dived for the other armed guard; Barr, with a yell and his teeth bared, had gone for the group of four with Jones and

Jackson. The lieutenant had dived for the pile of guns.
King had his man pinned and Wills was tearing the rifle off
his shoulder. The other one was shrieking on the ground
with the sergeant's knee in his back. There was a swirl of
bodies round Barr, Italians were dropping rapidly and then,
as suddenly as it had started, it was over. King, the lieutenant
and the sergeant had rifles, and the Italians were lying on the
sand looking terrified. Two of them were moaning, " Bambini. Bambini."

" What'll we do with them ? " the sergeant asked.

" We can't leave 'em here," the lieutenant said. " They'll
raise a hell of an alarm. We'll have to take 'em with us.
Come on, let's get going before anyone arrives."

They prodded the Italians with their own rifles towards the
lorry and the sergeant was nudging the driver back behind the
wheel when King and Barr in the same moment spotted the
two lorries coming down the road towards them. King
yelled, " Get 'em out of sight." They hustled the Italians
round to the side of the lorry farthest from the road, and the
lieutenant, swinging his rifle at their chests, hissed at them to
keep quiet. King and Barr lit cigarettes and sat against the
wheel of the lorry, trying to look natural. The dusk was
fairly deep now and there was not much chance of their
uniforms giving them away. The lorries were a hundred
yards away and King saw, with a stab of fright, that they were
pulling up. One after the other they braked to a stop fifteen
yards from him. He was thinking crazily, " If they speak in
Italian I'll try and talk German, and if they speak in German
I'll try and talk Italian."

No sound came from the lorries and the seconds dragged.
The front one suddenly revved up and started again, and both
of them rolled on along the road.

The lieutenant was encouraging the Italians to climb
hastily over the tailboard by some boot and butt work. The
others climbed in after them and the truck bumped south
away from the road. Not till they were well out in the
desert and cloaked in the darkness did King feel he could
relax. They slept out there in the truck, two of them staying
awake at a time to cover the Italians, who gradually stopped

their terrified pleadings as they realised they were not going to be shot.

At dawn they examined the lorry and found it was carrying only half a jerrycan of water, several jerrycans of petrol, but no food except a tin of meat and a little bread.

The lieutenant said that their best chance of avoiding the enemy was to go up to the top of the escarpment and turn east there. King said immediately, " Don't forget we haven't got a compass now. We'll have to navigate by the sun."

They bumped slowly over rough ground along the foot of the escarpment for an hour till they found a spot where the stony bed of a wadi led up to the top in a long slope. It was a hard climb even for the powerful truck, and when they reached the top steam was hissing out of the radiator cap. King dropped down to have a look at it, and it was then he found the radiator was leaking. The water was well down in it and they tried to plug the leaks with strips torn off their shirts, but some water still seemed to be seeping from hidden spots.

" Well, press on and hope we find a well," Barr grunted.

For the first half-hour's run east along the top of the escarpment the ground was flat and firm, and then they topped a small rise and saw spreading sand that lay in a great basin that ran for miles. They moved down to cross it and the lorry started ploughing through the soft sand that silted up the floor of the basin. It moved jerkily, wheels spinning in the sand, and the inevitable happened quite soon ; she stuck fast, axle-deep.

There were boards in the back of the lorry, obviously for this emergency. They all jumped out—Italians included— dug the wheels out and put the boards in front of them. Barr took the wheel, gave the lorry plenty of throttle and she jerked out ; he kept her moving to stop her sinking into the sand again while the others grabbed the boards, chased madly after the lorry, threw the boards aboard and scrambled over the tailboard. In five minutes they were axle-deep again.

That was the pattern of the morning. They were bogged five times and around noon when they came thankfully out of the thick sand the engine was boiling hard.

They waited for the engine to cool but that took a long time because the sun was beating down with midsummer strength and any metal parts were blisteringly hot to touch. There was no question of topping the radiator off with their half-jerrycan of water. They needed it themselves too much. King proposed a mouthful of water each, feeling that he could drink a jerrycan easily by himself. In the afternoon they ran into more sand and were bogged several times again, so that at dusk King estimated they had made only about twenty-five miles all day. At that rate he hardly needed to tell the others that the trip would take about ten days. With a mouthful, morning and evening, he thought the water might last them three days.

They huddled under the truck to try and keep warm that night and moved off at first light to get the benefit of the cooler hours. Barr found the sand firmer now and by noon they had made about thirty-five miles. They ate the last of their food then, and in the afternoon—more sand ; they were bogged again and as they came on to harder ground, King, sitting on a tarpaulin on the cab roof with his shirt covering his head, sighted a lorry ahead.

It seemed to be half on its side and they guessed—rightly —that it was a derelict. Barr drove up to it ; King jumped off and ran to the bonnet, tore off the radiator cap and cheered madly when he saw the radiator nearly full of rusty water. They drained it, filled their own radiator and had a little over to put in a jerrycan.

Half an hour later King sighted an untidy mess on the desert and, driving up to it, saw that it had been a food dump. Tins of vegetables and meat lay scattered on the ground but when they dived triumphantly on them they saw with over-whelming bitterness that every tin was punctured and the food destroyed.

" You always do that when you have to leave your stuff," the lieutenant said. " I don't think I could ever bear to do it again." Wills would not give up the search. He went rooting around in the faint hope of finding an unopened tin, and under a pile of tins (every one punctured) found two boxes of dried prunes. Grabbing a handful each they chewed them, though they were like leather and they could hardly swallow them because their throats were so dry. King thought they had made over fifty miles by dusk and guessed they had well over a hundred miles to go.

Next morning was flat, soft sand again, shimmering in heat so that they kept seeing the maddening mirages of lakes that vanished as they went up to them. Twice more they were bogged and King could see as they worked to dig the lorry out that they were all slowing up visibly. His mouth was like an old boot; he tried to stop thinking about water, but could not, and it was becoming an obsession. He thought it ironic that sweating to dig the lorry out was draining more moisture from their bodies, though he noticed now that little sweat was coming out of him. The jerrycan was nearly empty.

That morning he saw what looked like a mark on the desert ahead and as they came nearer it began to look like one of the posts that mark a water-hole. In the heat haze his eyes, aching from days of glare, could not be sure and he went through agony as they got nearer and nearer until he saw it *was* a water-hole and gave a croaking cheer. Barr drove for it. King jumped off with a jerrycan and ran, followed by the others. He flopped down by the rocky rim of the water-hole and looked stunned at the black sludge below. " It's oil," the lieutenant said quietly. " May have been done by our blokes in the retreat."

They went back and climbed into the lorry and lay there silently as it moved off again. Jackson was first to speak, saying, " It's a great life if you don't weaken," and King looked at him a little sourly. Jackson grinned and winked back with a little sideways nod of his head ; it was not much of a grin, more of a grimace on one side, but it was a good effort and oddly encouraging. It struck King how alike they all looked, burned nearly black by the days of the sun, scruffy with beard stubble and tangled hair, and with the fine sand caked at the corners of their eyes and mouths and in the nostrils. His lips were dry and cracking painfully. The army sergeant was still keeping a rifle by him but the Italians huddled apathetically in a corner of the truck.

At noon they stopped, had a mouthful of water and lay in

the shade under the lorry until Barr said, " No good hanging around here. Let's get cracking again." King climbed back on top of the cab and the effort and the sun beating on him made his head swim and his eyes hurt. As Barr was getting in behind the wheel King shouted, " Just a minute, Jock, I can see some water over there." He knew it could be only another mirage but it looked so real about two hundred yards off to the right that he started getting down from the cab.

The lieutenant said, " Take it easy, Johnny. We might come to a well soon," but King had dropped down from the lorry and was plodding over the sand. He heard someone saying wearily. " Don't be a bloody fool. Come back," but kept doggedly on. A detached corner of his mind knew it was stupid, but the rest was a woolly obsession about water.

Even when he was ten yards from the pool and it had not vanished he still did not really believe it. He had to get down on his knees and dip his hands in it before his mind cleared and he turned round and started shouting. They thought he was crazy until he threw some water in the air and they saw it sparkle, and came running across. There was a lot of shouting and they lay on their bellies by the edge, splashed their faces in it and sucked it up. The lieutenant said, " Don't drink it too fast."

The pool lay in a shallow saucer of sand about twenty yards across and the water was a milky colour from the sand grains in suspension. After stirring it up round the rim they kept moving about to clearer patches, dipping their heads in. Barr went back and drove the truck over and they filled all the empty jerrycans and the radiator, then took their clothes off and lay in it. Instead of being warm under the sun the water was surprisingly cool, and they never found out where it came from or how it happened to be there. The only possible explanation seemed to be that it came up through some spring in the rocky layers under the sand. As far as they were concerned it was a miracle, an explanation which the Italians seemed to accept devoutly.

They did not stay long by the pool ; everyone was keen to move and so elated and restored by the miracle that they felt that luck or some guardian angel was going to see them safe.

After so long in the empty desert King was feeling that they would go through without seeing an enemy. Only later he realised it was wishful thinking, shying away from the fear of what would happen if they were caught. The cowed Italians in the back of the truck would doubtless exaggerate what little violence there had been to excuse their own carelessness.

The lorry bogged in the sand two or three times more that afternoon, but no one minded so much now except the Italians who were elbowed out of the truck to help (rather lackadaisically) with the digging out.

That night they really began to feel hunger for the first time and King felt pinpricks of doubt sapping his new confidence. He had been praying for days that they would run into a stretch of hard smooth sand but it did not look likely now. He and Barr talked about moving down off the escarpment again but it would have meant running north towards Fuka, doubling their chances of meeting enemy patrols, so they shelved the idea.

More soft dunes in the morning and Barr flogged her across them in low gear. She ground up a long, eroded slope where the ground was hard and stony, dipped into more dunes and bogged again. They scrabbled the sand away, jammed the boards under the driving wheels and when Barr pressed the starter the engine turned gratingly but did not fire.

He tried again, and again and again, but there was only the metallic whining while the others stood round looking at the bonnet, willing it to start. King called, " Watch out for the battery. We can't push her here."

Barr swung out of the cab and hoisted the bonnet, and he, the lieutenant and the Italian driver poked about vainly trying to find out what was wrong. He tried the starter again but she would not fire.

" How far are we from the bomb-line ? " the lieutenant asked, and King said in a strained silence he thought about ninety miles. The butterflies were awake in his stomach again. Jackson said, " Taxi ! " but his voice sounded half-hearted.

" She's got to start," Barr said flatly, and went back to the engine. An hour later he looked up and shrugged.

They lay under the lorry and chewed some prunes. Afterwards all the mechanically-minded ones started systematically
taking the engine down, laying the pieces on a tarpaulin. It
felt better to be doing something. No one had started to talk
about the alternatives yet. In a way, there were no alternatives.

Wills suddenly said, " Hullo. Look at that ! " He stood up
and stared across the desert and the others looked and saw a
cloud of dust.

" M.T. of some sort," said the lieutenant.

King ran to the top of a hillock of sand a few yards from
the lorry. " There are two of 'em, whatever they are," he
said, and a minute later added grimly, " They're coming this
way." He could see the two dark shapes in front of the dust
trails and thought at first that they were tanks but they seemed
to be moving too nimbly. " Jeeps," he said at last. " They've
seen us all right. Heading straight for us."

" Get under the lorry," Barr yelled. " We might be able
to knock 'em off." He had one of the rifles and was jabbing
the Italians into movement. The jeeps were coming up fast.
King could see men in them ; realised how exposed he was
on the hillock and dropped down behind it. He had a wild
idea he might be able to start a diversion and wished he had
brought one of the rifles with him.

He could see the lorry round the side of the hillock, but not
the jeeps, though from the sound he knew the jeeps must be
less than a hundred yards away and his insides felt in a knot.
An Italian under the lorry started screaming for help and
suddenly the tearing clatter of machine-guns shocked the
ears.

Bullets were whanging against the truck and he pressed
himself instinctively against the hillock. A lull, then two more
quick bursts of machine-gun fire. Hoarse shouts came from
the lorry and edging round the hillock he saw the others
crawling out from under it with their hands up and one of the
Italians waving a dirty white handkerchief.

God, should he stay out and die of thirst or join them, and
a voice came from one of the jeeps saying, " What'll we do
with *this* bloody lot ? " It spoke in English.

A moment of stunned silence was broken by a babble of voices. Barr was shouting. " Hey, are you English ? "

" Don't move," a voice said. "Who are you ? "

" English . . . R.A.F. . . . we're escaping," Barr shouted. The babble broke out again and people started shouting wildly. King cautiously lifted his head above the sand and saw four British soldiers by the jeeps shaking hands with the others. He walked down the sand over to them. A burly man with captain's pips was explaining that they were a party of the Long Range Desert Group. King had heard a lot about their brazen sorties far into enemy territory.

Wills had an angry red bullet score across his back ; he had taken his shirt off and one of the soldiers was dabbing some stuff on it. He was the only casualty.

" You're pretty lucky," the captain was saying. " This wouldn't happen again in a million times. You're a hundred miles behind the line here. We only came out to look for a German officer who's escaped from us. We had him at our base so if we don't find him we'll have to pack up, or he'll give us away."

King asked where on earth they had come from, and Jellicoe, the captain, pointed behind and said vaguely. " A couple of miles back there." He added seriously, " Don't be too happy. You're not very safe out here with us, but we'll do our best for you. You'd better come back with us. That lorry won't go again."

King turned and saw the lorry's cab and bonnet riddled with bullet holes.

Jellicoe tossed the Italians a packet of iron rations, and the rest of them crammed somehow into the jeeps. After bumping several miles over the desert out of sight of the Italians, they turned inland, coming to rugged, hard country where the jeeps left no tracks.

Near a clump of rocks the two jeeps stopped, but King could see no signs of life anywhere. Jellicoe, beside the driver, was looking at another escarpment that rose steep and bare like a cliff out of the desert half a mile ahead. He murmured, " All right. Next point." The jeep moved off to the left a hundred yards and stopped again. In a few seconds Jellicoe said, " O.K.," and the jeeps moved on and stopped in another hundred yards. " All clear," Jellicoe said, and the jeeps moved on towards the cliff.

They were still fifty yards from the cliff and King was wondering what it was all about when he saw the face of the cliff at the base wrinkle and a part of it rose in the air, showing a dark space behind. He was looking at it goggle-eyed and Jellicoe was laughing as the two jeeps rolled into the cave and the sand-camouflage netting dropped behind them like a theatre curtain.

A very big man with a moustache, drill shorts and desert boots was there and Jellicoe introduced them to Colonel Stirling, leader of the Group. Nearly everyone in the Middle East had heard about Stirling but few people seemed to know him.

Behind the netting quite a lot of light filtered through and they could see that the cave was actually a wide, long space under an overhang of the cliff and there were another dozen soldiers and a lorry there. Stirling was saying wryly that it was not a very healthy spot at that moment.

" We'll try and get you back," he said, " but the Jerries have broken our supply route through the Depression and now that this Jerry has escaped we may have to evacuate this. Meantime we've got plenty of food, so relax and do just what we tell you."

King and the others did not move out of the cave for two days, though they were quite happy to lie there in the shade eating bully beef and pickled onions. The cave, the men and the operations fascinated them. The jeeps went out before dusk and in the morning they watched them coming back, stopping for a few seconds by the pile of rock half a mile away, turning to stop at the next check point and then the next, and moving on to the cave.

Nearly every time the machine-guns had to be cleaned. King gathered that the airfields around Fuka were the favourite hunting grounds.

Late on the third day Stirling said, " You're flying home to-night . . . I hope." He would not tell them how, but later motioned them into the truck and Jellicoe drove them out into the desert. At dusk they were moving along the smooth bed of a wadi that cut down to the flat coastal desert from the heights of the escarpment. By the time it was dark Jellicoe was heading confidently across the bare sand, steering by compass. About forty minutes later he stopped and some of the soldiers who had come in the truck spread out in the darkness with rags and tins of petrol.

It must have been two hours before they heard aircraft engines and soon the sound was circling somewhere overhead. Jellicoe flashed a torch and a line of flares sprang up along the sand where the soldiers had gone.

" Stick together and move smartly when I tell you to," Jellicoe was saying. " It's not healthy to waste time on these junkets."

They saw the big transport low, running up to the flare-path, and then it was trundling over the sand, braking hard. They were running towards it as it turned at the end of the lights ; a door in the side opened and one by one they were jumping through it like trained dogs going through a hoop. The engines blared and King felt the familiar bump and rumble of take-off; the propellers changed pitch and he knew they were flying.

He was lying between Jackson and Wills on some blankets on the floor feeling cold and restless. There was nothing to see out of the windows except blackness, but after half an hour he guessed they had crossed the line and leaned over and told Jackson.

" Yeah," Jackson said. " This junket's just about saved my bacon. I've got twelve days' pay coming."

(Less than a year later King was navigator of a Halifax flying from England, and on the eve of the thirteenth trip of his second tour of operations he felt the old premonition again. He gave his watch once more to the adjutant, talked a mess W.A.A.F. into bringing him two extra dinners and three hours later a fighter set them on fire over the Dutch border. This time he got out by parachute, lost his flying boots on the way down and landed in a field.

He had to get a pair of boots—that was the first thing—and then contact the Dutch Organisation. After an hour padding about in his socks he saw a white farmhouse, took the plunge and knocked on the door. A man opened it. " Are you Dutch ? " King asked.

" Ja, ja," the farmer said, and it was not till the German police arrived an hour later that he discovered that the farmer thought he had said " Deutsch."

He learned a lot more German behind barbed wire.)

.   .   .   .   .

In Stalag Luft III, King worked on the famous " X " Organisation, the escape society in the camp, though (perhaps luckily) he did not draw a " ticket " for the mass break-out of March, 1944, when the Gestapo murdered fifty out of seventy-six escaping Air Force officers. Freed eventually by the liberating armies, he left the R.A.F. in 1945 and married Diane, a Blandford girl whom he had known since he was a schoolboy. He became a teacher and the father of two daughters, but after four years of quiet country life went back to the Air Force, and when this was being written was a navigator (and adjutant) in No. 25 Squadron, flying jet night fighters from a base in Kent.

On May 21, 1952, he was in a Lancaster which caught fire in the air. The pilot tried to get down on West Malling airfield, but at one minute past midnight, half a mile short of the runway, the plane crashed into an orchard and King and three others were killed.

THE MAN WHO WENT PREPARED

John Whitley was born on September 7, 1905, and knew no permanent early home, because his father was a civil engineer and the family went with him from contract to contract all over the world. Whitley's mother died in Chile when he was five, and during World War I his father became a prisoner of the Turks, but the boy was, luckily, in England, being educated at Haileybury. He went into the R.A.F. in 1926. In 1931 he married and went to India as a flight lieutenant. By 1937, good-natured and briskly competent, he was a squadron leader at Bomber Command and was awarded the Air Force Cross. Later, as a flight commander in the V.I.P. flight at Hendon, he flew people like Chamberlain and Churchill. By 1940 he was a wing commander on a bomber squadron, and in the following year he became a group captain.

IN 1942 Group Captain John Whitley was prepared (though not eager) to be shot down and killed, if necessary, in air operations over Germany, but reacted violently against the idea of being captured. No regular group captain could equably contemplate emerging from the cage when the shooting was over to salute surviving contemporaries who were now air vice-marshals. It is not envy of contemporaries but knowledge that a man's greatest chance to fulfil his profession has been lost. A batsman might feel the same if in his first test match he made a pair of ducks.

When the R.A.F. became escape conscious before the war was half over, Whitley was an early disciple. Many airmen (bless their carefree hearts) liked to try and sleep during escape lectures, but Whitley rarely missed a word. As commander of a bomber airfield at Linton-on-Ouse he flew on operations a lot and knew that few of those who were shot down had much chance of using the tiny survival kit they all carried. He came to the conclusion that the best way to escape was (*a*) to avoid prompt capture, and (*b*) to fly always fully equipped to travel through enemy territory. So he evolved his own escape kit, and it was probably unexcelled in the history of the war.

First he tore the maker's tabs off a check lounge suit so that it could never betray him as English. He put a folded civilian tie in a pocket of the jacket, rolled it up and stowed it and a peaked cap in a little haversack. He sewed a strap on the haversack and thereafter kept the haversack with his parachute canopy pack so both could be clipped on his harness in a second. Whenever he went on a raid he wore the trousers of the lounge suit under his uniform trousers, and under his uniform shirt wore a blue check shirt with collar attached. In the pockets of his battledress blouse he carried a Rolls razor, tube of brushless shaving cream, toothbrush, tube of toothpaste, nail file and tiny compass. Among his aircrews the *ensemble* caused a lot of droll winks, shaking of heads and references to " kitchen sinks," but Whitley had enough blithe firmness not to be discouraged. He was at that time thirty-seven, lean and neat with a large, well-trained military moustache.

On the night of April 10, 1943, he flew in a Ruhr-bound Halifax of one of his squadrons, and about fifteen thousand feet over a corner of Belgium glowing balls of tracer streamed out of the darkness behind and the port wing flooded with fire as the tanks went up. Hull, the pilot, said quite calmly, " Bale out! Bale out! " He held the plane steady and the others clipped on their parachutes and crawled to the hatches. As Whitley slid through the hatch swung shut on his harness and he was hanging in the tearing slipstream about a foot under the fuselage. Ragged flame from the wing lit everything clearly. He clawed at the jammed hatch but the slipstream kept tearing his hand away. God, what a rotten end !

Suddenly he was falling gently away from the plane ; one end of his parachute canopy pack hit him under the chin and he saw that only one of the two hooks of the pack was attached to his harness. The strap of his escape haversack had apparently caught in the harness clip and eased the parachute hook out of it. As he fell he clearly recalled an inquiry he had once made into the death of a pilot who had baled out with only one hook clipped on the harness. The other hook had not held. Whitley kept trying to clip the hook on but it would not go, and he thought how bloody it was that the escape haversack that was to have got him back home should kill him instead.

Cloud closed round him, and he remembered that the cloud had been at seven thousand feet. Now he was half-way down and would be at terminal velocity. He stopped trying to clip the hook on and tried to get a firm hold on a strap at the side of the parachute pack, but his hand must have accidentally hooked the ripcord D-ring, because the parachute opened suddenly with a tremendous crack, and to his amazement (and gratification) it held.

Floating peacefully in the darkness he saw faint lights rising below. The lights were suddenly near and a voice shouted eerily beneath in German. He hit the ground hard and as the canopy crumpled saw he was in someone's garden, his back half supported by a wire fence. A yard away on either side two spiked iron posts supported the fence. It was a near thing. The Halifax was burning half a mile away.

A man's surprised voice cut the silence. It came from the house : " Eh bien, qu'est ce que c'est que cela ? "

Thank God ! Belgian or French.

Whitley said in a hoarse whisper, " Psst. Je suis aviateur Anglais."

A door opened, showing an oblong of light, a man came out and abruptly stopped, rigid with surprise. Grasping the situation, he said urgently, " Venez. Venez. Vitement." Whitley picked up his haversack and followed him into the house, asking in his schoolboy French, " Where is this place ? "

" Hirson," said the man.

" C'est Belgique ? "

" Mais non, m'sieur," the man said reproachfully. " Vous êtes en France."

They were in a big, low-ceilinged room that was kitchen and dining-room combined. A startled middle-aged woman, the Frenchman's wife, blinked at him in her dressing-gown, and then an old woman, apparently her mother, came in. They started firing questions at him so fast he could not understand. Haltingly he explained that he was " colonel " R.A.F., and their eyes widened. Several neighbours pushed excitedly in and everyone watched in amazement as Whitley took off his pants and revealed the lounge suit trousers underneath, then removed his blouse and Service shirt, exposing the check shirt. Opening the haversack, he pulled out the coat, extracted the tie from the pocket and put both tie and jacket on. Then he took the razor and the other things out of his blouse and stuffed them in his jacket pockets.

After a pop-eyed silence the old woman suddenly said dramatically, " Il est Allemagne ! "

Everyone started shushing her at once, shocked at the idea and assuring her that Whitley did not look German. Why, his parachute was in the garden. Was that not the proof? Whitley bent down to the old woman, curled the ends of his great moustache and said hopefully, " Anglais, n'est ce pas ? " but she shrank away, looked at him fearfully sideways, and as soon as he turned away started muttering again, " Allemagne. Allemagne. Prenez garde ! "

The Frenchman's wife brought him a bowl of milk and some biscuits and they were all chattering advice at him, saying things like " Take the five o'clock train to Paris." Then someone would hear something and say, " Ssssh," and everyone would all stop talking for a second, then start once more. Whitley found he had lost his peaked cap, so the Frenchman brought him an old black pork-pie hat. As there were Germans at the railway station two hundred yards away, he suggested that Whitley hide in a bombed house across the road till the curfew ended at dawn. All the women in the room (except the old one) kissed him on both cheeks ; he blushed, crept across the road and climbed in a broken window of the empty house. Broken glass cracked like pistol shots under his feet, so he took off his jacket, lay on it and tried to relax.

So far he had felt only confused relief, but a distant drone grew into the earth-shaking roar overhead of the bomber stream returning to England, filling him with lonely fury. Automatically his mind was dwelling on escape and it did not take him long to decide that he must try and contact the French Underground and make for Spain.

Too keyed up to sleep he lay in the darkness, thoughtfully tugging on his moustache, visualising the next twenty-four hours and trying to imagine the dangers so that he could forestall them. It came to him like a revelation that the very moustache he was stroking was a danger ; it must look very English. He fumbled in his pocket for his razor, assembled it in the dark and, flinching with the pain, shaved it off dry, trying to soften it with spittle to make it easier. Afterwards he fingered the spot, feeling naked and regretful. No razor had touched his lip for fifteen years.

At half-past five he noticed the darkness lifting and became restless. He was too close to the Germans and the wrecked aircraft and too many people knew he was there. Getting carefully to his feet he tip-toed to the door ; outside the street was dim and deserted, and with a sudden resolve he walked out into it and away from the railway station.

The light grew stronger as he left the houses of the village behind and walked between fields, grateful for the fresh dawn air. A mile out of the town a stream crossed the road, and he filled the rubber water-bottle from his " Pandora." The road was still deserted, but he felt he should hide during daylight. He found a double hedge near a wood off the road and settled between the rows.

Glad of something to do, he examined his pockets and, shrewdly alert for the future, scowled disapprovingly to see that his Horlicks and halazone tablets, matches and benzedrine had wrappers with instructions printed in English. After memorising the instructions, he took all the wrappers off and buried them. His tie slipped out of the fold of his jacket while doing this, and he noticed a tag on the tie that said, " Rankin and Co., Lahore and Delhi." He tore the tag off and buried it, then slid the little file between a seam at the top of his trousers and hid the compass in the seam of his fly.

It was bitterly cold on the damp ground in the shade between the two hedges and he sat, sleepless and miserable, with chattering teeth all day till, when it was nearly dusk, he walked out along the road again.

It was nearly deserted ; he passed a couple of people in the gloom and once muttered " Bonsoir " in reply to a casual greeting. Weariness was settling heavily on him, so that he began stumbling in the darkness and knew he could not go on indefinitely without getting help, even if it meant taking a risk. Passing a lonely farmhouse he heard French voices inside and stopped to listen. Tiredness drove him to a decision ; he picked up a stone and from the shadows about twenty yards away threw it at the front door. The door opened and a woman's angry voice said in French, " Who is there ? "

Whitley called back in schoolboy French, " Madame, I would like to speak to your husband."

" Monsieur is ill," she answered.

" Could I speak to you ? "

" What do you want ? "

He took the plunge, dropped his voice to a penetrating whisper and said, " I am an English airman. Can you give me shelter for the night ? "

Perhaps because of his accent, the woman said, " Come in quickly," and Whitley walked out of the gloom up to the door and into a large kitchen. The woman shut the door and they looked at each other for a moment in silence. She was a neat and competent-looking farmer's wife of about thirty. He started to say, " Merci. Merci beaucoup, madame," and she smiled and said that she expected he was hungry ; she was crossing to the stove as she said it, and a few minutes later laid a plate of bacon and eggs on the table for him. As he ate she said she had seen his plane going overhead in flames. She wanted to know when the war was going to end and how things were in England. (Whitley heard those same questions repeated many times in the next few weeks.) Her name was Madame Richet ; her husband was not ill, she said, but was a prisoner of war in Germany, and the only other people in the house were an evacuee boy of three and a wrinkled woman she called her " bonne." Composed and practical, she knew well enough that she would be shot if caught sheltering an Allied airman.

Later she showed him a bed in a spare room at the back.

Whitley tried to ask if he could visit the lavatory first but found he could not think of the word and floundered till, blushing, he had to explain in sign language. When he got into bed tiredness overwhelmed him and he slept dreamlessly for ten hours.

In the morning Madame told him to stay out of sight in the house while she visited her father, who lived in a village called Martigny, some three miles away. She rode off on a bicycle and was back an hour later smiling widely. Her father and another man would be round to see them that afternoon and everything would be " arranged."

Whitley said, hardly daring to hope, " L'Organisation? " Madame gave a little secret nod, as though reluctant to admit it openly, and Whitley felt a wonderful exhilaration. With little idea of how to contact the Organisation, he had wanted to find them so badly that he could hardly believe it had happened so easily and so quickly. He sat on the edge of the kitchen table talking light-heartedly to Madame when she went rigid and white, pointed dramatically through the window and said, " Les Boches! " Whitley jumped off the table and saw a little car with two men turning into the farmyard off the road.

He ran to a window that opened on to the other side of the house, heaved fiercely at it but it would not budge (it had not been opened for years), and for a moment had a panicky, rat-in-a-trap feeling. He heard the car stop in the yard and the doors bang, ran across to another window and yanked at it so hard that it shot up with a loud bang as the frame hit the top. He almost fell out of it, ran a few yards and dived into a bed of thick, tall nettles. They stung all over his face and hands, but he lay there with his head down for several minutes till he heard the doors bang again, the engine started and through the nettle stalks he saw the car gliding out of the yard.

Back at the house Madame was trembling but said that the Germans were not looking for him ; they were checking on hay stocks and were returning later. She took him round to the back of the house and showed him where he must hide in an old pigeon loft. He took his kit into the loft with him and, noticing that some of it still looked obviously English, filled in time scraping the print off the toothpaste and shaving cream tubes and filing the " Made in England " off his toothbrush and comb.

Later he heard the car in the yard again, and through a chink in the boards of the loft saw the Germans get out and knock on the door. They stood talking a few minutes with Madame Richet and drove off once more. A few minutes later she called him out of the loft and told him that lunch was ready.

That afternoon her father drove up in a battered old camionet. He was a little, wizened man with a walrus moustache, and into the house behind him walked a big man with a red, plump face and little bright eyes, the pork butcher Mahoudeaux.

Madame brought out wine ; they drank several toasts and then the two Frenchmen drove away. Whitley waited nervously in the house till the following night before Mahoudeaux came back for him in the camionet. He wanted to pay Madame Richet out of his escape money for looking after him, but she rattled off, " Non, non, non, non, non," waving her hands, palms outwards, so he gave her his gold and onyx R.A.F. cuff-links, and she said she would hide them for him till after the war.

The door of the old camionet was fastened with a bit of wire and the engine popped and clattered, but it jolted stiffly and noisily the three kilometres to the village of Leuze, and Mahoudeaux drove it into a little yard. " Follow me quickly," he said, and Whitley walked wordlessly after him through the door of a stone house. In the kitchen a stout woman with mousy hair caught neatly in a bun at the back bobbed and smiled warmly and shook his hand. She called him " M'sieur le colonel," and Whitley found she was intensely proud to have an R.A.F. " colonel " staying in the house. There was a daughter in the family, aged about twenty, plump like her mother, a good-looking boy called Roger, just past the pimples stage and preoccupied with one of the village girls, and a little boy of twelve with a sty in his eye who was utterly thrilled to meet Whitley.

Madame Mahoudeaux, who never stopped working, had an enormous veal steak on the table five minutes after Whitley arrived. She kept bustling around while all the others sat down and ate, and Whitley was embarrassed to take so long eating his veal because the others kept asking him questions and he had to get them to repeat them several times over and then laboriously think out the answers, finding alternative words for the ones he could not think of. Daniel, the little boy, sat breathlessly at his elbow all through the meal, as close as he could get, staring in awe.

In a little room upstairs with a high bed under a low ceiling he slept deeply, full of food and wine and dumb peace, feeling he was floating on a strong tide.

He was three weeks with the Mahoudeaux, feeling like Bonnie Prince Charlie hiding in the house of a loyal subject. He never quite got used to being a hero. Now and then they brought in chosen friends, who shook hands a little breathlessly and spent most of the time just looking at him. This worried him, because among themselves they were so talkative and he had an uncomfortable feeling that the exciting news of his presence was spreading far and wide through the friendly people of the surrounding country. The Mahoudeaux did not seem to mind, they were too proud of showing him off, but to Whitley they played their dangerous game in an undisciplined, dangerous way.

Little Daniel was the worst of the worshippers. He padded along beside Whitley wherever he went, never talking, never taking his eyes off him. Once he even tried to follow Whitley into the lavatory, but Whitley pushed him briskly outside, and Daniel waited by the closed door, occasionally flipping a stone companionably on to the corrugated iron roof. Papa Mahoudeaux sternly told Daniel that he must never open his mouth about " le colonel " outside the house, because if he did so the Germans would shoot Papa and Mama and send Genevieve, Roger and Daniel to a concentration camp (which was quite true), but Papa Mahoudeaux himself, bursting with importance, personally told nearly everyone in the village that his friend, the R.A.F. colonel, was staying with him.

For a couple of days Whitley sat contentedly enough in the

house, and then time began to drag more and more till it was nearly intolerable. He could not go out into the village because Germans were often there and he could not make much headway with the one or two ancient books in the house. There was a hutch of rabbits downstairs which he watched for hours at a time and then one day Mahoudeaux came in beaming with his hands behind his back, then with a flourish put one of his hands in front of Whitley, and in it was a dirty old pack of cards.

It was a rare and priceless gift. Whitley sat down to play patience and found instantly that all the twos, threes, fours, fives and sixes were missing. He revised the rules so he could play without them but found that like that the game came out easily every time and it became a sort of subtle torture. After a while he got to the point of nearly screaming with rage when the game came out and several times he almost tore the cards up. He tried to play to lose, then, but found he could not lose without cheating, and was maddened again.

The only bright part of the day was when Mahoudeaux turned the radio on softly in the evening and he heard the B.B.C. news.

The day Fontaine came he forgot his boredom. Fontaine was a local Resistance leader, a sturdy, short man of about forty ; Mahoudeaux brought him in and Fontaine said that Davies and Strange, two of Whitley's crew, were safe and hiding in other houses near the village. It gave Whitley a tremendous kick but he sobered as Fontaine said that three others of the crew had been found dead, and Hull, the pilot, was missing.

Fontaine said, picking his words carefully in stilted English, " We wait for orders to make travel for you. It will not be long." Whitley preferred to speak to him in French. After two weeks having to try and understand the Mahoudeaux and make himself understood, his French was improving unbelievably.

One night Fontaine walked in with a couple of self-conscious youths behind him and Whitley recognised Davies and Strange. They were in rough civilian clothes with berets and he started to laugh because Strange was wearing a ludicrous pair of tight black pants. Strange said sheepishly he had borrowed them from the local priest. They laughed at Whitley minus his moustache and uniform and almost forgot he was a group captain. The three of them talked volubly for hours while Fontaine and the Mahoudeaux family looked on benevolently and laughed when they did, though they had not the slightest idea what the jokes were. Afterwards Davies and Strange went back to their own houses.

Fontaine told Whitley about a curious new German installation in the vicinity and said that it might be important to get news of it back to England. In the morning he brought with him a tall, distinguished-looking grey-haired Frenchman whom he introduced as M'sieur Fournaise, Mayor of the nearby village of Aouste, and the three of them rode off on bicycles, pedalling along quiet lanes until on top of a cleared rise in the ground Whitley saw the thing that looked like a big framework for a hoarding, upright girders joined by cross-pieces and the whole lot rotating on a little circular track. Near it were barrack huts.

" It's a radar station all right," he said, confirming Fournaise's suspicions. They told him the local estimates of the Germans who lived on the site and he memorised it to take back to England.

Another day Fontaine and Fournaise took him on the bicycles again to another village where a dapper young man with a thin black moustache and riding breeches served them drinks from behind his bar and took Whitley into the village square and photographed him (in the presence of dozens of people) for his fake identity card.

" He is so bored," Fontaine said sympathetically, explaining that the young man was a de Gaullist lieutenant who had already made two secret trips to England and parachuted back. His only excitement for some time was the night a young man had sidled into the bar claiming to be a shot-down British airman trying to escape back to England. The lieutenant led him into the back parlour and decided, after a few sharp questions, that the " escaper " was a German plant trying to trace the escape channel. The lieutenant promised the man he would take " very good care " of him, and he did

—driving him out along the road to Paris and returning alone.

Whitley got very restive as the days passed and kept asking Fontaine when he could move on, but Fontaine only shrugged and said he did not know. On May 2 he infuriated Whitley by saying that Davies and Strange had been moved on the previous day and would be home in England in a week.

" Well, when the devil am I going ? " Whitley demanded. Fontaine shrugged again.

Two days later he came round early in the morning with an expansive grin and said he had just received a message that Whitley was to leave for Paris in the evening. His code name was " le gros gibier "—the big game.

For Whitley the day was a tumult of mounting excitement and towards dusk Fontaine drove up in the battered camionet. As Whitley was getting in Fontaine clapped the ball of his hand to his forehead and cried that he was an " imbecile." He had forgotten to bring Whitley's identity card.

" Well, we'll have to go back and get it, that's all," said Whitley. " There is no time," Fontaine shrugged. He added airily that it would be all right, but Whitley groaned with exasperation.

Mahoudeaux drove with them to the station at Aubenton ; Whitley thanked him warmly and climbed into a third-class carriage with Fontaine. After twenty uneventful minutes they changed trains at Liart and at ten-thirty steamed into Charleville Mezières. As Whitley followed Fontaine out of the station an elderly man joined Fontaine, who turned and beckoned to Whitley. The three of them walked about a mile till the elderly man led them in through a gate into a large house hidden in trees back from the road.

Whitley had a comfortable room to himself that night and at five o'clock the elderly man, whose name was Poinier, woke him and led the way back to the station where they left Fontaine and boarded the early train for Paris. Poinier said casually that the local chief of police was in the carriage to keep an eye on them in case of trouble, and Whitley had quite a shock when a dapper and rather effeminate little man came into the compartment and offered him a Gold Flake cigarette. It was his introduction to the police chief, who talked amusingly with a lisp but who was a nimble-witted little man who spent ten per cent. of his time rather clumsily " co-operating " with the Gestapo and the rest of the time sabotaging their efforts.

At noon the train drew into Paris and Whitley, uncomfortably aware of the beating of his heart, followed Poinier out of the Gare de l'Est into the Metro and out again at Les Invalides and into the streets that were full of people. He noted with dismay the numbers of German soldiers and felt rigid all over and quivering inside as he strode among them. None of them gave him a second glance, which was deeply satisfying, not just because he felt safer but because it was good to feel oneself hookwinking the enemy, moving inviolate among the unwitting soldiers on leave who were looking for interesting sights. Feeling a little more confident he thought that, if they only knew it, he was probably the most interesting sight for them. It would be funny to see their faces if they knew who he was, and then he thought that if they *did* find out, his own face would look rather peculiar.

Poinier turned in the door of a block of flats. " The lift is not working," he murmured and they walked up five flights of stairs. Whitley, panting, reached the top to see a flat door opening. He heard Poinier saying to a very dark, youngish man in the door, " Le gros gibier," and then Poinier was shaking his hand and smiling. He said " Bonne chance," and turned and walked back down the stairs.

" Do come in," said the dark young man in the door. " My name is Aimable." They shook hands and Whitley followed him into a lounge room where several young men were sitting. A little unsure of himself, Whitley said politely, " Bonjour, M'sieur," to the man nearest him and the man replied " Bonjour " in an atrocious accent. Whitley said, surprised, " Are you English ? "

" Yes, I am actually," said the young man. " Are you English, too ? "

Across the room Whitley saw Davies and Strange grinning at him and started laughing with the rest. There was a lot of chatter and then Aimable appeared in the doorway and said that lunch was ready. The others stood politely aside and let the group captain go first. Walking through the double glass doors he looked in amazement at the crisp white cloth over the big table, the centre-piece, patterned dinner service, silver and glasses. All through the excellent three-course lunch that Aimable brought in Whitley kept marvelling at the way they were all sitting down to a luncheon party under the noses of the Gestapo. After he had finished his coffee he said jovially to Aimable, " That was better than I could get in my own mess. Excellent. Very good, indeed."

" You are kind," Aimable murmured, and with a sly grin handed Whitley a tea-towel. " It is your turn to do the drying up," he said. " It is the custom."

Everyone laughed (including Whitley) and he and Laws, an English sergeant pilot who spoke almost perfect French, did the washing-up between them. Whitley thought that the kitchen was rather dirty and, in his usual thorough way, spent hours with Laws scrubbing it out and cleaning everything they could lay their hands on. Aimable threw up his hands with pleasure when he saw it and delighted Whitley with a spontaneous " Oo-la-la."

That afternoon a French girl called and took several of the young evaders on the next stage of their journey home. Whitley regretfully stayed behind with Laws, Davies and Strange, and at four-thirty Aimable brought them afternoon tea.

Paul, a French boy of about eighteen, came to the flat later and helped Aimable prepare dinner. Aimable said he had just that week started training Paul to be his assistant. " He is a good boy," he said thoughtfully, " devout and does not worry about women, and so I think he must be so high-principled that he will not break down easily if the Gestapo get him."

After dinner they all sat in the lounge and sipped cognac. Whitley wanted to know what the concierge of the building thought of all the nervous young men who kept coming and going in and out of Aimable's flat. " I suppose you've already thought of it," he said apologetically, " but I was wondering if he is safe. He must think we are a pretty dubious bunch."

" Oh, yes, he thinks you are all dubious," Aimable said

comfortably. " He will not even speak to you. You see, I am a trained nurse and I have told him you all have venereal disease and come here for treatment."

There were books and packs of cards in the flat and over the next few days Whitley did not find the time dragging so heavily as before. There was the feeling now, too, that they were in efficient hands and would be moved on as soon as it was safe. None of them felt any urge to leave the flat for a walk and Aimable locked them in every night when he went to work, telling them never to answer the door-bell if it rang. The gendarmes sometimes made checks and the gendarmes were dangerous. Aimable's job was looking after an eighty-year-old retired French admiral who was paralysed ; it was a " protected " job and gave him every excuse for coming and going at all hours.

He took Whitley and the others out one afternoon to the Bon Marché department store and down in the basement they sat in front of the photomaton for their new identity card pictures. A day or two later Aimable told Whitley and Laws that they would leave for Spain that evening. At six o'clock he handed them their new identity cards, and Whitley, the English officer and gentleman, grunted a little and then grinned when he looked at his card and saw that he was now a baker named Louis Bidet ! The door-bell rang and Aimable went out and let in a young, rather impassive Frenchman. " This is Jacques," he said. " He is your guide and you are to do exactly as he says."

He went into the kitchen and came back with two bottles of champagne and they ceremoniously drank to their success till the bottles were empty, so that they said a specially warm farewell to Aimable and followed Jacques down into the street with high morale.

They walked a long way to a railway station ; Jacques already had the tickets and the party walked wordlessly on to the platform and settled into reserved seats in a waiting train.

Whitley had just made himself comfortable when his heart lurched as a gendarme came into the compartment. The gendarme ignored them, settled in a seat opposite Whitley, and they sat in a strained silence. As the train pulled out the gendarme put his head back and shut his eyes. Soon he started to snore, and to Whitley it sounded like music.

The train was outside Paris now, rocking along fast in the darkness, and the rhythmic clickety-click and the swaying lulled the others into sleep. Whitley tried to sleep, too, but could not keep his eyes shut ; every minute or two he wanted to open them and see whether the gendarme was still asleep. His mind would not rest so he lay there with his eyes half closed, watching the gendarme. Around 3 a.m. the gendarme woke but took no interest in anyone, and then about an hour later the train pulled into Nantes and to Whitley's enormous relief the gendarme got up, yanked his valise off the rack and got off the train.

He slept fitfully after that and around noon they came to Bordeaux, where Jacques roused them and they followed him out of the station into a café. As they sat down a dark young Frenchman with a thin, almost cadaverous face, came over to their table and greeted them soberly as though he had known them for years.

" This is François," Jacques said. " He knows the frontier as well as anyone."

Jacques, François and Laws talked briskly in French, but Whitley found most of the conversation a shade too fast and sat somewhat isolated by the barrier of language, feeling awkward and conspicuous. Jacques leaned close and said more slowly that they were now in the dangerous frontier zone and must be very careful. They would travel by slow local trains because there were fewer checks on them.

That afternoon they went on to Dax by a local train and François led them through streets full of German soldiers to an hotel. He said he would leave them there for the night and as he booked rooms Whitley saw the manager looking hard at them. Jacques led them into the dining-room ; it was packed with noisy Germans and Whitley thought irritatedly that it was stupid to eat in such a dangerous place. They sat silently and self-consciously among the Germans and when the meal was over filed up to the shelter of their rooms. Though he had hardly slept the previous night Whitley knew he was too strung up to sleep. The border was only a few miles away and

Jacques kept harping on the scores of guards and checks they had to pass.

Whitley was in the lavatory, luckily, when he heard the knock on the door. Jacques and Laws had been talking and there was a dead silence after the knock. Whitley stayed in the lavatory. He heard steps and then a strange voice in the room. The voices were muffled and Whitley could not make out what was going on. He heard the voices of Jacques and Laws, raised a little, and knew unmistakably that they were arguing heatedly with someone. It seemed to go on and on and Whitley waited behind the lavatory door, keeping very still. After a long time he heard the outer door shut and then a knock on the lavatory door. He opened it. Jacques and Laws, both white faced, stood there.

" It was the bloody manager," Laws said. " We're supposed to fill in some rather tricky forms and show our passes. He was pretty suspicious."

" You didn't give him the passes, did you? " Whitley had already dubiously pointed out to Jacques that all their cards were supposed to come from different areas and they were all conspicuously in the same handwriting.

" No," Laws said. " He was getting a bit aerated for a while but Jacques told him we were Frenchmen making for the border and he seemed to take it all right."

" I do not think he will make trouble," Jacques said. " He seems to think we are all French."

Whitley told Jacques he thought it was madness to bring them to such an hotel and they had a long debate as to whether they should leave immediately in case the proprietor should report them before morning. In the end they decided to stay, but Whitley lay awake most of the night so he could make a break for it through the window in case the Germans came.

At dawn they were out of the hotel heading for the railway station, where François joined them. They caught the first train and came to Bayonne about an hour later. French gendarmes were checking papers at the barrier. Whitley showed his card as off-handedly as he could and was waved casually through. He was walking up to the others in the station yard when a German in a black uniform with a skull

and crossbones badge on his cap blocked his way and shot a
question at him in French. Whitley thought for a paralysing
moment that it was the Gestapo uniform (actually it was a
Panzer division) but gathered that the German was asking the
way to some street. With what he hoped was a Gallic shrug
he said, " Je ne sais pas, Monsieur."

" Ah," said the German, " vous ne savez pas, Monsieur,"
and walked away. Whitley, shaken, joined the others. François led them through the town, telling them to keep about
thirty yards behind. He kept looking round and waving them
back furtively and both Whitley and Laws wanted to kick him
because he was acting in an obviously suspicious way.
François finally turned into a large house and they followed
him up the stairs into a flat. François was fidgeting with
nerves. He told them they must keep absolutely quiet, so
they took off their shoes, tiptoed and spoke in whispers.
Every time they made the slightest sound François exploded
into a torrent of angry French, making much more noise
himself.

A young woman and a fat man came into the flat with a
covered basket of steak, roast potatoes and two bottles of red
wine. After eating they lay on mattresses on the floor and
subsided into a sort of coma until towards dusk when François
led them out of the house and back through the streets to the
station. He left them there but came back in a few minutes
with some bicycles, and soon they were cycling out of Bayonne
on the road towards the frontier.

They passed houses and occasional groups of German
soldiers, and nearly all the time François kept cursing Whitley
and Laws loudly in English for riding straight-backed like
Englishmen. Whitley tried bending low over the handlebars
but François still kept nagging at them. Whitley told him
angrily to speak in French—if he had to speak—but François
kept on in English until Whitley, seething with rage, told him
roughly to get a hold on his nerves and shut up.

By seven o'clock they were coming to St. Jean de Luz and
Whitley had to take a firm hold on his own feelings—rising
behind the town he saw the dark, wild slopes of the Pyrenees
and knew that just over the ridges lay neutral Spain. In

silence they ate omelettes in a little café in St. Jean de Luz and as they finished François handed them little tablets to swallow. He said it would give them strength for the climb, and Whitley assumed it was benzedrine.

After a stroll round the harbour wall François led them out on the other side of the town along a track under a railway embankment. Whitley saw a party of German soldiers walking along the embankment towards them ; he knew they must look suspicious walking out in the dusk towards the border and felt himself go cold all over. The Germans came abreast and the rearmost man stopped and looked down at them. Whitley waited for the hail, fighting against the impulse to break into a run. He walked on ; they were past the Germans now, but no hail came. A prickly feeling spread over the back of his neck and as they went round a slight curve they ran into some bushes beside the track and cut across some fields.

It was nearly midnight when François led them up to a farmhouse in the foothills and knocked on the door. A thick-set French peasant of about forty opened the door and let them in. François introduced him as Florentino, who was to guide them over the mountains. Florentino had bread and warm milk ready and handed each a pair of espadrilles—canvas shoes with rope soles—and in a few minutes they were climbing behind him up the easy slopes. François was still with them, but quieter now that the calm Florentino was in charge.

The slopes became steeper and steeper, and then they kept dipping into steep valleys and clambering up the other side. It was so dark that François, just behind Florentino, held the luminous dial of his watch at the back of his neck so the others could follow. Whitley and Laws kept tripping over unseen boulders and slipping down invisible slopes till they were both cut and bruised. Steadily they became wearier. Florentino stopped now and then so they could rest, but he said they had to keep moving fast because there was a long way to go and they must be well over the border by dawn. There was a rendezvous with another guide some miles inside the border, but if the Spanish police picked them up first they would end up in Miranda concentration camp.

Whitley felt physically sick at the thought. He had been keyed up to dodge the German frontier guards, and to pass them and end up in a neutral concentration camp would be an unbearable anti-climax.

They stumbled on hour after hour in the darkness. Whitley felt he was so exhausted and aching that he could not go on much longer, but the old discipline of being the senior officer and having to set an example kept him struggling on. About 4 a.m. Florentino turned and whispered that they were passing over the frontier, but Whitley and Laws were both too exhausted to feel any elation—and with what little feeling he had left Whitley was worrying about being caught by the Spanish.

Just before dawn they came to a brilliantly lit stone bridge. François said it was a Customs post and the only way to get across was to run for it into the far darkness before any Customs man on duty could intercept. It looked to be about two hundred yards to the shelter of darkness on the other side, and Whitley thought with despair that he could never raise a run. Florentino led the way, and then as Whitley started running his strength seemed to flood back. Within thirty yards he was leading the way and fairly pelted across the bridge. In the woods on the far side they lay and rested until Florentino said they must be moving before dawn. With a last effort they got up and followed him along a railway track as dawn was breaking.

A little way along the track Florentino felt under a bush, drew out a bottle of brandy and handed it to Laws and Whitley. He explained, grinning, that he kept it there to revive his clients, who were usually in a state of collapse at this stage.

Feeling better after a while, they moved on and managed to keep going till, about the middle of the morning, Florentino led them to an isolated farmhouse. Whitley dimly remembers stumbling up some steps and collapsing on some straw. A little later he had a terrible bout of dry retching. Florentino told them to rest for the next stage of the trip, but, in spite of all the exhaustion, Whitley found the benzedrine pills were still working and lay all day looking wide-eyed at the ceiling. He had had only six hours' sleep since leaving Paris three days before and almost groaned when Florentino came up at dusk and said they must move again.

It was agony setting out along the track ; Whitley felt his muscles were petrified, but after a while a sort of numbness came over him, and he went on and on like that till, hours later, they met François standing by a car on the edge of a village.

François said, " Get in," and, without asking questions, Whitley and Laws flopped on to the back seat. A dark Spaniard sat at the wheel. François got in beside him and they drove for a long time. Nearing San Sebastian two Spanish police with rifles stepped into the middle of the road in front of the headlights, and the driver pulled up. It was either that or running the police down. They came up to the car and Whitley heard the sharp questions in Spanish directed at the driver. He thought, " Oh, God, it can't end like this ! " and then the police were stepping back and the car moved on. François leaned back and said, " They were looking for black marketeers. It's all right."

They went through San Sebastian, and out on the road the other side Whitley kept hearing long peremptory hootings behind them. A big Renault slid past, still hooting. It crossed in front and began to slow, and Whitley's car pulled up behind it on the verge of the road. A man got out of the Renault and walked up to them. Whitley was looking at him, but his brain was not registering until he heard the man say, " Hello, chaps ; I'm going to take you to Madrid. You're all right now."

Ten days later the Dakota landed him at Hendon, London, ready to resume his profession, and that is the story of Group Captain (now Air Vice-Marshal) John Whitley.

(*Perhaps not quite all. He went back, when France was free, to thank the people who had helped him. Like all the others who came back via the Underground he knew that, in spite of all his own shrewd groundwork, he would have had little chance without their help. He found the people at Hirson were all right. Mahoudeaux was all right too, but*

Roger, his eldest son, was in Buchenwald. Fontaine was dead, caught by the Germans and shot in March, 1944. Fournaise, of Aouste, had frozen to death in a German cattle truck on his way to concentration camp. Poinier had died of starvation and torture in Charlevilles Prison. Aimable, of Paris, and Paul, the high-principled boy who had helped him, had been executed. So also Jacques. François was dying with tuberculosis in both lungs, and Florentino was a cripple—he had caught a burst of machine-gun fire in the legs.)

After his escape Whitley was decorated with the D.S.O., and a few months later promoted to air commodore. In February, 1945, he was promoted to air vice-marshal, in command of No. 4 (Bomber) Group, and later No. 8 Group (the Pathfinders). In this same year he was made a C.B.E. The following year he was honoured with the C.B., and after terms at the Air Ministry and the Imperial Defence College he went as Air Officer in charge of Administration to the 2nd Tactical Air Force in Germany.

HE RODE WITH THE COSSACKS

Cyril Rofe seldom feels strange in strange countries. Born in Cairo on April 11, 1916, he was educated at Clifton and Chillon College, trained for the hotel business at the Swiss Hotel School in Lausanne and, after a period at the May Fair Hotel in London, went to the Bristol, in Vienna, where he acquired a love of opera and ski-ing. He got out ten days after Hitler marched into Austria, and on the outbreak of war volunteered for aircrew. While waiting for training he joined the Scots Guards special ski battalion, which was intended for Norway, and when this was disbanded went into the Air Force and trained as an observer (navigator and bomb-aimer). Short, wiry and always determined, he was in the crew of a Wellington bomber of No. 40 Squadron which was shot down into the Maas Estuary on June 11, 1941.

THE first time he escaped Cyril Rofe tried walking to Switzerland, where his mother was living, but after ten days' tramping through woods and hills towards Czechoslovakia some week-end blackberry pickers pointed him out to a forester armed with a shotgun. Back in the cells at Lamsdorf, the Germans regarded him with the customary distaste shown to Palestinian soldiers in the British Army, unaware that the Jewish private whose name he had assumed was fraudulently bearing Rofe's name, rank and status as a flight-sergeant navigator in the well-guarded R.A.F. compound. Rofe, of course, like James Dowd, welcomed the soldier's obligation of going out on the lightly-guarded working parties.

His friends considered that, if he was so keen to escape by walking through Germany, it was asking for trouble to go as a Jewish soldier, but Rofe's attitude was a kind of stubborn loyalty to his race. He himself was an English Jew, though his small, wiry frame and broken nose looked untypical.

After the cells he went out with another working party to a Polish coal-mine, where, as a most reluctant miner, he took

to absenteeism and headed on foot for Danzig to stow away
on a boat for Sweden. Half-way to Danzig a Polish collabora-
tor gave him away and, back in the Lamsdorf cells, the
Germans said that if he made any more trouble he was liable
to find himself next time in one of the special camps for Jews.
Enough rumours had come out of Auschwitz to make their
meaning clear. A couple of guards hinted with satisfaction
that all Jewish prisoners would finish up in the special camps
anyway.

The winter stopped escape activities for a while, and in the
spring of 1944 the arm that was badly broken when he was
shot down gave him more trouble, so that it was summer
before he went out on another working party, this time to
help build wooden barracks near Schomberg and Kattowitz,
in the far east of Germany, the so-called " Little Ruhr "
where the borders of Poland and Czechoslovakia ran down
towards the Tatra Mountains.

It was a long way from either Switzerland or Sweden, and
he was wryly pondering that point when it occurred to him
that only two hundred miles to the east was the advancing
Russian Army, and that this distance was liable to be less
before long. He had been caught twice trying to escape in the
obvious direction ; why not, he thought, go the unexpected
way ? The longest way round might be the quickest way
home. He asked Karl Hillebrand, a thin, studious-looking
Palestinian corporal on the working party, if he would like to
try it with him.

" Might be Auschwitz if we're caught," Hillebrand said.

" It might be Auschwitz anyway," Rofe answered. " The
only way we can make sure of never seeing Auschwitz is to get
away from the Huns."

" What about getting through the German lines ? "

" Well, the whole area's chaotic. Even if we can't get
through we can hide up somewhere and wait till the Russians
bust through."

" O.K.," Hillebrand said, " I'm game."

By August 20, through exercising P.O.W. talents for
bribery, ingenuity and theft, they each had forged papers
showing them to be Belgian electrical workers with permits

to travel to Saybusch, a hundred marks and a store of chocolate, biscuits and cigarettes. Rofe had an old grey suit, grey trilby and a brief case, and Hillebrand had a black jacket, grey trousers and also a trilby.

At 5.30 a.m. on that day the German guard clumped through the barracks yelling, " Raus ! Raus ! " and as soon as he had gone they pulled their civilian clothes from under the wood-wool palliasses, put them on, pulled borrowed overalls over them and straggled out with the other hundred or so prisoners to the untidy patch where they had been (not very efficiently) putting up the prefabricated huts.

The others, well briefed, started milling around in confusion and Rofe and Hillebrand slipped into one of the finished huts, where they tore off the overalls, put on their hats and walked out of the hut like honest Germans. A couple of the prisoners winked, though most of them were clustering round the guards asking silly questions and diverting their attention. Rofe passed, poker-faced, within five yards of one of the guards, forcing himself to walk naturally, but the guard did not even look at him, and then he and Hillebrand had turned the corner of the last hut and were away.

They waited in the silent streets of Schomberg for the cross-country tram to Beuthen, and as a man walked down the street towards them Hillebrand quietly swore, grabbed Rofe's arm and swung him so that they both faced away. " He was working on the wiring at the huts the other day," Hillebrand hissed. " He would remember me."

The man stopped just behind them, and they stayed looking nervously and self-consciously the other way till the tram arrived and the man climbed into the front compartment. They got into the rear, and the man never glanced round all the way to Beuthen.

In Beuthen they were waiting for another tram to Kattowitz, and a policeman stopped and eyed them speculatively. Rofe turned half away and out of the corner of his eye saw the policeman walking towards him. Sometimes dread is paralysing and nauseous. The policeman was standing by his elbow and said something in German, evidently a question.

Rofe's German was not very good and he did not understand it. He looked dumbly.

The German spoke again, more slowly.

Ah, the time ! Rofe looked at his watch and said, with an attempt at a smile, " Sechs Uhr und Halb."

The policeman smiled ; he spoke slowly again and Rofe, incredulous, understood that he was apologising for not speaking German properly. He was Ukrainian, the policeman was saying, not German. It seemed to give him an inferiority complex.

Hillebrand, whose German was faultless, had moved to the rescue and was telling the policeman kindly that everyone could not be German. They chatted amiably until the tram arrived and the policeman got in with them and talked all the way to Kattowitz, which was reassuring when two more police got in at a little village and looked arrogantly round the tram.

At Kattowitz they boarded a train for Saybusch, and a woman in the opposite seat insisted on telling them about the time she was bombed out of Berlin and what she would do to any R.A.F. airman she got her hands on. Rofe left most of the talking to Hillebrand, bracing himself to agree with the woman now and then.

He thought they were getting away with it nicely, but that made the shock all the worse when a railway policeman swung through the far door and moved from person to person, examining travel permits. There was no escape and their papers were not expert ; when the man stood by the seat Rofe handed over the two permits, not bringing himself to look directly at him. The man looked and said something, and as Rofe lifted his eyes fearfully he vanished behind the seat with the papers.

They heard him in amazement talking to the people behind, explaining that these were the sort of papers they must have to travel, and they had better have them next time. And then the policeman was back, handing them their passes with a polite smile, and moving on.

At Saybusch they walked briskly east out of the town and not till they were out of sight of the houses did Rofe feel confidence seeping back into him. At dusk they slept in a

small wood and at dawn walked again, cutting across fields
towards the peak of Rabingora that rose out of the flat, Silesian
plain miles ahead. Somewhere near Rabingora Germany
ended, though their home-made map did not indicate exactly
where. Skirting fields where peasants worked, they came at
night to the foot of the mountain and rested.

At midnight Rofe woke Hillebrand ; a hush lay over the
country and a thin slice of moon shed just enough light to
outline the black tree-trunks. Hillebrand pulled on his boots
and they walked up the mountain. At first light they climbed
over a saddleback and came to a swathe about five yards wide
cut through the forest ; a few yards along it lay a white stone
shaped like a tiny pyramid. They could see the letter " D "
on the side facing them.

" This is it," Rofe said excitedly. He ran up to the stone
and saw on another side the letter " S," felt a momentary
dismay, and on the last side was " P."

" Polska," he said, as though he had found a gold-mine.
The " S," he guessed, was for Slowakei (Slovakia). They
must be a little south of course at the point where
Germany, Slovakia and Poland met. He kicked some dirt
over the letter " D," said " Good-bye, Deutschland " with
great feeling and they walked east through the trees into
Poland. Poland was thickly occupied by Germans and the
" Quisling " Polish police, but that could not damp the joy of
being out of Germany.

The next eight days were remarkable—not for narrow
escapes, but for swift progress and lack of drama. They
walked by day along dusty roads, across fields, through woods
and sometimes, boldly, through primitive little villages, and
nothing went wrong. They tramped steadily south-east
through the foothills of the Tatra Range, avoiding the main
roads to the north on the plain where the Germans were, and
in the quiet valleys behind the first ridges made good time
along the rough cart tracks, averaging nearly fifteen miles a day.

At night they slept, sometimes in woods and sometimes in
peasant barns and hayricks. Every day they walked boldly up
to lonely farmhouses and asked for food, finding the peasants
simple and friendly. After a day or two Rofe felt it was safe

enough to tell them that he was R.A.F., and the effect was invariably gratifying. The peasants almost worshipped him. They gave him and Hillebrand what food they could, but that was not much ; they had so little themselves. Usually it was a few potatoes and some milk ; sometimes a little bread. Rofe had never seen such poor people. Their houses were of baked mud, brick and thatch, usually divided into two rooms with hard earth floors, and the women went barefoot, dressed in shawls and simple homespun dresses that hung on them like sugar-bags.

The market town of Markowa straddled a valley road they were following and rather than climb out of the deep valley to go round it, Rofe suggested they walk straight through. It was the last time they made that mistake. Coming up to the town they saw an S.S. officer standing by the roadside. It was too late to turn back without looking guilty ; they walked on, passing within two yards of him and felt his eyes following them. For a terrifying moment he looked as though he were going to challenge them, and then he seemed to relax and they walked thankfully on through the town.

On the other side they were dismayed to see a line of German soldiers supervising gangs of Poles digging trenches— obviously a new defence line. Veering away from the road they found more Germans and Poles stretched across the valley and had to climb for two hours over the hills to the side before they struck a clear path through.

Some of the peasants spoke a little German and Rofe and Hillebrand had learned a few pat Polish phrases for asking food and shelter. Isolated in the valleys the farms were self-contained little units of life and in the first farm they tried after Markowa the peasant wife was sitting at a spinning wheel producing thread from flax grown by her husband ; she also weaved the thread herself and dyed it with home-made dyes. The husband grew his own tobacco and wore home-made slippers. Rofe and Hillebrand dined with this family, sitting round a big bowl of mashed potato. Each had a spoon and cup of milk, and dinner consisted of dipping the spoon in the communal bowl of potato and then dipping it again in one's own milk.

On the eighth morning, ambling casually through a wood, they heard voices through the trees over to the left and stopped abruptly, hunting for cover, but saw only the thin trunks of the pines where a cat could hardly have hidden. Through the trees three men in dark clothes filed into sight ; two of them carried rifles.

" Polish police," Rofe whispered in alarm. He grabbed Hillebrand and as they turned to run one of the men shouted. Two rifles were pointing at them and the third man with a revolver in his hand was running to cut them off.

" Take it easy. Don't run," Hillebrand said. Rofe hesitated a moment and then it was too late.

The one with the revolver, a tall man in his middle thirties, said something sharply in Polish. Rofe and Hillebrand shook their heads. Hillebrand said something in German and the man demanded (also in German), " Who are you ? "

Hillebrand said frankly, " Escaping British prisoners," and Rofe wanted to strangle him. He had braced himself to bluff it out and now, he thought bitterly, it was all over in a moment without even a show of fight. Hillebrand and the Pole were talking in German but it was too fast for Rofe to follow. Hillebrand handed over his P.O.W. identity disc ; the Pole looked at it and spoke again, and this time Rofe understood— " We will help you all we can," the Pole said, and Rofe gaped at him and turned to Hillebrand : " They're going to *help* us ? "

" Of course," Hillebrand said, puzzled. " We always thought the partisans would."

" They're *partisans* ? "

" Police have uniforms," Hillebrand said patiently. " These chaps don't. It's the first thing I noticed." He told the Pole with the revolver that Rofe had thought they were pro-German police and the Pole nearly wept with laughter, then shook his big fist at Rofe and said slowly in German that he was mortally offended. He introduced himself as Tadek and said he would lead them to a partisan hide-out. As they wound through the trees Tadek said they were lucky he had found them; a mile further on lay the wide Poprad River, swarming with Germans building a new defence line.

The hide-out was a small clearing where the partisans had built a wooden hut. Sentries were posted around in the woods and about six more men and a girl were in the hut. Rofe, as a member of the famous R.A.F., was given a hero's welcome ; Tadek brought out a bottle of brandy and they all drank individual toasts to the R.A.F. and themselves till the bottle was empty. The front line, according to Tadek, was about sixty kilometres away.

" We will try and get you across the Poprad," he said, " but it will be dangerous to try and get through the front. Why do you not stay with us till the battle goes past ? "

Neither Rofe nor Hillebrand would think about it. Having come more than a hundred miles in eight days they were too full of confidence, so Tadek shrugged and started telling them about a man called Kmicic who had a partisan band on a mountain called Jaworze, miles across the river.

At midnight, two nights later, he gave them a letter to Kmicic and led them through the woods to the river. The moon was like a cheddar cheese behind a veil of wispy cloud and they lay in the trees and watched a German patrol march along the river bank.

" Now," whispered Tadek, and they ran crouching through undergrowth, across newly-dug trenches, down to the water and into a punt. Tadek poled them across while others of his band watched over the gunwales with rifles at the ready. On the far bank Tadek briefly wished them luck and poled the punt back.

The first day was easy walking and that night the wind came from the east and they heard the rumble of guns. In the morning on a dust-laden road just below the foothills something stirred in the long grass beside the road and two German policemen rose up out of it, blinking sleep from their eyes. One of them called sharply and Rofe and Hillebrand stopped. There was no option. The police, suspicious from the start, demanded to know who they were, where they had come from, where going, what for, where they had slept the previous night and so on. They snapped the questions one after the other and Hillebrand, impassive but pale, was struggling to answer them. After seeing their papers the police wanted to know what two Belgians were doing so close to the East Front.

By some miracle Hillebrand knew the name of the next village and said they were detailed for work in Binczarowa. At that moment three Poles came along the road ; the police stopped them and asked if there was any work for electricians in Binczarowa and the Poles, after hesitating, said " Yes." God, the relief as the police sourly waved them all on.

For days the two of them tramped around Jaworze mountain, and one night, at a friendly farm, they came face to face with Kmicic, an elusive, blue-eyed, dynamic young man who was the hero of the district. Hearing that they wanted to get through to the Russians, he frowned and said they should wait till the Russian lines over-ran them. Only when both Rofe and Hillebrand insisted they were going through did he admit that there was, perhaps, one way. Both armies, he said, were massing for a battle round Tarnów, to the north, and due east of Jaworze was a hilly, wooded area where the front seemed to be fluid. One of his band, a Russian soldier called Achmetow who had escaped from the Germans, might be able to lead them through.

In another hut in the woods he introduced them to Achmetow, a cherubic little man in remnants of tattered Russian uniform. Achmetow spoke a little German and his round apple of a face grinned obligingly at the risky prospect of rejoining his own troops. Kmicic drew them a map and on the morning of September 17 Rofe, Hillebrand and Achmetow, keyed-up, started east. The guns were thumping louder at night now but still sounded far away.

All the first day they kept asking peasants where the line was, but the peasants shook their heads vaguely until a farmer who had lived years in America and spoke fluent English with an American accent, said, shrugging and throwing his hands out expressively, that there was no line. Some Russians had broken through not far away and scattered patrols of both sides were ranging over the country. Two days ago some Russians had been reported only three kilometres away. Rofe said, when they had left the farmer, " I don't like this. There must be a line somewhere."

" It can't be very near or we'd be seeing Germans," Hillebrand answered. " The guns must have been a good ten miles away last night."

A small river meandered across their path—the Visloka, according to the map—and they were walking along the winding bank when, a hundred yards ahead, three men stepped out of the shade of some trees and stared at them.

Rofe had stopped dead. " What sort of uniform is that ? " he asked. It was just too far to pick out the details.

" I don't know," Hillebrand said uncertainly.

Achmetow, very excited, swung round to them and said, " Russki ! Russki ! "

" They can't be," Rofe said, but Achmetow was running madly ahead. They watched him talking excitedly to the three men and then he turned and beckoned wildly. As he went cautiously forward Rofe could see that the three men had medals on both sides of their chests, black fur caps and dark uniforms with rather full-cut trousers tucked into riding boots.

" My God, they *are* Russians," he yelled, and broke into a run. He could make out the officer's tabs on their shoulders and as he came up to them one of them, a middle-aged man, said in German : " You are British ? "

" Royal Air Force," Rofe announced.

" We are the Red Army," declared the officer and Rofe said breathlessly, " Deutschland kaput! Deutschland kaput! " It was all he could think of to say. He was grinning and shaking hands and he and Hillebrand were both talking at once while the Russians regarded them tolerantly.

" I can't understand it," Rofe marvelled when things were a little quieter. " We've come right through the German lines and not seen a German. I thought it was terrible fighting on this front."

" This is not the front," said the middle-aged officer, shaking his head. " There are plenty of Germans back there." He turned and pointed behind, east, and added soberly, " We have been cut off for three weeks. The Germans are behind us trying to . . . " He pulled a finger across his throat, and Rofe felt as though he had been hit in the stomach. The Russian sensed the shock he had delivered and said cheerfully, " It is not the first time we have been cut off. The Cossacks are used to it."

" You are Cossacks ? " Hillebrand asked, and the Russian nodded and took off his black fur cap, showing the red top and the crossed gold braid over it. Waving his hand behind, he said that the rest of the Cossacks were camped in the fields and suggested they go back with Achmetow to join them. Rofe and Hillebrand said a wry farewell and walked off with Achmetow.

" No peace in this bloody war," Hillebrand said disconsolately and Rofe had to laugh at the unconscious humour. Half a mile on they came to the first Cossack units, scores of men in dark, coarse uniforms, lounging on the ground, nearly all with tommy guns beside them ; nearby were horse-lines and narrow farm-type waggons with sloping sides. Achmetow spoke to some of the men and they pointed down a cart track that cut between the fields.

For two hours they followed the track, staggered at the thousands of Russians camped in the fields. They looked so peaceful, as though no war existed and no enemy encircled them. Achmetow said they were a division of the Fourth Cossack Corps and he was trying to find division headquarters.

At a field kitchen a grinning Russian soldier with a three-days' beard stubble gave them hunks of bread and a plate of meat, and it occurred to Rofe that he, himself, must look even worse. He suggested to Hillebrand that they freshen up to meet the general and a little later, when they came to a stream, he made Achmetow wait while they stripped and swam and shaved.

In the shelter of a fringe of wood they came to a low, white farmhouse ; Achmetow vanished inside and a minute later Rofe was startled to see a girl coming out. She was about twenty-three, rather heavily built and dressed in the olive green officer's uniform, including riding boots, though instead of trousers she wore a neat pleated skirt. Walking straight up to them she introduced herself briskly in English as a headquarters' interpreter and asked, politely, if they would wait till the colonel was ready to see them.

Rofe mumbled facetiously about having nowhere else to go, but she did not seem to think that was particularly amusing. Rofe, trying hard, said he was surprised to see such a pretty girl in such a dangerous position in the front line of a war, but she took that solemnly, too, saying disconcertingly, " I am not pretty and I do not think it unusual that a Russian girl should be in the front line. There are many of us here. It is our duty." She wanted to know if they were " workers " and when Rofe virtuously said they were she smiled for the first time.

They waited a long time for the colonel. Dusk settled over the fields and they were still waiting when they heard the drone of aircraft, growing louder. The dark shape of what looked like a Dakota slid over the trees towards them and over the field a cloud of parachutes broke from the plane and floated down. A dozen more planes came over and dropped more supplies and then several antiquated single-engined biplanes puttered over the field. Someone flashed a torch at them and one by one they switched on landing lights, side-slipped steeply and made miraculous uphill dusk landings in the field. Under the wings on each side were little nacelles like overload tanks and Cossacks went up with stretchers of wounded men and loaded them into the nacelles like mummies. One by one the planes turned, roared over the field and lifted into the darkness. It was unbelievably quick and efficient.

The girl came out and led them into the house, and, in a low-ceilinged room, a dark, heavily-built colonel greeted them with grave friendliness. The girl interpreted while they told him of their trip, and in particular of the work of the partisans and the lack of Germans they had encountered. They talked for an hour before the colonel said, " Now you must eat." He called a soldier and they followed the soldier into the woods, coming after a while to another farmhouse. In a warm living room a dozen Russian officers crowded round them with dazzling smiles of welcome. Most were bemedalled and looking very spruce. One produced a bottle of schnapps and while they were drinking another officer brought in two plates of fresh meat and eggs, and bread and butter, and made Rofe and Hillebrand sit at the table and start eating. Rofe thought it was the best food he had eaten since he was shot down but one of the officers, a major called Fyodor, who spoke some German, apologised that it was the best they could do.

They talked for a couple of hours about their adventures and afterwards the major said, " Well, you are all right now. Enjoy yourselves."

" But we are cut off," Rofe said. " We can't very well relax yet, can we ? "

" Nichevo," said Major Fyodor explosively, rolling his eyes to the ceiling. He translated Rofe's words to the others and they laughed gaily. " We have been surrounded before," Fyodor said. " We will fight our way back."

" When ? " Rofe wanted to know and the major shrugged and said, " Soon. Very soon."

There were two small double beds in the house and around midnight Fyodor bowed Rofe and Hillebrand towards one of them. They both protested strongly, having seen two Russian officers lying on the bed before and guessing that the two usually slept there, but Fyodor insisted. He kept saying, " You are our guests. We will look after you."

Rofe and Hillebrand got on to the bed, almost purring with the luxury of it and thinking that the Russians would find a bed elsewhere. Again they were shaken to see the two displaced officers take off their boots, stretch out on the hard floor and pull blankets over themselves.

Hillebrand, the humble corporal, whispered to Rofe : " I was just trying to imagine a couple of Russian soldiers as grubby as us going up to a British officers' mess and getting this sort of thing."

In the morning an orderly brought them eggs and meat soup for breakfast. Another orderly came in with letters from home and newspapers for the Russians, dropped by the planes the previous night ; Rofe was most intrigued when the Russians, instead of reading the papers, tore them into strips, brought out tobacco pouches and began rolling cigarettes in the newsprint. One of them explained that they had already heard all the news on the radio.

Rofe and Hillebrand had many surprises in the next few days. After breakfast they went for a walk among the troops in the fields with a German-speaking Russian and gazed fascinated at the number of girl soldiers who had been lying down on their groundsheets to sleep among the other soldiers in the night.

They watched curiously, but apparently nothing questionable went on. Nothing came off either. The Russians explained that no one ever took their clothes off in the battle line. When they fought their way back, he said, they would all hand their clothes in to a depot, have a bath and be given new uniforms.

" The girls—they fight too ? " Rofe asked.

The Russian laughed and shook his head, explaining that they were headquarters' secretaries, nurses, interpreters and traffic controllers.

" No trouble among the men ? " Rofe persisted, and the Russian said solemnly : " There is no sex in battle. Russian girls in battle are comrades." He added, a little sadly, that things had not always been quite the same since the advance because the Russian girls had seen Polish girls with waved hair and cosmetics. " It has disturbed them a little," he lamented, and added gravely, " Some of them have been buying dresses."

Relations between the soldiers and the girls seemed completely impersonal. The girls never tried to be coquettish and the soldiers virtually ignored them. When Nature called, the girls went behind a hedge like the soldiers (though not the same hedge). Apart from the skirts they acted and looked just like the men ; like the men, too, some of them had lice, though there was nothing remarkable in that. They had not been able to take their clothes off for three weeks. Rofe had lice himself ; it was part of the life.

The whole scene seemed so strange and peaceful he could hardly believe they were surrounded by enemies until, on the way back to the farmhouse, heavy guns opened up somewhere across the woods and shells screamed overhead. The Russians paid no attention whatsoever.

More meat for lunch, more meat for supper and they were

just finishing when a tall Cossack officer wearing a beautifully cut astrakhan fur coat, sword and spurs clumped into the house and said that everyone must prepare to move.

They slept that night in their boots and at 5 a.m. Fyodor, unshaven and brisk, woke them and said, " We are going to break through."

Outside the door a convoy of waggons was assembling and Rofe and Hillebrand, tense and tingling, climbed into one of them. There was a lot of shouting and bustle and they were jolting over the fields on to a dirt road. Once they stopped and a patrol ran past carrying long, anti-tank rifles. Later, explosions and machine-gun fire sounded about a mile ahead and after a while the waggons moved on again. In the afternoon they sheltered in a wood and at darkness moved out along a road down into a valley. The moon was thin but bright and a mile or two away in front and on each side flares were bursting in the sky and distant thumps and the rattle of machine-guns reached them.

A quarter of a mile ahead a brilliant flash lit the darkness ; there was a heavy explosion and then more flashes and explosions. The drivers yelled and whipped at the horses and in a few seconds they were galloping ; Rofe crouched against the side of the waggon, clinging grimly as the waggon bucked on the rutted surface. He had a terrifying impression of flashes and explosions, shouts and hoofbeats and the clattering of wheels and then the convoy was slowing up ; the waggon stopped and the driver screamed at them to jump off. They did not know what he meant till they saw officers jumping off the other waggons and running up the hill towards the woods. They jumped off and ran after them, and in the cover of the trees found Fyodor, some of the other headquarters' men and several girl officers. In a long line they filed among the trunks up the steep side of the valley until the crashes of the shells sounded fainter and well below. Rofe was breathless and quiet but all the Russians—girls included—seemed to be in wonderful spirits, laughing and joking, straggling along as if they were on a midnight picnic.

Without warning, flashes winked a hundred yards ahead and a machine-gun rattled terrifyingly. Red streaks of tracer darted at them, the air was full of angry " zips " and Rofe instinctively dived to the side and went rolling down an embankment with the Russians. They lay in a huddle at the bottom. Fyodor was shouting and some Russians ran off into the trees.

A little later they heard a quick burst from the machine-gun and then cracks of rifle fire and some sharp explosions. Someone shouted from above and they were climbing back up the embankment. All the Russians were laughing cheer-fully again (including the girl officers) and Rofe gathered that an isolated German machine-gun post ahead had been wiped out. A little later more machine-gun fire rattled well ahead and Fyodor said they would lie down in the woods where they were and sleep.

Dawn broke grey and wet and they climbed to the heights over the valley and walked east for several miles till they reached a clear saddleback where a road ran just below. Almost immediately machine-gun bullets came at them from across the far heights and they scuttled over the saddleback and went on walking east. Rofe could not get over the attitude of the girls—they seemed as cheerful as ever and utterly oblivious of their danger. Tired and edgy, he found himself wishing he had their outlook.

At dusk they came down from the ridge to a farmhouse in the valley and there, unbelievably, were the waggons they had left the previous day. A field kitchen served meat stew ; they slept again in the woods and stayed there all the next day. Confused as to what was happening, Rofe could not shake off the fear that the purposeful Germans were closing in all round them.

They were. The attack came an hour after darkness. First there were some dull thumps a few hundred yards away. In a few seconds mortar bombs were bursting among the trees ; then the machine-guns started. Rofe heard shouting and the skin on the back of his neck crawled as he recognised German words. All round in the darkness the Cossacks were screech-ing. A bullet smacked into a tree-trunk two yards from his head. It seemed to go on unnervingly for a long time, and then gradually the firing and the shouting died away. He lay down to sleep but at midnight a Russian roused him and he and Hillebrand followed the others into the waggons which jolted off into the darkness.

At dawn they were sheltering on the edge of a birch wood when the Germans attacked again. First they were shelled, then mortared and then the machine-guns and shouting again. The shouts died away and some scattered German JU88's screamed over and the bombs fell. Most were wide but one exploded deafeningly fifty yards away and the blast knocked Rofe off his feet.

With a stub of pencil he noted on a scrappy diary he had started a few days before: " It is terrible being so helpless. I'm unarmed and don't understand a word that's being said so I don't know where we are or where we're going, or whether we'll ever get there. I do know that we're nearly out of ammunition."

He and Hillebrand spent another miserable wet and wakeful night among the birch trees and in the morning he could have wept with joy when a bloodstained and bandaged Achmetow walked up to them. They had not seen him for days and he said, not grinning quite so much now and so tired he could hardly stand, that he had been helping to man machine-guns. There were so many wounded now, he said, that the wounded had to fight too. Rofe could have guessed that ; he had watched the wounded being brought in and loaded into the waggons till the waggons were full. Achmetow said that the doctors had run out of medical supplies.

They moved off at noon, cramming into the waggons among the wounded and breaking out of the wood at a crazy gallop along a valley road. Machine-guns spat at them from the heights but the range was too far to be effective and the sweating horses dragged most of the waggons to a pinewooded ridge where they huddled again during the night.

It rained all night and Rofe lay awake the whole time, a groundsheet wrapped tightly round him like a shroud, but the rain soaked through so that he was lying in a puddle, shivering with cold. In the dawn he was stiff and muzzy with tiredness. A Russian gave him a piece of bread—it was the first food he had had for twenty-four hours. Chewing at the bread he walked briskly around with Achmetow to get warm; Hillebrand said he was too exhausted to walk so they left him propped against a tree trunk.

The earth in the woods was churned into mud by the rain, the waggons and the horses, and they slogged around the confused scene till they came to the fringe of the trees where the hillside sloped gently away to a broad meadowland, grey under mist. Achmetow pointed to a vague line of trees far across the fields and said, " Red Army . . . there." About a mile on each side the woods straggled down into broken ground, framing the meadows in a wide, shallow saucer. Achmetow waved vaguely from side to side, shrugged and said, " Germans." It looked deserted and peaceful. " We will know very soon," he added. " Perhaps by noon." He spoke stolidly but Rofe became conscious that the hollow feeling in his stomach was not only hunger. They turned back into the woods.

Shouts and the jingle of harness sounded through the trees ; they started running and saw officers cantering about yelling at the soldiers scattered thickly for hundreds of yards through the woods. Some of the waggons were already lurching through the mud, straggling into line and moving parallel to the edge of the woods. Rofe could not find the tree where he had left Hillebrand and ran anxiously through the mud looking for him, but Hillebrand had vanished. He met Fyodor who pointed ahead at the waggons and said he had seen Hillebrand moving up. Rofe ran along looking in the waggons and suddenly there was a tremendous explosion off to the right followed by the tearing sound of falling trees.

More shells came crashing into the woods and some of the horses were plunging about whinnying with fear. A waggon turned over, spilling the wounded into the mud ; the next two waggons picked them up. Rofe ran past two horses lying dead with their bellies ripped open, and then the pines opened into a small gully where a troop of about a hundred Cossacks sat quietly on their horses under the wet trees. On one of the horses Rofe recognised the tall officer in the astrakhan coat who had come into the divisional mess days ago. He ran across and asked if he had seen Hillebrand. The officer, who could apparently just understand the German, shook his head and as Rofe turned to follow the waggons the officer reached out of the saddle and grabbed his shoulder. He shouted something in Russian and one of the Cossacks walked his horse towards them, leading a brown mare with an empty saddle. The officer grinned gaily at Rofe and jerked his thumb towards the mare. He said in rough German, " Sie kommen mit uns."

Rofe tried to get his foot into the stirrup and a burly Cossack leaned over, grabbed his belt and hoisted him into the saddle. He grinned back at the Cossacks around him, trying to remember how long it was since he had last sat on a horse. They waited while the waggons went crashing past the gully and it must have been half an hour after the last one had gone that the officer stood up in his stirrups, raised his fist and waved it forward, and the troop moved off in single file through the trees.

They were heading a different way from the waggons and Rofe realised with a flutter round his heart that they were moving towards the fringe of the forest. The wet trees pressed all round and no one spoke. The mare seemed to sense the tension ; she was whinnying a little, pricking her ears and then laying them back.

They were moving downhill, the horses slithering on the slimy earth. Shots sounded in the distance. Some bodies of men and dead horses lay scattered among the trees and the mare shied nervously. The trees were thinning and the Cossacks started to fan out on each side. Rofe saw the officer ahead with his fist raised, motionless ; he veered to one side, reined in alongside the others and saw that they were lining up on the edge of the trees. Now the mist was gone and two miles across the sunlit meadows he saw clearly the trees where the Red Army was—and liberty. Over the flat fields there was no shred of cover. The horses were flank to flank, bobbing their heads nervously so that the harness jingled, and he had the weird feeling that he was in a Hollywood film that had suddenly become real.

Over to the left the tall officer had drawn his sabre ; he was waving it round his head so that the blade glinted in the sun and then with a wild yell he slashed it forward and spurred his horse. Wild shouts broke from the line and the horses surged forward, plunged out of the trees in a ragged line and galloped down the slope.

They rode like demons, yelling, spreading out in a long line. Rofe sensed the brutal strength of the mare's shoulders flexing under him, felt gladly that he was firm in the saddle and became conscious of his own yells in the wild chorus that mingled with the drumming of the hooves. Exhilaration swept him. A horse went down a few yards to one side and he saw fleetingly the rider rolling over and over.

Somewhere, heavy explosions were thumping and he bent lower in the saddle. Puffs of dirt spurted out of the ground and once he heard a " zip " past his ear. The Cossacks were waving their arms and the officer, drawn a little ahead on a beautiful black horse, slashed his sword in a circle over his head. They were pounding over the flat meadows full of fierce joy. The head of a Cossack in front seemed to split and his hat spun crazily back. A fleeting glimpse. Bullet or shell. He rolled sideways off the horse and the horse was galloping riderless with them. Two more horses went down and Rofe crazily thought he was part of a film again ; they were Red Indians, the Light Brigade, the gallant Six Hundred charging into the cannons and the cameras. And yet the taste of reality like iron on the tongue : an R.A.F. sergeant in a Cossack cavalry charge. Confusion, but madly, madly exciting. Something buzzed sharply by his ear ; another horse and rider were down. The mare was blowing hard but still stretched out in the mad gallop. Now only a spasmodic cry sounded and the rest was the thunder of hooves. He heard more bangs and was shocked to see a tank crawling over the grass ahead. Beyond it more tanks were crawling and beside him a Cossack was screaming : " Nasha ! Nasha ! " The shouting spread along the line and Rofe saw the big red stars on the side of the tanks. They raced straight for them and then they were past the first tank, weaving past the others and running up to the trees.

He was reining back and the half-crazed mare was breaking the gallop reluctantly, pulling iron-mouthed and slowly dropping to a canter while he dragged savagely on the reins. She broke down to a trot as she took him into the trees and he pulled her up and found he was perspiring and shaking. The Cossacks were milling around, laughing and shouting at Russian soldiers spread out in the woods. Rofe saw the slit trenches, a big mortar half hidden by branches, knew he was free, and felt warm joy soaking quietly through him.

An hour later he was drinking vodka with the riotously happy Cossacks in a large tent near a headquarters outside a village, and there, a couple of days later, he met Hillebrand, who had come through on the waggons.

Ten weeks later he was still waiting at another village a few miles back feeling he would go mad soon if something did not happen. The Russians kept saying, " Nichevo," claiming they must wait for orders from Moscow, and one day in December the orders came. A Russian Dakota flew them to Moscow, they went on by train to Murmansk and sailed aboard an aircraft carrier in a convoy. That was almost the worst part ; aircraft bombed them and then they ran into a U-boat pack and lost several ships. On Christmas Eve Rofe reached London and an intelligence officer, welcoming him with admirable detachment and no interest whatsoever, asked, " Have you come from the other side ? "

It sounded for a moment like " The Other Side," and Rofe said dryly, " Yes, I feel in a way I have."

———————————

Rofe was awarded the Military Medal for his escape and also commissioned. He joined Transport Command as a navigator, flying the Middle East routes with No. 216 Squadron, and it was during this period that he took some leave in Palestine after the war and met once more Hillebrand, still almost as thin as ever and now a lieutenant in the Israeli Army. Also on this leave he met again Kacenelenbeigen, the Jewish soldier with whom he first exchanged places at Lamsdorf, and Joseph

Luxemburg, his partner on his first abortive escape. He left the Air Force and got married, and he and his wife have taken over an inn near London. Rofe is now writing the full story of his escape, to be entitled " The Wrong Road Home."

IT FEELS LIKE THIS

Harry Wheeler's mother became critically ill at his birth in 1922 at Gatooma, in Southern Rhodesia, and Wheeler, of Irish-Scots descent, was brought up by a Dutch woman who had just lost her baby. He lived for a time near Johannesburg, and then with his father among the dusty, rough-and-ready gold mines of Southern Rhodesia, being educated at Prince Edward High School at Salisbury. The life made him a rather quiet, self-reliant youngster. Too young for the Forces in 1939, he became an apprentice electrician until he joined the R.A.F. in Rhodesia in 1942, qualified as a fighter pilot and left for England next day. He flew Typhoons with No. 266 Squadron, took part in the Invasion and a few weeks later was operating from Airstrip B3 on the Normandy Beach-head, doing close Army support, strafing tanks, transport and pillboxes. He was twenty-two when the following ordeal happened, a long, thin Rhodesian with deep-set eyes under hairy brows and a dry, composed manner. Always inclined to go his own way, he had a habit when flying of unclipping his oxygen mask and sucking at a tin of condensed milk. He wrote this when he came back, and it is so unusually vivid and unaffected that I have made few changes—a little trimming, a little added after talks with him, but that is all. It is as he saw it.

August, 1944, was my rugged month. On the 8th I was shot down by flak south of Caen but was able to crash-lob in a minefield behind our lines and got back to the squadron that night. Next day I was flying again and saw my pal " Pithie " get it on his twentieth birthday. He was in flames and I heard him saying over the R/T that he was going to bale out but he didn't make it.

On the 15th we were out beating up tanks and trucks in the Falaise Pocket. I was flying a new Typhoon, had a go with my rockets at a couple of heavy trucks and was pulling up through the thick flak when a shell exploded under my seat and the cockpit was full of smoke and shrapnel. I felt some of the shrap. get me in the back, the left arm and the left leg and saw a lot of flames flaring under my seat.

I couldn't have been more than about fifteen hundred feet then and knew pretty soon that the " Tiffie " had had it. She was out of control, the port wing was dropping and nothing happened when I pulled the stick over except that she winged over some more and the nose started dropping. She was going down steeper and steeper and there wasn't much time.

I remember I tried to call up over the R/T and say I was hopping out but my left arm wouldn't move so I couldn't get it up to press the transmission switch. Anyway I'd no sooner thought of it than I knew I didn't have time. I pulled the hood jettison but she wouldn't go, it was stuck somehow from the explosion and I thought I was trapped and hammered at the side panel like a madman with my right arm which was all right.

I got a grip on the panic and bashed away some more and the forward end of the hood opened a shade and the slipstream ripped it clear away. I was going nearly straight down now, must have been hitting over three hundred miles an hour and had a hell of a time trying to force myself out of the cockpit. It was all happening at a terrible speed, only a few seconds for the whole lot, and I was trying to do it all at once and not panic.

I got my head out and the air felt fluid at that speed and pressed me back into the cockpit. I was panicking again, rammed up with my legs, got my head and shoulders out and the slipstream sucked me out suddenly and my boots flew off. Just for a moment I was frightened I was going to hit the tail, but I did not. I was falling face down, spreadeagled, saw the ground rushing up at me, pulled the ripcord and thankfully felt a terrific jerk as the parachute opened.

I only floated for about four or five seconds, I was so low. The aircraft hit the ground and exploded into flames with a great roar and I felt sick because I was so close to being in it, no longer myself, a living being, but a mangled, charred monstrosity burning fiercely with the aircraft, the fats of my body providing the fuel to feed the fires of self-destruction.

I am told this is so. It is not a pleasant thought but I had no time to dwell on it, because I hit the deck in my socks.

I saw I was in a little field with a high hedge all round it and the Jerries who had been shooting at me on the way down were still shooting. The bullets were zipping through the hedges and though they were shooting blindly it didn't feel too good. I pulled out my revolver and ran and dived through the hedge on the other side, squeezed through all the sticks and leaves and got an awful shock to see a little Nazi standing beside me with a gun as I stood up. He was the first one I had seen and he was a little rat-faced sod in a green uniform screaming something at me.

A lot of other Germans were running up so I didn't feel inclined to shoot the little one but he looked as though he was going to shoot me. I think he thought I should have put my hands up but I couldn't move my left arm. I put my gun in my belt and was quite satisfied to go quietly, being wounded and having no boots and surrounded—I'm no hero—but he started taking aim from about a foot away, or that is, going through the motions of shooting from that range—it's hard to describe—so I got hold of his gun barrel with my good hand and pointed it to one side. He started swearing but he was only a little guy so he couldn't do much else for the moment. I was too scared just to stand there and be shot and then a big English-speaking Westphalian came running up and told him to ease up. I was glad of that.

There now, that's how I was captured and the amazing thing is how fast it all happened—say six seconds for getting out of the plane, two seconds for falling free, gloriously aware of the cool, liquid air flowing past me, snatching at my clothes (I remember liking that), five seconds for the time I hung on silk and thirty seconds for the confused business on the ground up till the time the Westphalian came up—about forty-five seconds from the time I was sitting serenely in the aircraft and was hit. It does not seem possible it could all happen so fast. I was pretty sure the squadron would think I was dead (and, as a matter of fact, they did—they reported me " Missing, believed killed "). All they'd see was the kite on fire very low and the explosion and smoke when it hit.

I do not know the Westphalian's name but shall call him Hans. I daresay that will do. I always connect the name with German wood-choppers. He was a big fellow with a heavy face and mousy hair and looked as though he had a lot of kids. He spoke a bit of rough English and stood no nonsense from the other Germans. He was a sergeant.

Hans went away, I think to report my arrival somewhere, and the other Jerries pinched my watch and things. I was feeling pretty dizzy and faint now and simply stood still with my left arm dangling down watching the blood drip from my finger tips on to my left foot, soaking my sock. It struck me as being rather funny that I should be standing there in my socks surrounded by men whose language I could not understand staring at me, some with hatred in their eyes and others mildly curious.

The little sod who had captured me had not yet stopped cursing me. I wondered when he would run out of swear words but he did not do so in my presence. I shan't soon forget his expression of loathing, how he circled round me cursing me all the time and then saying, " Amerikana ? Tormie ? " and when I said " Tommy " he wanted to shoot me again. I did not like him either. It was all very frightening and I did not want to die.

Hans came back and suggested I sit on the grass while he took my name and number and so on. It was a small enough humanitarian gesture but it was a change from the cursing and it cheered me up a lot.

The dizzy sensation started passing away and when I really knew I was alive the sun seemed brighter and the grass greener, and my wounds did not seem to hurt so much. I could breathe without it hurting so I knew the shrap. in my back had not gone through my lungs, and that was a relief.

A Volkswagen pulled up and Hans told me to get in. Driving out of the field a gate barred our way. Jerry would not be stopped by the gate, oh no—the driver drove straight into it but it would not give and we were all thrown forward violently. He backed the car away and tried again but the gate held again. He did that three times in all but the rickety old gate held so the driver climbed out and opened it, looking very foolish. It seemed funny to me and I grinned, and he gave me a dirty look.

They took me to a dressing station in an old farmhouse. It was full of badly wounded men, most of them in a filthy condition and the stink was awful. There were a lot of yells and moans coming out of one room, and I saw some surgeons come out of it looking weary and overworked, and peeling dripping rubber gloves from their hands, well smeared with gore. (I fully expected to see a trolley load of arms and legs being wheeled out.)

Anyway, I decided to tell them I was very fit and after some bandaging they took me away in the Volkswagen again. I was feeling a bit revolted. It was my first view of the side of war we don't like to think about. Ground fighting is an unpleasant, messy business.

Hans took me in the Volkswagen to his C.O. and on the way I saw a Yank pilot in a Lightning buy it. He came down much the same way as I did and burst into flames, but the difference was he didn't get out. The Heinies cheered wildly. Hans did not. He said, " Your Kamerad was not as lucky as you."

His C.O. was a scrawny, hard-looking individual. He was sitting in a tent and shot a few questions at me through Hans which I wouldn't answer and then he made me wait outside the tent. I heard him nattering on the phone inside. I can speak Afrikaans which is a bit like German in a way, but all I could make out of what he was saying on the phone sounded like, " Maak die Man dood." In Afrikaans that means, " Make the man dead—shoot the man," and I did not feel too good. He was having a heated argument with someone over the phone and I hoped like hell that the guy at the other end was better at arguing than he was. It was not very funny to stand there and listen to two men arguing as to whether I should die or not. It was nearly too much for me.

He put the phone down and called me into the tent. Hans stood very gravely beside me, at attention. The C.O. asked for my identity card. I handed it to him, he glanced at it and threw it in the dirt. I suppose I was expected to pick it up but left it lying there. Hans picked it up and we loped off.

When we got back in the car I asked, " Am I going to be

shot?" but Hans didn't answer, he only shrugged, and I started feeling pretty sick. I didn't want to die. I knew I would not be shot normally but these were anything but normal times. These Germans were being trapped in the shambles of the Falaise Pocket. They were in a desperate position and not likely to bother overmuch with prisoners— particularly someone who had been strafing them with rockets and cannon, and they surely hated us in Typhoons. I did not know what the verdict was for certain, but was pretty sure I was for it.

Hans drove me to another tent and three more German officers interrogated me, wanting to know about the buzz-bombs and all that sort of thing. One of them accused me of resisting capture and I guessed they were going to use that as flimsy excuse for shooting me. When they tried to search me I turned out the front pockets of my battledress jacket and told them that if they wanted my emergency kit they'd have to look in the dinghy pack on my parachute. I argued with them about that so that they forgot to search my pants and I kept all my survival kit in my pants pockets.

After that they took me out into a field and some soldiers came up with rifles and a pick and shovel and started digging a hole. I tried to remain outwardly calm and watched them digging. One of them was cursing me all the time until Hans told him to shut up, and then I saw that the hole was not oblong, it was a round sort of shape. I don't know what it was for but I sighed very deeply. Hell, I was frightened.

Then Hans drove me to a German army barbed-wire cage for prisoners but the Germans refused to take me, saying I was the Luftwaffe's responsibility. Hans looked pretty grim at that and we drove off again and after a lot of trouble he found two German officers in a staff car who said they would whip me back to a rear prison camp in their car. Hans looked pretty relieved and from a couple of little things he said at the time about being lucky to have found them I gathered I was to have been shot if I'd had to stay in the front area that night. Hans wished me luck then and loped off. He was a good Jerry and I was lucky to have fallen into his hands.

The two Jerry officers were all right, neither friendly nor

unfriendly, in fact they rather ignored me. Now that the shock was wearing off a bit I was thinking about escape. I thought if I could give these two the slip I might be able to filter through the lines back to the squadron, or lie up somewhere till our advance overtook me. So I was particularly glad when they said it was too late to drive to the rear areas that night and they parked under a tree with a couple more German officers and brought out some bottles of champagne. They offered me some and it was very good, particularly as my back and left shoulder were getting very painful and I needed a bit of a pick-me-up. The Heinies kept polishing off bottles of the stuff, sitting under a tree and getting merrier and merrier. They kept offering me more but I said no. I was hoping they would get good and bottled and pass out, so I could mosey off into the woods, but one sly blighter stayed sober and after a couple of hours he hauled me off to a nearby barn and locked me in for the night.

My wounds were getting worse and worse and I had to keep sitting up all night to ease the pain. The rain was pouring down outside and I could see my escape plans getting dimmer.

In the morning they drove me off in the car through Falaise, which was a shambles. It had been bombed and shelled a few hours before and the dust was still settling over the dead ruins. You didn't see a soul. The buildings reeled drunkenly and the shop windows were bursting open, spilling all the odds and ends over the rubble on the pavements. We went straight through it and I was keeping a crafty check on where we were going with my compass and map.

It was a lovely day—for air operations—and I was hoping we'd be spotted and attacked so I could run for it in the general confusion. We saw a lot of kites about—ours—but none of them made a pass at us. I suppose if they had attacked I'd have soon changed my mind about being glad of it.

Once we had to get out and walk up a stony hill that was too steep for the little car and I hurried on ahead thinking I might get far enough away for a dash, but one of the guards kept up with me. He must have been a thought-reader.

My back was getting worse than ever and it was swelling up

a lot so that I began to look as if I'd flake out any moment.
The Jerries called in at a field hospital so my back could be
dressed. They were rather decent about it. It was a big tent
with a lot of wounded lying about on cots and on the ground,
and a general noise and smell. I lost my compass here. I
had it tucked into the bandage on my arm and forgot it when
a German orderly unbandaging it found the compass. He
didn't know what it was and I tried to pass it off as a joke,
saying it was a lucky souvenir, but the doctor recognised it and
said he would keep it for a lucky souvenir himself.

He had one look at my back and arm and put on that
solemn look that doctors do when they don't like what they
see. He said something and I gathered I was in for the knife.
The Jerries in the car said they would wait, which was decent
of them, though I think they were glad of the chance to sit
down and do nothing.

A young S.S. fellow was having a boil lanced just before
my turn. They had to hold him down and he made a hell of
a din about it which made me laugh openly, and he saw this
and took exception to it. When they let him off the slab he
came across to me and looked me over. I did likewise. He
told me he had killed four " Tormies," holding up four fingers
and saying " Tormie " and drawing his finger across his throat
and pointing to himself. He seemed very proud of himself.
I thought it would not be good policy to tell him how many
Jerry troops I had belted with rockets and cannon. I saw no
reason to be proud of it in any case.

The little S.S. type swaggered round and the others thought
him pretty good. There was a band round his forearm with
" Hitler " written on it. When it came to my turn on the slab
he looked on with great interest, hoping I'd yell out, no doubt,
but I was determined not to. The doc probed a bit in the hole
in my back but it did not hurt. I screwed up my face as if it
did hurt, but did not make a sound and the Jerry looked
disappointed. I chuckled to myself because it seemed funny
and then the Jerry loped off. The doc said I had a big piece
near the lung and a couple of dozen pieces in the arm, and they
would have to be done somewhere else. He gave me a shot
in the arm and I drifted off into unconsciousness. When I

woke up some time later I asked for more. I'd easily become addicted to drugs. Must watch that.

They put me back in the car and drove me a few more miles to a base hospital at Evreau. The drug had made me feel dopey and a woman threw a bucket of water in my face to wake me up. There were hundreds of wounded Jerries about and they put me on the slab again and gave me chloroform. I don't like chloroform.

When I woke up I was all bandaged and they were loading me into an ambulance. That ride from Evreau to Paris was the worst thing I've ever had. I can still hear, if I allow myself to, the moans and cries of the Luftwaffe pilot above me who kept thrashing around in his agony. He was burned all over his head and body and wrapped in paper bandages (all the Jerries had) which had come undone, exposing the burned flesh.

There was the Yank whose system was poisoned by a gangrenous hand and who kept shouting out in delirium to someone called " Mike " or " Mac," telling him to look out. Then he'd clap his swollen and good hands together spasmodically and lash out at the fellow next to him. This boy was an Englishman with an amputated leg and the Yank kept kicking it. He would yell and curse horribly. I asked the Heinies to let me change places with him, even though the Yank's wound smelt putrid, but they would not let me. This din went on for about six hours. The roads were blocked with a lot of horse-drawn carts the Jerries were using, and we went pretty slowly. About six in the evening we got to the Hôpital de la Pitié in Paris. I was very tired.

They took me up to the top floor where all the prisoner patients were, and it was crammed to the eyebrows. The wards were overfull of serious cases and scores of double-decker bunks lined the cold white walls of the corridors to take the overflow. No one seemed to know what was happening. There were no doctors, only a skeleton staff of German and French nurses and dull-looking German guards leaning lazily against the walls There didn't seem to be much in the way of medical supplies.

I found a bunk for myself in one of the corridors, peeled off my battledress and piled in, beginning to feel pretty good again because in all this confusion it ought to be a piece of cake to escape. What I wanted more than anything was some shoes or boots to make me mobile.

In the morning when I woke up my pants and battlejacket were gone so it looked as if I was stuck, unless I could swipe someone else's. All I had then was a rather bloody shirt, some underpants and my big green silk scarf which we all wore on the squadron to prevent the chafing of " weaver's neck " . . . looking around all the time when you're flying.

On the bunk next to mine I noticed a munt getting dressed in a lazy way. He was very black. I thought he was an American negro at first but then I wasn't sure. He was slender with an aquiline nose and an aristocratic sort of face, and was sitting there very composed, not saying a word and looking rather lonely, and I saw he was putting on a ragged British battledress.

I spoke to him in English but he looked baffled, so I tried him in " kitchen kaffir," which I speak a bit, and his eyes lit up like a lamp-post. He started nattering away, looking terribly glad, and it turned out that he came from Nyasaland. I talk that language very well so we nattered for a long time.

He'd been caught in Tobruk nearly three years before and all that time he'd been a prisoner in Europe, cut off by language and class and all that sort of thing, terribly lonely and homesick and not knowing what it was all about or when it was going to end, if ever. He had been utterly forlorn, not able to talk to anyone, but in some funny way it had broadened his mind immensely so that I could not help wondering at it. Yet he was a simple, sincere munt for all that and had not developed any of the unpleasant traits you get in some of the educated munts from the mission schools back home. He had learned in a far harder school. If he got home all right I'm afraid he would have found himself a misfit, though I hope he receives a square deal. I sincerely hope that.

His name was Kbwana Yusuf and he told me how he was being marched from Chartres towards Paris when a lorry ran over his guard and himself, he being pinned under his guard as the wheel passed over them, killing the guard. He was a young fellow and I asked him if he would like to try and escape with me and come and be a batman on the squadron. He said, " Inde, chabwino Bwana "—(meaning that he'd like to very much).

As he was quite fit and I could not use my left arm I asked him if he would wash my clothes, and he did so cheerfully ; I gave him two hundred francs from my escape money as a " bonsella." The day passed almost pleasantly talking to Kbwana and I forgot all about the war. It took my mind right back home again. I thought I would like to have him work for me after the war. He said he would like to and I gave him my name and address but I guess he has forgotten it. I should have written it down for him.

The Germans never gave us any rations as they were supposed to, but they brought us round Red Cross parcels that day and we would have been in Queer Street without them. Kbwana did not like the chocolate in them. He said he'd give a lot for a pot of sadza instead. Sadza is a mess of ground maize, a staple diet for the munts, and it does not taste too good. I gave Kbwana my cigarettes for his chocolate.

I didn't get to meet many of the other prisoners at this stage. They seemed to be all sorts, mostly foreign, though a few were English and Dominion and American. I talked to a couple but there were no Air Force people among them and most of them anyway were too sick to talk. Still it was a great relief to feel that there were some of my own kind around.

A rumour started flying around that afternoon that the Allies were within two days of reaching Paris and all the boys started to feel a bit cheerful. If only we could be left there long enough, I thought. If only . . .

About four o'clock a bunch of Heinies came in and took away a lot of the less seriously wounded men. My name was not on the list, thank God, and I found out that the list had been made up the previous day. I guess that's what saved me that time. If they had known I was a pilot they'd have nabbed me right away. I'd like to thank the unknown thief who pinched my battlejacket with the wings on it. Maybe they saw him with it and took him because of the wings. That would be funny. Poetic justice.

They took Kbwana away with this first lot. I was having a look at the washing at the time and did not know he was taken or I would have tried to hide him away. I was sorry to see him go. How strange it was that he should have been there, he who had no real ideas about the war, the reasons for fighting it, but only had an idea that he liked the English and disliked the Germans. He had seen enough of them. He wanted to go home. How strange it was that we should have sat there, he translating what the Germans said to me (he could understand some but not speak it) and I translating English to him. Now he was gone and I don't suppose I will ever see that rather quaint munt again. Life is queer.

The Heinies had said they would be coming back for more and we were all hoping and hoping that we, individually, would be left behind. I had been limping around a bit but now I climbed back into my bunk ready to look very sick when they came back. I took off my vest so my wounded back would show more, spread the bandages on my arm and leg as far as I could and tore up my " Verwundet " card with all the details of my wounds on them. Unfortunately I was caught on the wrong foot. The Heinies came back sooner than I thought they would and they ran in and saw me sitting up on my bunk talking to the chap two bunks along.

They came straight for me and indicated I must walk downstairs to the ambulance. I pointed to my leg, showing the bandages and shook my head. They pointed to a stretcher and I asked " Deutschland ? " They said, " Ja," and I said, " Nein," very emphatically, and two of them grabbed hold of me to hoist me away. I hung on to the bed with both hands, groaning, and they tugged and tugged but I wouldn't let go.

I thought it was pretty safe to do that—they didn't have any pistols on them so they'd have had to take the bunk as well as me to get me. They tried persuading me, saying that everyone was going, so I told them in Afrikaans (which they could understand a bit) that they could take everyone else in the hospital first and then I would go They looked bewildered for a while, they just did not seem to know what to do in these circumstances, so they turned and took some other guys who did not seem to know how to argue.

The fun was not over yet. The chap I'd been talking to (his leg was badly shattered) kept telling me to hide quickly, but I didn't dare get off the bed because the Heinies were clumping about the place and would grab me if I did. So I lay there hoping and hoping they would not return and then two more came along and told me to get up and move. They had guns.

I was lying down when they came up and was pretty sure these particular two had not seen me sitting up before so I started drooling at the mouth and breathing in short, sharp gasps as I'd seen a fellow breathing earlier in the day, dying with a hole through his lung.

I looked at them as one does when thinking hard, without seeing them, so to speak, and murmured " Loong " (lung) and " Blut " (blood), pointing to my mouth and coughing, and then pointing to the hole in my back.

They nodded and looked quite sympathetic and then they walked away. God, it was a tense moment. I suppose they thought I'd soon be dead. All the lung cases there died, as far as I know. I suppose it was only because they were half drunk they fell for it, because they hustled away a lot of chaps who weren't fit to be moved.

It felt pretty good after they had gone. I didn't think I could have bluffed them so easily. And then an English-speaking French padre came round and said the Jerries would not be coming back and that the S.S. were machine-gunning the streets to clear them of civilians. We could hear the bursts of fire out in the streets and knew we looked like being in the thick of a battle for Paris, but it still felt pretty good. I was quite happy and terribly pleased with myself.

We started organising ourselves then and an English army officer with his arm lashed in a steel and leather cradle round his shoulder took charge of the place. There were three hundred of us left and we moved out of the corridors into the wards, those who could walk, like me, helping those who could not. We cleaned the place up as it was pretty filthy and a few of us tried to do what we could for the helpless ones. There was not much we could do. The Germans had taken all the medical supplies. Anyway, I carried bedpans and did what

I could and that night none of us got much sleep because the gunfire in the streets had worked up to quite a pitch.

There was a fight going on outside the hospital somewhere. The French Resistance boys had come out into the open. You could always pick out the Jerry machine-guns, their rate of fire was so fast it sounded like calico tearing, but much louder of course. The French had mostly the slower firing British guns. The Jerries had some of their wicked 88 mm. mobile guns and they bellowed forth from time to time. After a while I dropped into a half-doze, but there was an engine in the hospital laundry going and its chug-chug-chug worked into my dreams and then another burst from the guns would wake me up in a fright. Now and then you could hear the crunch crunch of Germans marching in the street. The fires in the boiler house sent flickering shadows dancing across the walls, and then someone banged loudly on a door below.

It must have been the butt of a rifle. There were some sharp shouts in German, then silence again. I got all tight inside again. More loud bangs and then a hell of a crash as though the door had been smashed open. Then silence— nothing else, just silence. It was very weird.

I dropped into a sort of sleep again and woke up with a heavy thump. I was lying on the floor, my back wound hurting terribly. I had fallen or jumped out of bed in my sleep. I'm always doing that. I crawled back into bed feeling like a goat and shivered till morning.

That was the first of the ten nights we had there while Paris was falling. I got used to the shooting after that and slept through it all, though most of the others had hell every night.

There's no use telling all that happened in the next days. First, some French doctors and nurses came in about the third day, having dodged the bullets in the streets. They had heard we were there and wanted to look after us and as we were the first Allied men they had seen they made a wonderful fuss of us. The nurses came round kissing us all in turn and from somewhere they brought out bottles of champagne and some wonderful grub. The doctors all seemed to be specialists and the nurses were all very pretty. They did a wonderful job with the sick but it didn't stop people dying all the time.

I helped to carry some of the bodies down and put them in the coffins and one of the boys used to read something from a French bible over them. Unfortunately no one knew which part of the burial ceremony to read so it meant the guy had to read it all and it was very long. A few of us used to try and stick around in the mortuary till he had finished reading to give the man some sort of send-off, and then it was all over bar the banging in of the nails. We had to leave them in the mortuary and it was midsummer, which was not too good after a while. It seemed so damn silly that all these men should be dying. War is a fool business to be sure.

I used to feel a bit silly at these " funerals " because, having no pants, I couldn't very well stand there in underpants, so I wrapped my green silk scarf round my waist like a sarong. The nurses all thought it was funny as hell and said " Oo-la-la " whenever they passed me. I kept wishing my legs weren't so long and thin.

The French brought in their wounded from the street fighting, and brought in wounded Germans, too, and when a German died his mates took their turn behind us to take him down to the mortuary and read the service over him.

We waited and waited in the hospital while the shooting went on all round and it was getting pretty tense. People were looking thin-lipped and edgy. We kept on hoping the Germans would not come back into the hospital and wondering where the Allies were. The battle was still going on noisily in the city and a Frenchman brought in a radio and tuned it in to London. It was strange to hear the B.B.C. announcer's voice echoing round the wards, but the strangest part was when he said the fighting in Paris had now ceased. There were some horse-laughs round the ward and then a particularly vicious burst of machine-gun fire outside the grounds. The Jerries never got back into the hospital in strength. A sniper broke in one night and shot a doctor, and another night two nurses were shot standing too near a window.

The morning after that I heard a tremendous commotion in the street, a lot of shouting and roaring rolling along nearer

and nearer. I pinned my sarong on and ran down and
through the front door and there was an armoured car tearing
along with a French tricolour waving over it and French
soldiers leaning out of it, waving and grinning. French people
were pouring into the street from their houses where they'd
been hiding in the cellars for days and they were screaming
and jumping and kissing and waving flags they'd been storing
up for years and years for this moment. My God, the steam
had really blown the safety valve and they were going crazy.
A lot of them were crying and then they found that I was an
R.A.F. pilot and a mob got round me and a lot of girls were
kissing me and an old man was kissing me on both cheeks (his
breath wasn't too good) and the noise was a roar all round.

More armoured cars rolled down the street and it was
obvious that the boys were here to stay. I got myself away
from the French, went back into the hospital and walked
round telling everyone that the boys were here and that Paris
was free. A man in my ward who was dying said, " Thank
God." He was crying. The man in the next bed, who was
going to live, said, " Christ, about time, too."

I got hold of a pair of pants and a jacket from someone who
had just died and went out back into the street and got as far
as the Champs-Elysées and the Unknown Soldier's tomb in
the Arc de Triomphe. It was a pretty mad day. Snipers
were still around and the occasional rattle of shots sent us
ducking for cover, but outside that it was mostly kisses and
champagne till I got sick of it and crawled back to the hospital.
Some of the boys were carried in on stretchers, completely
bottled. God, I was tired and limp. It was a little too much
to realise we were free. All I could feel then was that I
wanted to get back to the squadron as soon as I could because
I was pretty sure I'd been reported as probably killed.

That was my last night in Paris, and that night the Jerries
bombed us. A stick of bombs straddled the hospital, blowing
in the windows and shaking up some of the sick boys pretty
badly. We thought we'd all better beat it down to the cellars
till it was over. We carried the sick ones down. I carried a
French-Canadian called Maurice and it was a bit of a strain
on my back and leg and arm. We stayed down there the whole

night waiting for more bombs and I spent most of the time chatting with a very pretty little French nurse. The French shot her next day for collaborating with the Germans. Poor kid. She was only about eighteen and her collaboration consisted of sleeping with a few Germans. She was too young— certainly when the Germans arrived—to be really responsible for her actions, but there was not much justice in Paris at this time. It was like the tumbrils in the revolution.

I'd had enough of Paris now. All I wanted to do was get back to the squadron and let the people know I was alive before the boys auctioned my kit. There were some American ambulances arrived that day and I hitched a lift a few miles back out of Paris on one. Then I hitched with an American negro driver taking a truck back along the " red ball " (priority) route. He drove all night and kept falling asleep at the wheel, so I had to stay awake and grab the wheel every time his head dropped.

At sunrise I tagged a Yank in a jeep heading for Cherbourg. He didn't have a map, but I did, so I directed him a long way off his road till we went through Caen where the squadron used to be and I hopped off there before he found out how far I'd led him astray.

I walked out of town across the fields to where the airfield used to be, and there it was, still there, with the kites at dispersal. I spotted the familiar " ZH " on the side of the kites and that was a good moment. I'd been afraid the squadron might have moved on. I wandered in casually around the back of the dispersals and came on old Dave Morgan suddenly. Someone was shooting the place up and I asked Dave what was to do. Were they leaving?

He looked frightened for a moment and then he said, " Wait a minute, Harry, what are you doing here? You're dead ! " He looked thunderstruck as though he'd seen a ghost. I said I wasn't dead and he came out of his trance and said, " Jesus, it's good to see you. Where've you come from? What the hell happened? We thought you were dead." He turned round and screamed, " Hey, Dinkery, look who's here."

Dinkery came running up and said, " Christ . . . Harry . . . No ! " Paddy Culligan came out of the mess, and so on.

It was very strange indeed. It's good to have people look so pleased to see you after they thought you were dead.

Pithie had not got back. Royce had got the chop in a dog-fight against a swarm of Heinies. But oh, I was so pleased to see all the others again. The wingco, Johnny Baldwin, had a bath fixed up for me. Barney Wright, my C.O., who is a "press-on" type, said, "Would you like a week's leave?" and I said "No. I've got a hole in my back. I'd like more than that." The doc looked me over and said I ought to have twenty-eight days.

That night I was in Ted Donne's tent and got to sleep quite early, but not for long. Little Joe, Zombie Laing, Ginger Cunnison (who had watched my aircraft fly into the deck and explode) and Henderson turned up after a visit to the front line, and hearing I was back came across to see for themselves that it was true.

They asked me what had happened and I tried to tell them. I got so far and then my mind went blank—I simply could not think or talk intelligently. Try as I might. Being woken suddenly when I was so very, very tired was a bit of a shock and my body started to tremble violently all over and my face to twitch. I tried to say I'd tell them in the morning and then Ted told them to leave me.

I lay there trying to stop my fool body from twitching and trembling and my mind from wandering off along endless channels of thought. At one time I felt I was being wrapped in cotton wool. Then my mind, my being, seemed to grow smaller and smaller till I became a mere speck burning within my head. This frightened me and I fought against that train of thought. My body would not stop trembling so I let it do so. I concentrated on making it tremble till I grew tired, but this took a long time.

Eventually I slept for a while, only to be woken by the sound of the Typhoons being started and run up very early in the morning before it grew light. The explosions of the Koffman starters sent my mind racing back to Paris and the street fighting. My body started trembling again and I grew annoyed. I was like an old woman. I did not like my face to twitch. I thought the tendency might stay with me, but it has not done so since that night, I am glad to say.   It was just that I was very tired.

Wheeler was a ferry pilot for six weeks after his escape until, bored by that, he got himself posted back to his old squadron. Commissioned then, he stayed on operations till the end of the war. He returned to South Africa in September, 1945, did a four-year degree course in electrical engineering at the University of Cape-town, then a two-year post-graduate course in England.   Now he is a professional engineer in Southern Rhodesia, still a bachelor.